Rick Steves'

Portuguese

Phrase Book & Dictionary
First Edition

AVALON
TRAVEL

Avalon Travel Publishing, 1400 65th Street, Suite 250,
Emeryville, CA 94608, USA

Avalon Travel Publishing is a division of Avalon
 Publishing Group, Inc.

Printed in the United States of America by Worzalla.
First edition. First printing May 2003.

ISBN 1-56691-547-3

Europe Through the Back Door Managing Editor:
 Risa Laib
Europe Through the Back Door Editors:
 Cameron Hewitt, Jill Hodges
Avalon Travel Publishing Editor: Matt Orendorff
Translation: Maria Antonia Campota Mafi,
 Luis F. Gonçalves Conde
Phonetics: Risa Laib, Cameron Hewitt
Production & Typesetting: Matt Orendorff
Cover Design: Kari Gim
Maps & Graphics: David C. Hoerlein, Zoey Platt
Photography: Rick Steves, Dominic Bonuccelli
Front cover photos:
 foreground– © Getty Images, Inc.
 background–Torre Belém, Lisbon © Getty Images, Inc.

Distributed to the book trade by Publishers Group
West, Berkeley, California

Other ATP travel guidebooks by Rick Steves

Rick Steves' Best of Europe
Rick Steves' Europe 101: History and Art for the Traveler
  (with Gene Openshaw)
Rick Steves' Europe Through the Back Door
Rick Steves' Mona Winks (with Gene Openshaw)
Rick Steves' Postcards from Europe
Rick Steves' France (with Steve Smith)
Rick Steves' Germany, Austria & Switzerland
Rick Steves' Great Britain
Rick Steves' Ireland (with Pat O'Connor)
Rick Steves' Italy
Rick Steves' Scandinavia
Rick Steves' Spain & Portugal
Rick Steves' Amsterdam, Bruges & Brussels
  (with Gene Openshaw)
Rick Steves' Florence (with Gene Openshaw)
Rick Steves' London (with Gene Openshaw)
Rick Steves' Paris (with Steve Smith and Gene Openshaw)
Rick Steves' Rome (with Gene Openshaw)
Rick Steves' Venice (with Gene Openshaw)
Rick Steves' Phrase Books: French, German, Italian,
  Spanish, and French/Italian/German

For the latest on Rick's lectures, guidebooks, tours, and public
television series, contact Europe Through the Back Door, Box
2009, Edmonds, WA 98020, tel. 425/771-8303, fax 425/771-
0833, www.ricksteves.com, or e-mail: rick@ricksteves.com.

CONTENTS

Illustrations

Maps

Hi, I'm Rick Steves.

I'm the only monolingual speaker I know who's had the nerve to design a series of European phrase books. But that's one of the things that makes them better.

You see, after 25 summers of travel through Europe, I've learned first-hand: (1) what's essential for communication in another country, and (2) what's not. I've assembled the most important words and phrases in a logical, no-frills format, and I've worked with native Europeans and seasoned travelers to give you the simplest, clearest translations possible.

But this book is more than just a pocket translator. The words and phrases have been carefully selected to help you have a smarter, smoother trip in Portugal. The key to getting more out of every travel dollar is to get closer to the local people, and to rely less on entertainment, restaurants, and hotels that cater only to foreign tourists. This book will not only help you order a meal at a locals-only Lisbon restaurant—it will help you talk with the family who runs the place . . . about their kids, social issues, travel dreams, and favorite *música*. Long after your memories of museums have faded, you'll still treasure the personal encounters you had with your new Iberian friends.

A good phrase book should help you enjoy your Iberian experience—not just survive it—so I've added a healthy dose of humor. A few phrases are just for fun and aren't meant to be used at all. Most of the phrases are for real and should be used with "please" (*por favor*). I know you can tell the difference.

To get the most out of this book, take the time to internalize and put into practice my Portuguese pronunciation tips. Don't worry too much about memorizing grammatical rules, like the gender of a noun—the important thing is to communicate!

This book has a handy dictionary and a nifty menu decoder. You'll also find tongue twisters, international words, telephone tips, and a handy tear-out "cheat sheet." Tear it out and keep it in your pocket, so you can easily memorize key phrases during otherwise idle moments. As you prepare for your trip, you may want to read this year's edition of my *Rick Steves' Spain & Portugal* guidebook.

The Portuguese speak less English than their European neighbors. But while the language barrier may seem a little higher, the locals are happy to give an extra boost to any traveler who makes an effort to communicate.

My goal is to help you become a more confident, extro-verted traveler. If this phrase book helps make that happen, or if you have suggestions for making it better, I'd love to hear from you. I personally read and value all feedback. My address is Europe Through the Back Door, P.O. Box 2009, Edmonds, WA 98020, tel. 425/771-8303, fax 425/771-0833, e-mail: rick@ricksteves.com.

Happy travels,

Rick Steves

GETTING STARTED

Portuguese

...is your passport to Europe's bargain basement. For its wonderful pricetag, you'll enjoy piles of fresh seafood, brilliant sunshine, and local character that often feels decades behind the rest of Europe. With its Old World charm comes a bigger language barrier than you'll find elsewhere in Europe. A phrase book is of greater value here than anywhere else in western Europe.

Here are a few tips on pronouncing Portuguese words:

C usually sounds like C in cat.
> But C followed by E or I sounds like S in sun.
Ç sounds like S in sun.
CH sounds like SH in shine.
G usually sounds like G in go.
> But G followed by E or I sounds like S in treasure.
H is silent.
J sounds like S in treasure.
LH sounds like LI in billion.
NH sounds like NI in onion.
R is trrrilled.
S can sound like S in sun (at the beginning of a word),
> Z in zoo (between vowels), or SH in shine.
SS sounds like S in sun.

Portuguese vowels:

A can sound like A in father or A in sang.
E can sound like E in get, AY in play, or I in wish.
É sounds like E in get.
Ê sounds like AY in play.
I sounds like EE in seed.
O can sound like O in note, AW in raw, or OO in moon.
Ô and *OU* sound like O in note.
U sounds like OO in moon.

As with any Romance language, sex is important. A man is *simpático* (friendly), a woman is *simpática.* In this book, we show bisexual words like this: *simpático[a].* If you're speaking of a female (which includes females speaking about themselves), use the *a* ending. It's always pronounced "ah." A word that ends in *r*, such as *cantor* (singer), will appear like this: *cantor[a].* A *cantora* is a female singer. A word ending in *e*, such as *interessante* (interesting), applies to either sex.

Adjectives agree with the noun. A clean room is a *quarto limpo,* a clean towel is a *toalha limpa. Quartos limpos* have *toalhas limpas.* You'll be quizzed on this later.

If a word ends in a vowel, the Portuguese usually stress the second-to-last syllable. Words ending in a consonant are stressed on the last syllable. To override these rules, the Portuguese add an accent mark (such as ´, ~, or ^) to the syllable that should be stressed, like this: *rápido* (fast) is pronounced **rah**-pee-doo.

Just like French, its linguistic buddy, Portuguese has nasal sounds. A vowel followed by either *n* or *m* or topped with a ~ (such as *ã* or *õ*) is usually nasalized. In the phonetics, nasalized vowels are indicated by an underlined **n** or **w**. As you say the vowel, let its sound come through your nose as well as your mouth.

Here are the phonetics for nasal vowels:

ay<u>n</u>	nasalize the AY in day.
oh<u>n</u>	nasalize the O in bone.
oo<u>n</u>	nasalize the O in moon.
o<u>w</u>	nasalize the OW in now.

Some words have only a slight nasal sound. To help you pronounce these words, I add an *ng* or *n* in the phonetics: *sim* (meaning "yes") is pronounced seeng, and *muito* (meaning "very") like **mween**-too.

Here's a quick guide to the rest of the phonetics used in this book:

a	like A in sang.
ah	like A in father.
ay	like AY in play.
ee	like EE in seed.
eh	like E in get.
ehr	sounds like "air."
g	like G in go.
i	like I in hit.
ī	like I in light.
o	like AW in raw.
oh	like O in note.
oo	like OO in moon.
or	like OR in core.
ow	like OW in now.
oy	like OY in toy.
s	like S in sun.
zh	like S in treasure.

Too often tourists insist on speaking Spanish to the Portuguese. Your attempts at Portuguese will endear you to the locals. And if you throw in *"por favor"* (please) whenever you can, you'll eat better, sleep easier, and make friends faster.

PORTUGUESE
BASICS

In 1917, according to legend, the Virgin Mary visited Fatima using only these phrases.

Meeting and Greeting

Hello.	*Olá.*	oh-**lah**
Good morning.	*Bom dia.*	bohn **dee**-ah
Good afternoon.	*Boa tarde.*	boh-ah **tar**-deh
Good evening. / Good night.	*Boa noite.*	boh-ah **noy**-teh
Welcome!	*Bem-vindo[a]!* *	behm-**veen**-doo
Mr.	*Senhor*	sin-**yor**
Mrs.	*Senhora*	sin-**yoh**-rah
Miss	*Menina*	meh-**nee**-nah
How are you?	*Como está?*	**koh**-moo ish-**tah**
Very well.	*Muito bem.*	**mween**-too bayn
Thank you. (said by a male)	*Obrigado.*	oh-bree-**gah**-doo
Thank you. (said by a female)	*Obrigada.*	oh-bree-**gah**-dah
And you? (formal / informal)	*E você? / E tú?*	ee voh-**say** / ee too

* Males use the "*o*" ending (*Bem-vindo*) when speaking; females use the "*a*" ending (*Bem-vinda*).

4

My name is ___.	Chamo-me ___.	**shah**-moo-meh
What's your name?	Como se chama?	**koh**-moo seh **shah**-mah
Pleased to	Prazer em	prah-**zehr** ayn
meet you.	conhecer.	kohn-yeh-**sehr**
Where are	De onde é que	deh **ohn**-deh eh keh
you from?	você é?	voh-**say** eh
I am / We are /	Estou / Estamos /	ish-**toh** / ish-**tah**-moosh /
Are you...?	Estás...?	ish-**tash**
...on vacation	...de férias	deh **feh**-ree-ahsh
...on business	...em negócios	ayn neh-**gos**-ee-oosh
So long!	Até logo!	ah-**teh log**-oo
Goodbye.	Adeus.	ah-**deh**-oosh
Good luck!	Boa sorte!	**boh**-ah **sor**-teh
Have a good trip!	Boa-viagem!	boh-ah-vee-**ah**-zhayn

BASICS

The Portuguese say "*Bom dia*" (Good morning) until noon, "*Boa tarde*" (Good afternoon) until dark, and "*Boa noite*" (Good evening) after dark. In Portugal, a woman who looks over 35 years old is addressed as *senhora*, younger than 35 as *menina*. Good luck.

Essentials

Hello.	Olá.	oh-**lah**
Do you speak	Fala inglês?	**fah**-lah een-**glaysh**
English?		
Yes. / No.	Sim. / Não.	seeng / now
I don't speak	Não falo	now **fah**-loo
Portuguese.	português.	poor-too-**gaysh**
I'm sorry.	Desculpe.	dish-**kool**-peh
(said by a male)		
I'm sorry.	Desculpa.	dish-**kool**-pah
(said by a female)		
Please.	Por favor.	poor fah-**vor**
Thank you.	Obrigado[a].	oh-bree-**gah**-doo
It's (not) a problem.	(Não) á problema.	(now) ah proo-**blay**-mah

Good / Great / Excellent.	Óptimo / Muito bom / Exelente.	**ot**-tee-moo / **mween**-too boh<u>n</u> / ehsh-eh-**layn**-teh
You are very kind.	É muito simpatico[a].	eh **mween**-too seeng-**pah**-tee-koo
Excuse me. (to pass)	Com licença.	koh<u>n</u> li-**sehn**-sah
Excuse me. (to get attention)	Desculpe[a].	dish-**kool**-peh
It doesn't matter.	Não faz mal.	no<u>w</u> fahsh mahl
You're welcome.	De nada.	deh **nah**-dah
Sure.	Claro.	**klah**-roo
O.K.	Está bem.	ish-**tah** bay<u>n</u>
Let's go.	Vamos.	**vah**-moosh
Goodbye.	Adeus.	ah-**deh**-oosh

Where?

Where is...?	Onde é que é...?	**ohn**-deh eh keh eh
...the tourist information office	...a informação turistica	ah een-for-mah-**sow** too-**reesh**-tee-kah
...the train station	...a estação de comboio	ah ish-tah-**sow** deh koh<u>n</u>-**boy**-yoo
...the bus station	...a terminal das camionetas	ah tehr-mee-**nahl** dahsh kahm-yoo-**neh**-tahsh
...a cash machine	...uma caixa automática	**oo**-mah **kī**-shah ow-toh-**mah**-tee-kah
...the toilet	...a casa de banho	ah **kah**-zah deh **bahn**-yoo
men / women	homens / mulheres	**ah**-may<u>n</u>sh / mool-**yeh**-rish

You'll find some Portuguese words are similar to English if you're looking for a *hotel*, *restaurante*, *supermercado*, *banco*, or *farmacia*.

How Much?

| How much is it? | Quanto custa? | **kwahn**-too **koosh**-tah |
| Write it? | Escreva? | ish-**kray**-vah |

Is it free?	É grátis?	eh **grah**-teesh
Is it included?	Está incluido?	ish-**tah** een-kloo-**ee**-doo
Do you have...?	Tem...?	tayn
Where can I buy...?	Onde posso comprar...?	**ohn**-deh pos-soo kohn-**prar**
I would like...	Gostaria...	goosh-tah-**ree**-ah
We would like...	Gostaríamos...	goosh-tah-**ree**-ah-moosh
...this.	...isto.	**eesh**-too
...just a little.	...só um bocadinho.	soh oon boo-kah-**deen**-yoo
...more.	...mais.	mī sh
...a ticket.	...um bilhete.	oon beel-**yeh**-teh
...a room.	...um quarto.	oon **kwar**-too
...the bill.	...a conta.	ah **kohn**-tah

BASICS

How Many?

one	um	oon
two	dois	doysh
three	três	traysh
four	quatro	**kwah**-troo
five	cinco	**seeng**-koo
six	seis	saysh
seven	sete	**seh**-teh
eight	oito	**oy**-too
nine	nove	**nah**-veh
ten	dez	dehsh

You'll find more to count on in the Numbers section beginning on page 14.

When?

At what time?	A que horas?	ah kee **oh**-rahsh
open / closed	aberto / fechado	ah-**behr**-too / feh-**shah**-doo
Just a moment.	Um momento.	oon moo-**mayn**-too

Now.	*Agora.*	ah-**goh**-rah
Soon.	*Breve.*	**bray**-veh
Later.	*Mais tarde.*	mī sh **tar**-deh
Today.	*Hoje.*	**oh**-zheh
Tomorrow.	*Amanhã.*	ah-ming-**yah**

Be creative! You can combine these phrases to say: "Two, please," or "No, thank you," or "Open tomorrow?" or "Please, where can I buy a ticket?" Please is a magic word in any language. If you want to buy something and you don't know the word for it, just point and say *por favor* (please). If you know the word for what you want, such as the bill, simply say, "*A conta, por favor*" (The bill, please). If you add *por favor* to most of the phrases in this book, you'll have a smoother trip.

Struggling with Portuguese

Do you speak English?	*Fala inglês?*	**fah**-lah een-**glaysh**
A teeny weeny bit?	*Um pouquinho?*	oon poh-**keen**-yoo
Please speak English.	*Por favor fale inglês.*	poor fah-**vor fah**-leh een-**glaysh**
You speak English well.	*Fala bem inglês.*	**fah**-lah bayn een-**glaysh**
I don't speak Portuguese.	*Não falo português.*	now **fah**-loo poor-too-**gaysh**
We don't speak Portuguese.	*Não falamos português.*	now fah-**lah**-moosh poor-too-**gaysh**
I speak a little Portuguese.	*Falo um pouco em português.*	**fah**-loo oon **poh**-koo ayn poor-too-**gaysh**
Sorry, I speak only English.	*Desculpe[a], só falo inglês.*	dish-**kool**-peh soh **fah**-loo een-**glaysh**
Sorry, we speak only English.	*Desculpe, só falamos inglês.*	dish-**kool**-peh soh fah-**lah**-moosh een-**glaysh**
Does somebody nearby speak English?	*Alguem aqui fala inglês?*	**ahl**-kayn ah-**kee fah**-lah een-**glaysh**

BASICS

Who speaks English?	Quem fala inglês?	kayn **fah**-lah een-**glaysh**
What does this mean?	O que quer dizer isto?	oo keh kehr dee-**zehr eesh**-too
What is this in Portuguese / English?	Como se diz isto em português / inglês?	**koh**-moo seh deez **eesh**-too ayn poor-too-**gaysh** / een-**glaysh**
Repeat?	Repita?	ray-**pee**-tah
Please speak slowly.	Por favor fale devegar.	poor fah-**vor fah**-leh deh-vah-**gar**
Slower.	Mais devagar.	mĩ sh deh-vah-**gar**
I understand.	Compreendo.	kohn-pree-**ayn**-doo
I don't understand.	Não compreendo.	now kohn-pree-**ayn**-doo
Do you understand?	Compreende?	kohn-pree-**ayn**-deh
Write it?	Escreva?	ish-**kray**-vah

BASICS

Handy Questions

How much?	Quanto custa?	**kwahn**-too **koosh**-tah
How many?	Quantos?	**kwahn**-toosh
How long...?	Quanto tempo...?	**kwahn**-too **tayn**-poo
...is the trip	...é a viagem	eh ah vee-**ah**-zhayn
How many minutes / hours?	Quantos minutos / horas?	**kwahn**-toosh mee-**noo**-toosh / **oh**-rahsh
How far?	A que distância?	ah keh deesh-**tahn**-see-ah
How?	Como?	**koh**-moo
Can you help me?	Pode ajudar-me?	**pod**-eh ah-zhoo-**dar**-meh
Can you help us?	Pode ajudar-nos?	**pod**-eh ah-zhoo-**dar**-noosh
Can I / Can we...?	Posso / Podemos...?	**pos**-soo / poo-**day**-moosh
...have one	...ter um	tehr oon
...go free	...ir gratis	eer **grah**-teesh
...borrow that for a moment / an hour	...emprestar isto por um momento / uma hora	ayn-prehsh-**tar eesh**-too poor oon moh-**mayn**-too / **oo**-mah **oh**-rah
...use the toilet	...usar a casa de banho	oo-**zar** ah **kah**-sah deh **bahn**-yoo

English	Portuguese	Pronunciation
What? (didn't hear)	*Diga?*	**dee**-gah
What is this / that?	*O que é isto / aquilo?*	oo keh eh **eesh**-too / ah-**kee**-loo
What is better?	*O que é melhor?*	oo keh eh mil-**yor**
What's going on?	*Que se passa?*	keh seh **pah**-sah
When?	*Quando?*	**kwahn**-doo
What time is it?	*Que horas são?*	kee **oh**-rahsh sow
At what time?	*A que horas?*	ah kee **oh**-rahsh
On time?	*Pontual?*	pohn-too-**ahl**
Late?	*Atrasado?*	ah-trah-**zah**-doo
How long will it take?	*Quanto tempo leva?*	**kwahn**-too **tayn**-poo **leh**-vah
What time does this open / close?	*A que horas é que abre / fecha?*	ah kee **oh**-rahsh eh keh **ah**-breh / **fay**-shah
Is this open daily?	*Está aberto todos os dias?*	ish-**tah** ah-**behr**-too **toh**-doosh oosh **dee**-ahsh
What day is this closed?	*Que dia fecha?*	keh **dee**-ah **feh**-shah
Do you have...?	*Tem...?*	tayn
Where is...?	*Onde é...?*	**ohn**-deh eh
Where are...?	*Onde estão...?*	**ohn**-deh ish-**tow**
Where can I find...?	*A onde posso encontrar...?*	ah **ohn**-deh **pos**-soo ayn-kohn-**trar**
Where can we find...?	*A onde podemos encontrar...?*	ah **ohn**-deh poo-**day**-moosh ayn-kohn-**trar**
Where can I buy...?	*A onde posso comprar...?*	ah **ohn**-deh **pos**-soo kohn-**prar**
Where can we buy...?	*A onde podemos comprar...?*	ah **ohn**-deh poo-**day**-moosh kohn-**prar**
Is it necessary?	*É necessário?*	eh neh-seh-**sah**-ree-oo
Is it possible...?	*É possível...?*	eh **pos**-see-vehl
...to enter	*..entrar*	ayn-**trar**
...to picnic here	*...fazer picnic aqui*	fah-**zehr peek**-neek ah-**kee**
...to sit here	*...sentar aqui*	sayn-**tar** ah-**kee**
...to look	*...olhar*	ohl-**yar**
...to take a photo	*...tirar uma foto*	tee-**rar oo**-mah **foh**-toh
...to see a room	*...ver um quarto*	vehr oon **qwar**-too

Who?	*Quem?*	kayn
Why?	*Porquê?*	poor-**kay**
Why not?	*Porquê não?*	poor-**kay** now
Yes or no?	*Sim ou não?*	seeng oh now

To prompt a simple answer, ask, "*Sim ou não?*" You can turn a word or sentence into a question by asking it in a questioning tone. "*Isso é bom*" (It's good) becomes "*Isso é bom?*" (Is it good?).

Yin and Yang

cheap / expensive	*barato / caro*	bah-**rah**-too / **kah**-roo
big / small	*grande / pequeno*	**grahn**-deh / pay-**kay**-noo
hot / cold	*quente / frio*	**kayn**-teh / **free**-oo
cool / warm	*fresco / quente*	**frehsh**-koo / **kayn**-teh
open / closed	*aberto / fechado*	ah-**behr**-too / feh-**shah**-doo
push / pull	*empurre / puxe*	**ayn**-poor / push
entrance / exit	*entrada / saída*	ayn-**trah**-dah / sah-**ee**-dah
arrive / depart	*chegar / partir*	shay-**gar** / par-**teer**
early / late	*cedo / tarde*	**say**-doo / **tar**-deh
soon / later	*breve / mais tarde*	**bray**-veh / mĩ sh **tar**-deh
fast / slow	*rápido / lento*	**rah**-pee-doo / **layn**-too
here / there	*aqui / ali*	ah-**kee** / ah-**lee**
near / far	*perto / longe*	**pehr**-too / **lohn**-zheh
indoors / outdoors	*dentro / fora*	**dayn**-troo / **for**-ah
good / bad	*bom / mau*	bohn / mow
best / worst	*melhor / pior*	mil-**yor** / pee-**yor**
a little / lots	*um pouco / muito*	oon **poh**-koo / **mween**-too
more / less	*mais / menos*	mĩ sh / **may**-noosh
mine / yours	*meu / vosso*	**meh**-oo / **vas**-soo
this / that	*isto / aquilo*	**eesh**-too / ah-**kee**-loo
everybody / nobody	*toda gente / ninguem*	**toh**-dah **zhayn**-teh / neeng-**gayn**
easy / difficult	*fácil / difícil*	**fah**-seel / dee-**fee**-seel
left / right	*esquerda / direita*	ish-**kehr**-dah / dee-**ray**-tah

BASICS

up / down	cima / baixo	**see**-mah / **bī**-shoo
above / below	em cima / em baixo	ay<u>n</u> **see**-mah / ay<u>n</u> **bī**-shoo
young / old	jovem / velho	**zhav**-ay<u>n</u> / **vehl**-yoo
new / old	novo / velho	**noh**-voo / **vehl**-yoo
heavy / light	pesado / leve	peh-**zah**-doo / **leh**-veh
dark / light	escuro / claro	ish-**koo**-roo / **klah**-roo
happy / sad	feliz / triste	feh-**leesh** / **treesh**-teh
beautiful / ugly	lindo / feio	**leen**-doo / **fay**-oo
nice / mean	boa / má	**boh**-ah / mah
smart / stupid	inteligente / estúpido	in-teh-leh-**zhayn**-teh / ish-**too**-pee-doo
vacant / occupied	livre / ocupado	**lee**-vreh / oh-koo-**pah**-doo
with / without	com / sem	koh<u>n</u> / say<u>n</u>

Big Little Words

I	eu	**eh**-oo
you (formal)	você	voh-**say**
you (informal)	tu	too
we	nós	nohsh
he	ele	**eh**-leh
she	ela	**eh**-lah
they	eles	**eh**-lish
and	e	ee
at	á	ah
because	porque	**poor**-keh
but	mas	mahsh
by (via)	via	**vee**-ah
for	para	**pah**-rah
from	de	deh
here	aqui	ah-**kee**
if	se	seh
in	em	ay<u>n</u>
it	isto	**eesh**-too
not	não	now
now	agora	ah-**goh**-rah

BASICS

only	*só*	soh
or	*ou*	oh
that	*aquilo*	ah-**kee**-loo
this	*isto*	**eesh**-too
to	*para*	**pah**-rah
very	*muito*	**mween**-too

Perfectly Portuguese Expressions

Fantastic!	*Fantástico!*	fahn-**tahsh**-tee-koo
Perfect.	*Perfeito.*	pehr-**fay**-too
Wow!	*Fiche!*	**fee**-sheh
Good!	*Porreiro! Óptimo!*	poo-**ray**-roo, **ot**-tee-moo
Congratulations!	*Parabéns!*	pah-rah-**baynsh**
Really?	*A sério?*	ah **seh**-ree-oo
That's life.	*É a vida.*	eh ah **vee**-dah
No problem.	*Não tem problema.*	no<u>w</u> tay<u>n</u> proo-**blay**-mah
O.K.	*Está bem.*	ish-**tah** bay<u>n</u>
Good luck!	*Boa-sorte!*	boh-ah-**sor**-teh
Let's go!	*Vamos!*	**vah**-moosh

COUNTING

Numbers

0	*zero*	**zeh**-roo
1	*um*	oo<u>n</u>
2	*dois*	doysh
3	*três*	traysh
4	*quatro*	**kwah**-troo
5	*cinco*	**seeng**-koo
6	*seis*	saysh
7	*sete*	**seh**-teh
8	*oito*	**oy**-too
9	*nove*	**nah**-veh
10	*dez*	dehsh
11	*onze*	**ohn**-zeh
12	*doze*	**doh**-zeh
13	*treze*	**tray**-zeh
14	*catorze*	kah-**tor**-zeh
15	*quinze*	**keen**-zeh
16	*dezasseis*	deh-**zah**-saysh
17	*dezassete*	deh-zah-**seh**-teh
18	*dezoito*	deh-**zoy**-too
19	*dezanove*	deh-zah-**nah**-veh
20	*vinte*	**veen**-teh

21	*vinte e um*	**veen**-teh ee oo<u>n</u>
22	*vinte e dois*	**veen**-teh ee doysh
23	*vinte e três*	**veen**-teh ee traysh
30	*trinta*	**treen**-tah
31	*trinta e um*	**treen**-tah ee oo<u>n</u>
40	*quarenta*	kwah-**rayn**-tah
41	*quarenta e um*	kwah-**rayn**-tah ee oo<u>n</u>
50	*cinquenta*	seeng-**kwayn**-tah
60	*sessenta*	seh-**sayn**-tah
70	*setenta*	seh-**tayn**-tah
80	*oitenta*	oy-**tayn**-tah
90	*noventa*	noh-**vayn**-tah
100	*cem*	say<u>n</u>
101	*cento e um*	**sayn**-too ee oo<u>n</u>
102	*cento e dois*	**sayn**-too ee doysh
200	*duzentos*	doo-**zayn**-toosh
1000	*mil*	meel
2000	*dois mil*	doysh meel
2001	*dois mil e um*	doysh meel ee oo<u>n</u>
2002	*dois mil e dois*	doysh meel ee doysh
2003	*dois mil e três*	doysh meel ee traysh
2004	*dois mil e quatro*	doysh meel ee **kwah**-troo
2005	*dois mil e cinco*	doysh meel ee **seeng**-koo
2006	*dois mil e seis*	doysh meel ee saysh
2007	*dois mil e sete*	doysh meel ee **seh**-teh
2008	*dois mil e oito*	doysh meel ee **oy**-too
2009	*dois mil e nove*	doysh meel ee **nah**-veh
2010	*dois mil e dez*	doysh meel ee dehsh
million	*milhão*	mil-**yow**
billion	*bilhão*	bil-**yow**
number one	*número um*	**noo**-meh-roo oo<u>n</u>
first	*primeiro*	pree-**may**-roo
second	*segundo*	seh-**goon**-doo
third	*terceiro*	tehr-**say**-roo
once / twice	*uma vêz / duas vezes*	**oo**-mah vayz / **doo**-ahsh **veh**-zehsh

a quarter	um quarto	oo<u>n</u> **kwar**-too
a third	um terço	oo<u>n</u> **tehr**-soo
half	metade	meh-**tah**-deh
this much	esta	**ehsh**-tah
	quantidade	kwahn-tee-**dah**-deh
a dozen	uma dúzia	**oo**-mah **dooz**-yah
some	alguns	**ahl**-goonsh
enough	suficiente	soo-fee-see-**yayn**-teh
a handful	uma porção	**oo**-mah poor-**sow**
50%	cinquenta	seeng-**kwayn**-tah
	per cento	pehr **sayn**-too
100%	cem per cento	**sayn** pehr **sayn**-too

Money

Where is a cash machine?	Onde está uma caixa automática?	**ohn**-deh ish-**tah** **oo**-mah **kī**-shah ow-toh-**mah**-tee-kah
My ATM card has been...	O meu cartão ATM foi...	oo **meh**-oo kar-**tow** ah tay em foy
...demagnetized.	...desmagnetizado.	dish-mag-neh-tee-**zah**-doo
...stolen.	...roubado.	roh-**bah**-doo
...eaten by the machine.	...prêso na maquina.	**preh**-zoo nah **mah**-kee-nah
Do you accept credit cards?	Aceitam cartões de credito?	ah-say-**tayn** kar-**towsh** deh **kreh**-dee-too
Can you change dollars?	Pode trocar dollares?	**pod**-eh troo-**kar** **dol**-ah-rehsh
What is your exchange rate for dollars...?	Qual é a taxa de câmbio para o dollar...?	kwahl eh ah **tah**-shah deh **kahm**-bee-oo **pah**-rah oo **dol**-lar
...in traveler's checks	...em cheque de viagem	ayn **sheh**-keh deh vee-**ah**-zhayn
What is the commission?	Qual é a comissão?	kwahl eh ah koo-mee-**sow**

Any extra fee?	À taxa extra?	ah **tah**-shah **ish**-trah
Can you break this? (large to small bills)	Pode trocar?	**pod**-eh troo-**kar**
I would like...	Gostaria...	goosh-tah-**ree**-ah
...small bills.	...notas pequenas.	**not**-ahsh peh-**kay**-nahsh
...large bills.	...notas grandes.	**not**-ahsh **grahn**-dish
...coins.	...moedas.	moo-**eh**-dahsh
€ 50	cinquenta euros	seeng-**kwayn**-tah **yoo**-roosh
Is this a mistake?	Isto é um erro?	**eesh**-too eh oon **eh**-roo
This is incorrect.	Isto está incorreto.	**eesh**-too ish-**tah** een-koo-**rehk**-too
Did you print these today?	Foi imprimido hoje?	foy eem-pree-**mee**-doo **oh**-zheh
I'm broke.	Estou teso[a].	ish-**toh tay**-zoo
I'm poor.	Sou pobre.	soh **pob**-reh
I'm rich.	Sou rico[a].	soh **ree**-koo
I'm Bill Gates.	Sou o Bill Gates.	soh oo "Bill Gates"
Where is the nearest casino?	Onde é o casino mais próximo?	**ohn**-deh eh oo kah-**zee**-noh mīsh **proh**-see-moo

Portugal uses the euro currency. Euros (€) are divided into 100 cents. Use your common cents—cents are like pennies, and the currency has coins like nickels, dimes, and half-dollars.

Money Words

euro (€)	euro	**yoo**-roh
cents	cent	sehnt
money	dinheiro	deen-**yay**-roo
cash	dinheiro	deen-**yay**-roo
cash machine	caixa automática, Multibanco	**kī**-shah ow-toh-**mah**-tee-kah, mool-tee-**bahng**-koo
bank	banco	**bang**-koo
credit card	cartão de crédito	kar-**tow** deh **kreh**-dee-too

COUNTING

change money	troca de dinheiro	**troo**-kah deh deen-**yay**-roo
exchange	troca	**troo**-kah
buy / sell	comprar / vender	koh<u>n</u>-**prar** / vay<u>n</u>-**dehr**
commission	comissão	koo-mee-**sow**
traveler's check	cheques de viagem	**sheh**-kehsh deh vee-**ah**-zhay<u>n</u>
cash advance	levantamento em caixa automática	leh-vahn-tah-**mayn**-too ay<u>n</u> **kī**-shah ow-toh-**mah**-tee-kah
cashier	caixa	**kī**-shah
bills	notas	**not**-ahsh
coins	moedas	moo-**eh**-dahsh
receipt	recibo	reh-**see**-boo

COUNTING

Commissions for changing traveler's checks can be steep in Portugal. It's easier and cheaper to use your ATM or debit card to withdraw cash from a *caixa automática* or *Multibanco* (cash machine). Cash machines are multilingual, but if you like to experiment, *anular* means "cancel," *corrigir* is "correct," and *continuar* means "continue."

KEY PHRASES: MONEY

euro (€)	euro	**yoo**-roh
money	dinheiro	deen-**yay**-roo
cash	dinheiro	deen-**yay**-roo
credit card	cartão de crédito	kar-**tow** deh **kreh**-dee-too
bank	banco	**bang**-koo
cash machine	caixa automática, Multibanco	**kī**-shah ow-toh-**mah**-tee-kah, mool-tee-**bahng**-koo
Where is a cash machine?	Onde está uma caixa automática?	**ohn**-deh ish-**tah** **oo**-mah **kī**-shah ow-toh-**mah**-tee-kah
Do you accept credit cards?	Aceitam cartões de credito?	ah-say-**tayn** kar-**towsh** deh **kreh**-dee-too

Time

What time is it?	*Que horas são?*	kee **oh**-rahsh sow
It's...	*São...*	sow
...8:00 in the morning.	*...oito horas da manhã.*	**oy**-too **oh**-rahsh dah ming-**yah**
...16:00.	*...dezasseis horas.*	deh-zah-**saysh oh**-rahsh
...4:00 in the afternoon.	*...quatro da tarde.*	**kwar**-too dah **tar**-deh
...10:30 (in the evening).	*...dez horas e meia (da noite).*	dehsh **oh**-rahsh ee **may**-ah (dah **noy**-teh)
...a quarter past nine.	*...nove e um quarto.*	**nah**-veh ee oon **kwar**-too
...a quarter to eleven.	*...um quarto para as onze.*	oon **kwar**-too **pah**-rah ahz **ohn**-zeh
...noon.	*...meio-dia.*	may-oo-**dee**-ah
...midnight.	*...meia-noite.*	may-ah-**noy**-teh
...early / late.	*...cedo / tarde.*	**say**-doo / **tar**-deh
...on time.	*...pontual.*	pohn-too-**ahl**
...sunrise.	*...nascer do sol.*	**nahsh**-sehr doo sohl
...sunset.	*...por do sol.*	poor doo sohl
It's my bedtime.	*Está na hora de dormir.*	ish-**tah** nah **oh**-rah deh dor-**meer**

COUNTING

KEY PHRASES: TIME

minute	*minuto*	mee-**noo**-too
hour	*hora*	**oh**-rah
day	*dia*	**dee**-ah
week	*semana*	seh-**mah**-nah
What time is it?	*Que horas são?*	kee **oh**-rahsh sow
It's...	*São...*	sow
...8:00.	*...oito horas.*	**oy**-too **oh**-rahsh
...16:00.	*...dezasseis horas.*	deh-zah-**saysh oh**-rahsh
What time does this open / close?	*A que horas é que abre / fecha?*	ah kee **oh**-rahsh eh keh **ah**-breh / **fay**-shah

Timely Expressions

I'll return / We'll return at 11:20.	Volto / Voltamos as onze e vinte.	**vohl**-too / vohl-**tah**-moosh ahz **ohn**-zeh ee **veen**-teh
I'll / We'll be there by 18:00.	Vou / Vamos estar lá por volta das dezoito horas.	voh / **vah**-moosh ish-**tar** lah poor **vohl**-tah dahsh deh-**zoy**-too **oh**-rahsh
When is checkout time?	Qual é a hora da saída?	kwahl eh ah **oh**-rah dah sah-**ee**-dah
What time does...?	A que horas...?	ah kee **oh**-rahsh
...this open / close	...é que abre / fecha	eh keh **ah**-breh / **fay**-shah
...this train / bus leave for ___	...este comboio / auto-carro parte para ___	**ehsh**-tah koh<u>n</u>-**boy**-oo / ow-too-**kah**-roo **par**-teh **pah**-rah
...the next train / bus leave for ___	...o próximo comboio / auto-carro parte para___	oo **proh**-see-moo koh<u>n</u>-**boy**-oo / ow-too-**kah**-roo **par**-teh **pah**-rah
...the train / bus arrive in ___	...o comboio / auto-carro chega em ___	oo koh<u>n</u>-**boy**-oo / ow-too-**kah**-roo **shay**-geh ay<u>n</u>
I want / We want to take the 16:30 train.	Quero / Queremos apanhar o comboio das dezesseis e trinta.	**kay**-roo / keh-**ray**-moosh ah-payn-**yar** oo koh<u>n</u>-**boy**-oo dahsh deh-zah-**saysh** ee **treen**-tah
Is the train...?	O comboio está... ?	oo koh<u>n</u>-**boy**-oo ish-**tah**
Is the bus...?	O auto-carro está...?	oo ow-too-**kah**-roo ish-**tah**
...early / late	...adiantado / atrasado	ah-dee-ahn-**tah**-doo / ah-trah-**zah**-doo
...on time	...na hora	nah **oh**-rah

In Portugal, the 24-hour clock (or military time) is used mainly for train, bus, and ferry schedules. Informally, the Portuguese use the same 12-hour clock we do.

About Time

minute	minuto	mee-**noo**-too
hour	hora	**oh**-rah
in the morning	da manhã	dah ming-**yah**
in the afternoon	da tarde	dah **tar**-deh
in the evening	da noite	dah **noy**-teh
night	noite	**noy**-teh
at 6:00 sharp	as seis horas em ponto	ahsh saysh **oh**-rahsh ayn **pohn**-too
from 8:00 to 10:00	das oito ás dez	dahz **oy**-too ahzh dehsh
in half an hour	daqui a meia hora	dah-**kee** ah **may**-ah **oh**-rah
in one hour	em uma hora	ayn **oo**-mah **oh**-rah
in three hours	em trez horas	ayn traysh **oh**-rahsh
anytime	a qualquer hora	ah kwahl-**kehr oh**-rah
immediately	imediatamente	ee-meh-dee-ah-tah-**mayn**-teh
every hour	todas as horas	**toh**-dahsh ahsh **oh**-rahsh
every day	todos os dias	**toh**-doosh oosh **dee**-ahsh
last	último	**ool**-tee-moo
this	este	**ehsh**-teh
next	próximo	**proh**-see-moo
May 15	quinze de Maio	**keen**-zeh deh **mah**-yoo
high season	época alta	**eh**-poh-kah **ahl**-tah
low season	época baixa	**eh**-poh-kah **bī**-shah
in the future	no futuro	noo foo-**too**-roo
in the past	no passado	noo pah-**sah**-doo

The Day

day	dia	**dee**-ah
today	hoje	**oh**-zheh
yesterday	ontem	**ohn**-tayn

COUNTING

tomorrow	amanhã	ah-ming-**yah**
tomorrow	amanhã de	ah-ming-**yah** deh
morning	manhã	ming-**yah**
day after	depois de	day-**pwaysh** deh
tomorrow	amanhã	ah-ming-**yah**

The Week

week	semana	seh-**mah**-nah
last week	na semana passada	nah seh-**mah**-nah pah-**sah**-dah
this week	esta semana	**ehsh**-tah seh-**mah**-nah
next week	para a próxima semana	**pah**-rah ah **proh**-see-mah seh-**mah**-nah
Monday	segunda-feira	seh-goon-dah-**fay**-rah
Tuesday	terça-feira	tehr-sah-**fay**-rah
Wednesday	quarta-feira	kwar-tah-**fay**-rah
Thursday	quinta-feira	keen-tah-**fay**-rah
Friday	sexta-feira	saysh-tah-**fay**-rah
Saturday	sábado	**sah**-bah-doo
Sunday	domingo	doo-**meeng**-goo

The Month

month	mês	maysh
January	Janeiro	zhah-**nay**-roo
February	Fevereiro	feh-veh-**ray**-roo
March	Março	**mar**-soo
April	Abril	**ah**-breel
May	Maio	**mah**-yoo
June	Junho	**zhoon**-yoo
July	Julho	**zhool**-yoo
August	Agosto	ah-**gohsh**-too
September	Setembro	seh-**tayn**-broo
October	Outubro	oh-**too**-broo
November	Novembro	noo-**vayn**-broo
December	Dezembro	deh-**zayn**-broo

COUNTING

The Year

year	*ano*	**ah**-noo
spring	*primavera*	pree-mah-**veh**-rah
summer	*verão*	veh-**row**
fall	*outono*	oh-**toh**-noo
winter	*inverno*	een-**vehr**-noo

Holidays and Happy Days

holiday	*feriado*	feh-ree-**ah**-doo
national holiday	*feriado*	feh-ree-**ah**-doo
	nacional	nah-see-oo-**nahl**
religious holiday	*feriado*	feh-ree-**ah**-doo
	religioso	ray-lee-zhee-**oh**-zoo
Is today / tomorrow	*Hoje / Amanhã*	**oh**-zheh / ah-ming-**yah**
a holiday?	*é feriado?*	eh feh-ree-**ah**-doo
Is a holiday	*Há um feriado*	ah oon feh-ree-**ah**-doo
coming up	*em bréve?*	ayn **breh**-veh /
soon? When?	*Quando?*	**kwahn**-doo
What is the	*Qual é o*	kwahl eh oo
holiday?	*feriado?*	feh-ree-**ah**-doo
Merry Christmas!	*Feliz Natal!*	feh-**leesh** nah-**tahl**
Happy New Year!	*Feliz Ano Novo!*	feh-**leesh** ah-noo **noh**-voo
Easter	*Páscoa*	**pahsh**-kwah
Happy wedding	*Feliz*	feh-**leesh**
anniversary!	*aniversário*	ah-nee-vehr-**sah**-ree-oo
	de casamento!	deh kah-zah-**mayn**-too
Happy birthday!	*Feliz*	feh-**leesh**
	aniversário!	ah-nee-vehr-**sah**-ree-oo

The Portuguese sing "Happy Birthday" to the same tune we do, but they sing the tune twice, using these words: *Parabéns a você, nesta data querida, muitas felicidades, muitos anos de vida. Hoje é dia de festa, cantam as nossas almas, para* (fill in name), *uma salva de palmas!* Whew!

Portugal celebrates its Independence Day on December 1. Other major holidays include Liberty Day (April 25), Good Friday and Easter, Camões Day (June 10, in honor of the Portuguese poet Luis de Camões), Assumption of Mary (August 15), and Republic Day (October 5).

TRAVELING

Flights

All airports post bilingual signs in the local language and in English. Also, nearly all airport service personnel and travel agents speak English these days. Still, these words and phrases could conceivably come in handy.

Making a Reservation

I'd like to... my reservation / ticket.	*Quero... minha reserva / bilhete.*	**kay**-roo... **meen**-yah ray-**zehr**-vah / beel-**yeh**-teh
We'd like to... our reservation / ticket.	*Queremos... nossa reserva / bilhetes.*	keh-**ray**-moosh... **noh**-sah ray-**zehr**-vah / beel-**yeh**-tish
...confirm	*...confirmar*	kohn-feer-**mar**
...change	*...mudar*	moo-**dar**
...cancel	*...cancelar*	kahn-seh-**lar**
aisle seat	*assento à janela*	ah-**sayn**-too ah zhah-**neh**-lah
window seat	*assento sobre o corredor*	ah-**sayn**-too **soh**-breh oo koo-ray-**dor**

25

At the Airport

Which terminal?	Qual terminal?	kwahl tehr-mee-**nahl**
international flights	vôos internacionais	vohz **een**-tehr-nah-see-oh-nī sh
domestic flights	vôos internos, vôos domesticos	vohz een-**tehr**-noosh, vohzh doh-**maysh**-tee-koosh
arrival	chegada	shay-**gah**-dah
departure	partida	par-**tee**-dah
baggage check or claim	bagagem	bah-**gah**-zhay<u>n</u>
check in	check in	"check in"
Nothing to declare.	Nada a declarar.	**nah**-dah ah deh-klah-**rar**
I have only carry-on luggage.	Só tenho bagagem de mão.	soh **tayn**-yoo bah-**gah**-zhayn deh mo<u>w</u>
flight number	numero do vôo	**noo**-meh-roh doo voh
departure gate	porta de partida	**por**-tah deh par-**tee**-dah
duty free	imposto não pago, tax free	eem-**pohsh**-too no<u>w</u> **pah**-goo, "tax free"
luggage cart	carrinho de malas	kah-**reen**-yoh deh **mah**-lahsh
jet lag	jet lag	"jet lag"

Getting to/from the Airport

Approximately how much is a taxi ride to...?	Mais ou menos quanto custa a viagem por taxi para...?	mī sh oh **may**-noosh **kwah**<u>n</u>-too **koosh**-tah ah vee-**ah**-zhay<u>n</u> poor **tahk**-see **pah**-rah
...downtown	...o centro	oo **sayn**-troo
...the train station	...a estação de comboio	ah ish-tah-**sow** deh koh<u>n</u>-**boy**-yoo
...the airport	...o aeroporto	oo ah-roh-**por**-too
Does a bus (or train) run...?	O auto-carro (o comboio) vai...?	oo ow-too-**kah**-roo (oo koh<u>n</u>-**boy**-yoo) vī

TRAVELING

...from the airport	...do aeroporto	doo ah-roh-**por**-too
to downtown	até o centro	ah-**tay** oo **sayn**-troo
...to the airport	...para o aeroporto	**pah**-rah oo ah-roh-**por**-too
from downtown	do centro	doo **sayn**-troo
How much is it?	Quanto custa?	**kwahn**-too **koosh**-tah
Where does it leave from...?	De onde parte...?	deh **ohn**-deh **par**-teh
Where does it arrive...?	De onde chega...?	deh **ohn**-deh **shay**-gah
...at the airport?	...no aeroporto?	noo ah-roh-**por**-too
...downtown?	...no centro?	noo **sayn**-troo
How often does it run?	Com que frequência passa?	kohn keh freh-**kwayn**-see-ah **pah**-sah

Trains

The Train Station

Where is the...?	Onde é a...?	**ohn**-deh eh ah
...train station	...estação de comboio	ish-tah-**sow** deh kohn-**boy**-yoo
Portuguese State Railways	Caminhos de Ferro	kah-**meen**-yoosh deh **fehr**-roo
train information	informação sobre comboios	een-for-mah-**sow** **soh**-breh kohn-**boy**-yoosh
train	comboio	kohn-**boy**-yoo
high-speed train	comboio expresso	kohn-**boy**-yoo ish-**pray**-soo
fast / faster	rápido / mais rápido	**rah**-pee-doo / mī sh **rah**-pee-doo
arrival	chegada	shay-**gah**-dah
departure	partida	par-**tee**-dah
delay	atraso	ah-**trah**-zoo

TRAVELING

toilet	casa de banho	**kah**-zah deh **bahn**-yoo
waiting room	sala de espera	**sah**-lah deh ish-**peh**-rah
lockers	depósito de bagagem	day-**poh**-see-too deh bah-**gah**-zhayn
baggage check room	despacho de bagagem	dish-**pah**-shoo deh bah-**gah**-zhayn
lost and found office	perdidos e achados	pehr-**dee**-doosh ee ah-**shah**-doosh
tourist information	informação turistica	een-for-mah-**sow** too-**reesh**-tee-kah
to the trains	para os comboios	**pah**-rah oosh kohn-**boy**-yoosh
to the platforms	acesso ão cais	ah-**seh**-soo ow kī sh
platform	cais	kī sh
track	linha	**leen**-yah
train car	carruagem	kar-**wah**-zhayn
dining car	carruagem restaurante	kar-**wah**-zhayn rish-toh-**rahn**-teh
sleeper car	carruagem cama	kar-**wah**-zhayn **kah**-mah
conductor	condutor	kohn-doo-**toor**

Trains in Portugal come in several types. Along with the various local and milk-run trains (*Regional, Suburbano*), there are:

• the slow *Interregional* (IR) trains,
• the medium-speed *Intercidades* (IC) trains, and
• the fast *Alfa Pendular* (AP) train between Lisbon and Porto.

Faster trains are more expensive, but all are cheaper per mile than their northern European counterparts. Off the main Lisbon-Coimbra-Porto train lines, buses are usually a better bet. In cases where buses and trains serve the same destination, the bus is often more efficient, offering more frequent connections and sometimes a more central station.

KEY PHRASES: TRAINS

train station	*estação de comboio*	ish-tah-**sow** deh kohn-**boy**-yoo
train	*comboio*	kohn-**boy**-yoo
ticket	*bilhete*	beel-**yeh**-teh
transfer (verb)	*mudar*	moo-**dar**
supplement	*suplemento*	soo-pleh-**mayn**-too
arrival	*chegada*	shay-**gah**-dah
departure	*partida*	par-**tee**-dah
platform	*cais*	kī sh
track	*linha do comboio*	**leen**-yah doo kohn-**boy**-yoo
train car	*carruagem*	kar-**wah**-zhayn
A ticket to ___.	*Um bilhete para ___.*	oon beel-**yeh**-teh **pah**-rah
Two tickets to ___.	*Dois bilhetes para ___.*	doysh beel-**yeh**-tish **pah**-rah
When is the next train?	*Quando é o próximo comboio?*	**kwahn**-doo eh oo **proh**-see-moo kohn-**boy**-oo
Where does the train leave from?	*De onde é que parte o comboio?*	deh **ohn**-deh eh keh **par**-teh oo kohn-**boy**-yoo
Which train to ___?	*Que comboio para ___?*	keh kohn-**boy**-yoo **pah**-rah

TRAVELING

Getting a Ticket

Where can I buy a ticket?	*Onde posso comprar um bilhete?*	**ohn**-deh **pos**-soo kohn-**prar** oon beel-**yeh**-teh
A ticket to ___.	*Um bilhete para ___.*	oon beel-**yeh**-teh **pah**-rah
Where can we buy tickets?	*Onde podemos comprar bilhetes?*	**ohn**-deh poo-**day**-moosh kohn-**prar** beel-**yeh**-tish
Two tickets to ___.	*Dois bilhetes para ___.*	doysh beel-**yeh**-tish **pah**-rah

English	Portuguese	Pronunciation
Is this the line for...?	Esta é a fila para...?	**ehsh**-tah eh ah **fee**-lah **pah**-rah
...tickets	...bilhetes	beel-**yeh**-tish
...reservations	...reservas	reh-**zehr**-vahsh
How much is a ticket to ___?	Quanto custa o bilhete para ___?	**kwahn**-too **koosh**-tah oo beel-**yeh**-teh **pah**-rah
Is this ticket valid for ___?	Este bilhete é válido por___?	**ehsh**-teh beel-**yeh**-teh eh **vah**-lee-doo poor
How long is this ticket valid?	Por quanto tempo é válido o bilhete?	poor **kwahn**-too **tayn**-poo eh **vah**-lee-doo oo beel-**yeh**-teh
When is the next train?	Quando é o próximo comboio?	**kwahn**-doo eh oo **proh**-see-moo kohn-**boy**-oo
Do you have a schedule for all trains departing for ___ today / tomorrow?	Você tem o horário dos comboios que partem para ___ hoje / amanhã?	voh-**say** tayn oo oh-**rah**-ree-oo doosh kohn-**boy**-oosh keh **par**-tayn **pah**-rah ___ **oh**-zheh / ah-ming-**yah**
I'd like to leave...	Gostaria de partir...	goosh-tah-**ree**-ah deh par-**teer**
We'd like to leave...	Gostaríamos de partir...	goosh-tah-**ree**-ah-moosh deh par-**teer**
I'd like to arrive...	Gostaria de chegar...	goosh-tah-**ree**-ah deh shay-**gar**
We'd like to arrive...	Gostaríamos de chegar...	goosh-tah-**ree**-ah-moosh deh shay-**gar**
...by ___.	...por ___.	poor
...in the morning.	...de manhã.	deh ming-**yah**
...in the afternoon.	...de tarde.	deh **tar**-deh
...in the evening.	...ao anoitecer.	ow ah-noy-teh-**sehr**
Is there a...?	Há um...?	ah oon
...earlier train	...comboio mais cedo	kohn-**boy**-oo mī sh **say**-doo
...later train	...comboio mais tarde	kohn-**boy**-oo mī sh **tar**-deh
...overnight train	...comboio durante a noite	kohn-**boy**-oo doo-**rayn**-teh ah **noy**-teh

...cheaper train	...comboio mais barato	koh<u>n</u>-**boy**-oo mī sh bah-**rah**-too
...local train	...comboio local	koh<u>n</u>-**boy**-oo loo-**kahl**
...express train	...comboio rápido (expresso)	koh<u>n</u>-**boy**-oo **rah**-pee-doo (ish-**pray**-soo)
Is there a cheaper option?	Há um opção mais barata?	ah oo<u>n</u> ohp-**sow** mī sh bah-**rah**-tah
What track does it leave from?	De que linha parte?	deh keh **leen**-yah **par**-teh
What track?	Que linha sai?	keh **leen**-yah sī
On time?	Pontual?	poh<u>n</u>-too-**ahl**
Late?	Atrasado?	ah-trah-**zah**-doo

Reservations, Supplements, and Discounts

Is a reservation required?	É preciso reservar?	eh preh-**see**-zoo reh-zehr-**var**
I'd like to reserve a...	Gostaria de reservar um...	goosh-tah-**ree**-ah deh reh-zehr-**var** oo<u>n</u>
...seat.	...assento.	ah-**sayn**-too
...berth (couchette).	...lugar sentado.	loo-**gar** say<u>n</u>-**tah**-doo
...sleeper.	...camarote.	kah-mah-**roh**-teh
...the entire train.	...o comboio todo.	oo koh<u>n</u>-**boy**-oo **toh**-doo
We'd like to reserve...	Gostaríamos de reservar...	goosh-tah-**ree**-ah-moosh deh reh-zehr-**var**
...two seats.	...dois lugares.	doysh loo-**garsh**
...two berths (couchettes).	...dois lugares sentados.	doysh loo-**garsh** say<u>n</u>-**tah**-doosh
...two beds in a sleeper car.	...dois camarotes.	doysh kah-mah-**roh**-tish
Is there a supplement?	Há um suplemento?	ah oo<u>n</u> soo-pleh-**mayn**-too
Does my railpass cover the supplement?	O meu passe cobre os extras?	oo **meh**-oo **pah**-seh **koh**-breh ooz **ish**-trahsh

Is there a discount for...?	*Tem desconto para...?*	tay<u>n</u> dish-**koh<u>n</u>**-too **pah**-rah
...youth	*...jovens*	**zhah**-vay<u>n</u>sh
...seniors	*...pessoas de terceira idade*	peh-**soh**-ahsh deh tehr-**say**-rah ee-**dah**-deh
...families	*...familia*	fah-**meel**-yah

Ticket Talk

ticket window	*bilhetes, bilhetaria*	beel-**yay**-tish, beel-yeh-tah-**ree**-ah
reservations window	*reservas*	reh-**zehr**-vahsh
national / international	*nacional / internacional*	nah-see-oh-**nahl** / **een**-tehr-nah-see-oh-nahl
ticket	*bilhete*	beel-**yeh**-teh
one way	*uma ida*	**oo**-mah ee-**dah**
roundtrip	*ida e volta*	**ee**-dah ee **vohl**-tah
first class	*primeira classe*	pree-**may**-rah **klah**-seh
second class	*segunda classe*	seh-**goon**-dah **klah**-seh
non-smoking	*não fumar*	no<u>w</u> foo-**mar**
validate	*validade*	vah-lee-**dah**-deh
schedule	*horário*	oh-**rah**-ree-oo
departure	*partida*	par-**tee**-dah
direct	*directo*	dee-**reh**-too
transfer (verb)	*mudar*	moo-**dar**
connection	*conexão*	koo-nehk-**sow**
with supplement	*com suplemento*	koh<u>n</u> soo-pleh-**may<u>n</u>**-too
reservation	*reserva*	ray-**zehr**-vah
seat...	*assento...*	ah-**say<u>n</u>**-too
...by the window	*...à janela*	ah zhah-**neh**-lah
...on the aisle	*...sobre o corredor*	**soh**-breh oo koo-ray-**dor**
berth	*beliche*	beh-**lee**-sheh
...upper	*...em cima*	ay<u>n</u> **see**-mah
...middle	*...no meio*	noo **may**-oh
...lower	*...em baixo*	ay<u>n</u> **bī**-shoo
refund	*reembolso*	reh-ay<u>n</u>-**bohl**-soo
reduced fare	*tarifa reduzida*	tah-**ree**-fah reh-doo-**zee**-dah

Changing Trains

Is it direct?	*É directo?*	eh dee-**reh**-too
Must I transfer?	*É preciso mudar?*	eh preh-**see**-zoo moo-**dar**
Must we transfer?	*Precisamos*	preh-see-**zah**-moosh
	de mudar?	deh moo-**dar**
When? Where?	*Quando? Onde?*	**kwahn**-doo / **ohn**-deh
Do I / Do we	*Faço / Fazemos*	**fah**-soo / fah-**zeh**-moosh
change	*mudança*	moo-**dahn**-sah
here for ___?	*aqui para ___?*	ah-**kee pah**-rah
Where do I / do we	*Onde faço /*	**ohn**-deh **fah**-soo /
change for ___?	*fazemos*	fah-**zeh**-moosh
	mudança para ___?	moo-**dahn**-sah **pah**-rah
At what time...?	*A que horas...?*	ah kee **oh**-rahsh
From what track	*De qual linha a*	deh kwahl **leen**-yah ah
does my / our	*minha / nossa*	**meen**-yah / **noh**-sah
connecting train	*conexão parte?*	koo-nehk-**sow par**-teh
leave?		
How many	*Quantos*	**kwahn**-toosh
minutes in ___ to	*minutos em ___*	mee-**noo**-toosh ayn ___
change trains?	*para mudar de*	**pah**-rah moo-**dar** deh
	comboios?	kohn-**boy**-oosh

On the Platform

Where is...?	*Onde é...?*	**ohn**-deh eh
Is this...?	*Isto é ...?*	**eesh**-toh eh
...the train to ___	*...o comboio para ___*	oo kohn-**boy**-yoo **pah**-rah
Which train to ___?	*Que comboio para ___?*	keh kohn-**boy**-yoo **pah**-rah
Which train	*Que carruagem*	keh kar-**wah**-zhayn
car for ___?	*para ___?*	**pah**-rah
Where is	*Onde é a*	**ohn**-deh eh ah
first class?	*primeira classe?*	pree-**may**-rah **klah**-seh
...front / middle /	*...frente / meio /*	**frayn**-teh / **may**-oh /
back	*trás*	trahsh
Where can I	*Onde posso*	**ohn**-deh **pos**-soo
validate	*validar o*	vah-lee-**dar** oo
my ticket?	*meu bilhete?*	**meh**-oo beel-**yeh**-teh

On the Train

Is this (seat) free?	*Está livre?*	ish-**tah** lee-vreh
May I / May we...?	*Posso / Podemos...?*	**pos**-soo / poo-**day**-moosh
...sit here (I / we)	*...sentar-me / sentar-nos aqui*	say<u>n</u>-**tar**-meh / say<u>n</u>-**tar**-nooz ah-**kee**
...open the window	*...abra a janela*	**ah**-brah ah zhah-**neh**-lah
...eat your meal	*...coma a sua comida*	**koh**-mah ah **soo**-ah koh-**mee**-dah
Save my place?	*Guarde o meu lugar?*	**gwar**-deh oo **meh**-oo loo-**gar**
Save our places?	*Guarde os nossos lugares?*	**gwar**-deh oosh **nos**-oosh loo-**garsh**
That's my seat.	*Este é o meu lugar.*	**ehsh**-teh eh oo **meh**-oo loo-**gar**
These are our seats.	*Esses são os nossos lugares.*	**ays**-sehsh so<u>w</u> oosh **nos**-oosh loo-**garsh**
Where are you going?	*Onde é que vai?*	**ohn**-deh eh keh vī
I'm going to ___.	*Vou para ___.*	voh **pah**-rah
We're going to ___.	*Nós vamos para ___.*	nohsh **vah**-moosh **pah**-rah
Tell me when to get off?	*Diga-me quando devo sair?*	**dee**-gah-meh **kwahn**-doo **deh**-voo sah-**eer**
Tell us when to get off?	*Diga-nos quando devemos sair?*	**dee**-gah-noosh **kwahn**-doo deh-**veh**-moosh sah-**eer**
Where is a (good-looking) conductor?	*Onde está o condutor (bonitaô)?*	**ohn**-deh ish-**tah** oo kohn-doo-**toor** (boo-nee-to<u>w</u>)
Does this train stop in ___?	*Esse comboio para em ___?*	**ays**-seh koh<u>n</u>-**boy**-oo **pah**-rah ay<u>n</u>
When will it arrive in ___?	*Quando chega em ___?*	**kwahn**-doo **shay**-gah ay<u>n</u>
When will it arrive?	*Quando é que vai chegar?*	**kwahn**-doo eh keh vī shay-**gar**

TRAVELING

Major Rail Lines in Iberia

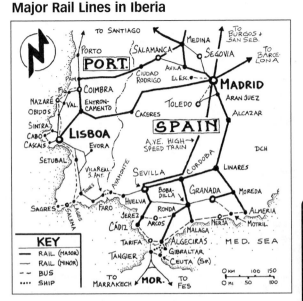

Reading Train and Bus Schedules

até	until
atrasado	late
chegada	arrival
de	from
destino	destination
diário	daily
dias	days
dias de semana	weekdays
domingos e feriados	Sundays and holidays
excepto	except
hora	time

linha		track
para		to
partida		departure
sabádo		Saturday
só		only
também		also
todo		every
1-5, 6, 7		Monday-Friday, Saturday, Sunday

Going Places

Portugal	*Portugal*	poor-too-**gahl**
Lisbon	*Lisboa*	leezh-**boh**-ah
Spain	*Espanha*	ish-**pahn**-yah
Morocco	*Marrocos*	mah-**rak**-oosh
Gibraltar	*Gibraltar*	zhee-brahl-**tar**
Austria	*Austria*	**owsh**-tree-ah
Belgium	*Belgica*	behl-**zhee**-kah
Czech Republic	*Republica Checa*	reh-**poob**-lee-kah **sheh**-kah
France	*França*	**frahn**-sah
Germany	*Alemanha*	ah-leh-**mahn**-yah
Great Britain	*Inglaterra*	eeng-glah-**tehr**-rah
Greece	*Grécia*	**gray**-see-ah
Ireland	*Irlanda*	eer-**lahn**-dah
Italy	*Italia*	ee-**tahl**-yah
Netherlands	*Holanda*	oh-**lahn**-dah
Scandinavia	*Escandinavia*	ish-kan-dee-**nahv**-yah
Switzerland	*Suiça*	**swee**-sah
Turkey	*Turkia*	**toor**-kee-ah
Europe	*Europa*	eh-oo-**roh**-pah
EU (European Union)	*UE (União Europeia)*	oo eh (oo-nee-**ow** eh-oo-roh-peh-**ee**-ah)
Russia	*Russia*	**roo**-see-ah
Africa	*Africa*	**ah**-free-kah
United States	*Estados Unidos*	ish-**tah**-doosh oo-**nee**-doosh
Canada	*Canadá*	kah-nah-**dah**
the world	*o mundo*	oo **moon**-doo

TRAVELING

Buses and Subways

At the Bus Station or Metro Stop

ticket	*bilhete*	beel-**yeh**-teh
city bus	*autocarro*	ow-too-**kah**-roo
long-distance bus	*camioneta*	kahm-yoo-**neh**-tah
bus stop	*paragem de autocarro*	pah-**rah**-zhayn deh ow-too-**kah**-roo
bus station	*terminal das camionetas*	tehr-mee-**nahl** dahsh kahm-yoo-**neh**-tahsh
subway	*metro*	**meh**-troo
subway station	*estação do metro*	ish-tah-**sow** doo **meh**-troo
subway map	*mapa do metro*	**mah**-pah doo **meh**-troo
subway entrance	*entrada do metro*	ayn-**trah**-dah doo **meh**-troo
subway stop	*paragem do metro*	pah-**rah**-zhayn doo **meh**-troo
subway exit	*saída do metro*	sah-**ee**-dah doo **meh**-troo
direct	*directo*	dee-**reh**-too
connection	*conexão*	koo-nehk-**sow**
pickpocket	*carteirista*	kar-tay-**rish**-tah

TRAVELING

Taking Buses and Subways

How do I get to ___?	*Como vou para ___?*	**koh**-moo voh **pah**-rah
How do we get to ___?	*Como vamos para ___?*	**koh**-moo **vah**-moosh **pah**-rah
How much is a ticket?	*Quanto custa um bilhete?*	**kwahn**-too **koosh**-tah oon beel-**yeh**-teh

Where can I buy a ticket?	A onde posso comprar um bilhete?	ah **ohn**-deh **pos**-soo koh<u>n</u>-**prar** oo<u>n</u> beel-**yeh**-teh
Where can we buy tickets?	Onde podemos comprar bilhetes?	**ohn**-deh poo-**day**-moosh koh<u>n</u>-**prar** beel-**yeh**-tish
Is this ticket valid (for ___)?	Este bilhete é válido (por ___)?	**ehsh**-teh beel-**yeh**-teh eh **vah**-lee-doo (poor)
Is there a one-day pass?	Há bilhetes para um dia inteiro?	ah beel-**yeh**-tish **pah**-rah oo<u>n</u> **dee**-ah een-**tay**-roo
Which bus to ___?	Que autocarro para ___?	keh ow-too-**kah**-roo **pah**-rah
Does it stop at ___?	Para em ___?	**pah**-rah ay<u>n</u>
Which metro stop for ___?	Qual é a paragem para ___?	kwahl eh ah pah-**rah**-zhay<u>n</u> **pah**-rah
One ticket, please.	Um bilhete, por favor.	oo<u>n</u> beel-**yeh**-teh poor fah-**vor**
Two tickets.	dois bilhetes.	doysg beel-**yeh**-tish
Must I transfer?	É preciso mudar?	eh preh-**see**-zoo moo-**dar**
Must we transfer?	Precisamos de mudar?	preh-see-**zah**-moosh deh moo-**dar**
When does the... leave?	Quando é que... parte?	**kwahn**-doo eh keh... **par**-teh
...first	...o primeiro	oh pree-**may**-roo
...next	...o próximo	oh **proh**-see-moo
...last	...o último	oh **ool**-tee-moo
...bus / subway	...autocarro / metro	ow-too-**kah**-roo / **meh**-troo
What's the frequency per hour / day?	Quantas vêzes por hora / dia?	**kwahn**-tahsh **vay**-zish poor **oh**-rah / **dee**-ah
Where does it leave from?	De onde parte?	deh **ohn**-deh **par**-teh
What time does it leave?	A que horas parte?	ah kee **oh**-rahsh **par**-teh
I'm going to___.	Vou para ___.	voh **pah**-rah

We are going to___.	Nós vamos para ___.	nohsh **vah**-moosh **pah**-rah
Tell me when to get off?	Diga-me quando devo sair?	**dee**-gah-meh **kwahn**-doo **deh**-voo sah-**eer**
Tell us when to get off?	Diga-nos quando devemos sair?	**dee**-gah-noosh **kwahn**-doo deh-**veh**-moosh sah-**eer**

KEY PHRASES: BUSES AND SUBWAYS

bus	auto-carro	ow-too-**kah**-roo
subway	metro	**meh**-troo
ticket	bilhete	beel-**yeh**-teh
How do I get to ___?	Como vou para ___?	**koh**-moo voh **pah**-rah
How do we get to ___?	Como vamos para ___?	**koh**-moo **vah**-moosh **pah**-rah
Which stop for ___?	Qual é a paragem para ___?	kwahl eh ah pah-**rah**-zhayn **pah**-rah
Tell me when to get off?	Diga-me quando devo sair?	**dee**-gah-meh **kwahn**-doo **deh**-voo sah-**eer**
Tell us when to get off?	Diga-nos quando devemos sair?	**dee**-gah-noosh **kwahn**-doo deh-**veh**-moosh sah-**eer**

TRAVELING

Taxis

Getting a Taxi

Taxi!	*Táxi!*	**tahk**-see
Can you call a taxi?	*Pode chamar um táxi?*	**pod**-eh shah-**mar** oo<u>n</u> **tahk**-see
Where is a taxi stand?	*Onde é uma paragem de táxis?*	**ohn**-deh eh **oo**-mah pah-**rah**-zhay<u>n</u> deh **tahk**-seesh
Where can I get a taxi?	*Onde posso apanhar um táxi?*	**ohn**-deh **pos**-soo ah-pahn-**yar** oo<u>n</u> **tahk**-see
Where can we get a taxi?	*Onde podemos apanhar um táxi?*	**ohn**-deh poo-**day**-moosh ah-pahn-**yar** oo<u>n</u> **tahk**-see
Are you free?	*Está livre?*	ish-**tah lee**-vreh
Occupied.	*Ocupado.*	oo-koo-**pah**-doo
To ___, please.	*Para ___, por favor.*	**pah**-rah ___ poor fah-**vor**
To this address.	*Para este endereço.*	**pah**-rah **ehsh**-teh ay<u>n</u>-deh-**ray**-soo
Take me to ___.	*Leve-me para ___.*	**leh**-veh-meh **pah**-rah
Take us to ___.	*Leve-nos para ___.*	**leh**-veh-noosh **pah**-rah
Approximately how much will it cost to go to...?	*Mais ou menos quanto custa a viagem para...?*	mī sh oh **may**-noosh **kwahn**-too **koosh**-tah ah vee-**ah**-zhay<u>n</u> **pah**-rah
...the airport	*...o aeroporto*	oo ah-roh-**por**-too
...the train station	*...a estação do comboio*	ah ish-tah-**sow** doo koh<u>n</u>-**boy**-oo
...this address	*...este endereço*	**ehsh**-teh ay<u>n</u>-deh-**ray**-soo
Any extra supplement?	*Alguma tarifa extra?*	ahl-**goo**-mah tah-**ree**-fah **ish**-trah
Too much.	*É muito caro.*	eh **mween**-too **kah**-roo
Can you take ___ people?	*Pode levar ___ pessoas?*	**pod**-eh leh-**var** ___ peh-**soh**-ahsh
Any extra fee?	*À taxa extra?*	ah **tah**-shah **ish**-trah
How much per hour?	*Quanto é por hora?*	**kwahn**-too eh poor **oh**-rah

How much for a one-hour city tour?	Quanto custa por visitar a cidade durante uma hora?	**kwahn**-too **koosh**-tah poor vee-zee-**tar** ah see-**dah**-deh doo-**rahn**-teh **oo**-mah **oh**-rah

If you have trouble flagging down a taxi, ask for directions to a *paragem de táxis* (taxi stand). The simplest way to tell a cabbie where you want to go is by stating your destination followed by "please" (*Belém, por favor.*) Tipping isn't expected, but it's polite to round up. So if the fare is €19, round up to €20.

In the Taxi

The meter, please.	O medidor, por favor.	oo may-dee-**dor** poor fah-**vor**
Where is the meter?	Onde está o medidor?	**ohn**-deh ish-**tah** oo may-dee-**dor**
I'm / We're in a hurry.	Estou / Estamos com presa.	ish-**toh** / ish-**tah**-moosh kohn **preh**-zah
Slow down.	Mais devagar.	mī sh deh-vah-**gar**
If you don't slow down, I'll throw up.	Se não for mais devagar, vou vomitar.	seh no<u>w</u> for mī sh day-vah-**gar** voh voo-mee-**tar**
Right / Left / Straight.	Direita / Esquerda / Em frente.	dee-**ray**-tah / ish-**kehr**-dah / ayn **frayn**-teh
I'd like / We'd like to stop here briefly.	Gostaria / Gostaríamos de parar aqui por uns minutos.	goosh-tah-**ree**-ah / goosh-tah-**ree**-ah-moosh deh pah-**rar** ah-**kee** poor oonsh mee-**noo**-toosh
Please stop here for ___ minutes.	Por favor, pare aqui por ___ minutos.	poor fah-**vor pah**-reh ah-**kee** poor ___ mee-**noo**-toosh
Can you wait?	Pode esperar?	**pod**-eh ish-peh-**rar**
Crazy traffic, isn't it?	Este trânsito é doido, não é?	**ehsh**-teh **trayn**-see-too eh **doy**-doo, no<u>w</u> eh

You drive like ...	O senhor conduz como...	oo sin-**yor** koh<u>n</u>-**doosh koh**-moo
...a madman!	...um louco!	oo<u>n</u> **low**-koo
...Michael Schumacher.	...Michael Schumacher.	"Michael Schumacher"
You drive very well.	O senhor conduz muito bem.	oo sin-**yor** koh<u>n</u>-**doosh mween**-too bay<u>n</u>
Where did you learn to drive?	Onde é que aprendeu a conduzir?	**ohn**-deh eh keh ah-**prayn**-doo ah koh<u>n</u>-doo-**zeer**
Stop here.	Pare aqui.	**pah**-reh ah-**kee**
Here is fine.	Aqui está bom.	ah-**kee** ish-**tah** boh<u>n</u>
At this corner.	Nesta esquina.	**nehsh**-tah ehsh-**kee**-nah
The next corner.	Na próxima esquina.	nah **proh**-see-mah ehsh-**kee**-nah
My change, please.	O meu troco, por favor.	oo **meh**-oo **troh**-koo poor fah-**vor**
Keep the change.	Fique com o troco.	**fee**-keh koh<u>n</u> oo **troh**-koo
This ride is / was more fun than Disneyland.	Esta viagem é / foi mais agradavel do que na Disneyland.	**ehsh**-tah vee-**ah**-zhay<u>n</u> eh / foy mī sh ah-grah-**dah**-vehl doo keh nah "Disneyland"

KEY PHRASES: TAXIS

Taxi!	Táxi!	**tahk**-see
Are you free?	Está livre?	ish-**tah** **lee**-vreh
To ___, please.	Para ___, por favor.	**pah**-rah ___ poor fah-**vor**
meter	medidor	may-dee-**dor**
Stop here.	Pare aqui.	**pah**-reh ah-**kee**
Keep the change.	Fique com o troco.	**fee**-keh koh<u>n</u> oo **troh**-koo

TRAVELING

Driving

Rental Wheels

car rental agency	companhia de carros de aluguel	kohn-pahn-**yee**-ah deh **kah**-roosh deh ah-loo-**gehl**
I'd like to rent...	Gostaria de alugar...	goosh-tah-**ree**-ah deh ah-loo-**gar**
We'd like to rent...	Gostaríamos de alugar...	goosh-tah-**ree**-ah-moosh deh ah-loo-**gar**
...a car.	...um carro.	oon **kah**-roo
...a station wagon.	...uma carrinha.	**oo**-mah kah-**reen**-yah
...a van.	...uma furgoneta.	**oo**-mah foor-goo-**nay**-tah
...a motorcycle.	...uma mota.	**oo**-mah **moh**-tah
...a motor scooter.	...uma motocicleta.	**oo**-mah moh-toh-see-**kleh**-tah
How much...?	Quanto custa...?	**kwahn**-too **koosh**-tah
...per hour	...á hora	ah **oh**-rah
...per half day	...por meio-dia	poor may-oh-**dee**-ah
...per day	...ao dia	ow **dee**-ah
...per week	...á semana	ah seh-**mah**-nah
Unlimited kilometers?	Quilômetragem ilimitada?	kee-**loh**-meh-trah-zhayn ee-lee-mee-**tah**-dah
When must I bring it back?	Quando é para devolver?	**kwahn**-doo eh **pah**-rah deh-vohl-**vehr**
Is there...?	Há...?	ah
...a helmet	...um capacete	oon kah-pah-**say**-teh
...a discount	...um desconto	oon dish-**kohn**-too
...a deposit	...um depósito	oon deh-**poh**-zee-too
...insurance	...seguro	say-**goo**-roo

At the Gas Station

gas station	stação de gasolina	ish-tah-**sow** deh gah-zoo-**lee**-nah
The nearest gas station?	A próxima estação de gasolina?	ah **proh**-see-mah ish-tah-**sow** deh gah-zoo-**lee**-nah

Self-service?	*Self-service?*	"self-service"
Fill the tank.	*Abastecer o carro.*	ah-bahsh-teh-**sehr** oo **kah**-roo
Wash the windows.	*Lave os vidros do carro.*	**lah**-veh oosh **veed**-roosh doo **kah**-roo
I need...	*Preciso...*	preh-**see**-zoo
We need...	*Precisamos...*	preh-see-**zah**-moosh
...gas.	*...gasolina.*	gah-zoo-**lee**-nah
...unleaded.	*...sem chumbo.*	say<u>n</u> **shoon**-boo
...regular.	*...normal.*	nor-**mahl**
...super.	*...super.*	soo-**pehr**
...diesel.	*...diesel.*	dee-**zehl**
Check...	*Verifique...*	vehr-ee-**feek**
...the oil.	*...o óleo.*	oo **ahl**-yoh
...the air in the tires.	*...o ar nos pneus.*	oo ar noosh **pehn**-yoosh
...the battery.	*...a bateria.*	ah bah-teh-**ree**-ah
...the sparkplugs.	*...as velas.*	ahsh veh-**lahsh**
...the headlights.	*...os faróis da frente.*	oosh fah-**roysh** dah **frayn**-teh
...the tail lights.	*...as luzes traseiras.*	ahsh **loo**-shish trah-**zay**-rahsh
...the directional signal.	*...o pisca-pisca.*	oo **pish**-kah-**pish**-kah
...the brakes.	*...os travões.*	oosh trah-**vowsh**
...the transmission fluid.	*...o óleo de transmissão.*	oo **ahl**-yoh deh trah<u>ns</u>-mee-**show**
...the windshield wipers.	*...o para-brisas.*	oo pah-rah-**bree**-zahsh
...the fuses.	*...o fussil.*	oo **foo**-zeel
...the fan belt.	*...a correia de ventoinha.*	ah koh-**ray**-ah deh vehn-toh-**een**-yah
...the radiator.	*...o radiador.*	oo rah-dee-ah-**dor**
...my pulse.	*...a minha pulsação.*	ah **meen**-yah pool-sah-**sow**
...my husband / my wife.	*...meu marido / minha mulher.*	**meh**-oo mah-**ree**-doo / **meen**-yah mool-**yehr**

Euros and liters replace dollars and gallons. If a euro is equal to a dollar and there are about four liters in a gallon, gas costing €1 a liter = $4 a gallon.

Car Trouble

accident	*acidente*	ah-see-**dayn**-teh
breakdown	*parado*	pah-**rah**-doo
dead battery	*sem bateria*	sayn bah-teh-**ree**-ah
funny noise	*barulho estranho*	bah-**rool**-yoo ish-**trahn**-yoo
electrical problem	*problema elétrico*	proo-**blay**-mah eh-**leh**-tree-koo
flat tire	*pneu furado*	**pehn**-yoo foo-**rah**-doo
shop with parts	*loja de peças*	**loh**-zhah deh **peh**-sahsh
My car won't start.	*O meu carro não arranca.*	oo **meh**-oo **kah**-roo now ah-**rang**-kah
My car is broken.	*Meu carro está avariado.*	**meh**-oo **kah**-roo ish-**tah** ah-vah-ree-**ah**-doo
This doesn't work.	*Isto não funciona.*	**eesh**-too now foon-see-**oh**-han
It's overheating.	*Está muito quente.*	ish-**tah mween**-too **kayn**-teh
It's a lemon (rattletrap).	*É um calhambeque.*	eh oon kahl-yahm-**beh**-keh
I need...	*Preciso...*	preh-**see**-zoo
We need...	*Precisamos...*	preh-see-**zah**-moosh
...a tow truck.	*...um reboque.*	oon reh-**bah**-keh
...a mechanic.	*...um mecânico.*	oon meh-**kah**-nee-koo
...a stiff drink.	*...whiskey.*	"whiskey"

For help with repair, look up "Repair" on page 159 in the Services chapter.

Parking

parking lot	*(parque de) esta-cionamento*	(**par**-keh deh) ish-tah-see-oo-nah-**mayn**-too
parking garage	*garagem*	gah-**rah**-zhayn
Where can I park?	*Onde é que posso estacionar?*	**ohn**-deh eh keh **pos**-soo ish-tah-see-oo-**nar**

Is parking nearby?	*O estaciona-mento é perto de aqui?*	oo ish-tah-see-oo-nah-**mayn**-too eh **pehr**-too deh ah-**kee**
Can I park here?	*Posso estacionar aqui?*	**pos**-soo ish-tah-see-oo-**nar** ah-**kee**
Is this a safe place to park?	*É seguro estacionar aqui?*	eh say-**goo**-roo ish-tah-see-oo-**nar** ah-**kee**
How long can I park here?	*Quanto tempo posso estacionar aqui?*	**kwahn**-too **tayn**-poo **pos**-soo ish-tah-see-oo-**nar** ah-**kee**
Must I pay to park here?	*É preciso pagar para estacionar aqui?*	eh preh-**see**-zoo pah-**gar pah**-rah ish-tah-see-oo-**nar** ah-**kee**
How much per hour / day?	*Quanto é por hora / dia?*	**kwahn**-too eh poor **oh**-rah / **dee**-ah

There are no parking meters in Portugal; instead, you'll find machines (*bilhete de estacionamento*) from which you purchase timed tickets to place inside your car.

Finding Your Way

I'm going to ___.	*Vou para ___.*	voh **pah**-rah
We're going to ___.	*Nós vamos para ___.*	nohsh **vah**-moosh **pah**-rah
How do I get to ___?	*Como vou para___?*	**koh**-moo voh **pah**-rah
How do we get to ___?	*Como chegamos a ___?*	**koh**-moo shay-**gah**-moosh ah
Do you have a...?	*Tem um...?*	tayn oon
...city map	*...mapa da cidade*	**mah**-pah dah see-**dah**-deh
...road map	*...mapa da estrada*	**mah**-pah dah ish-**trah**-dah
How many minutes / hours...?	*Quantos minutos / horas...?*	**kwahn**-toosh mee-**noo**-toosh / **oh**-rahsh
...on foot	*...a pé*	ah peh

...on bicycle	...de bicicleta	deh bee-see-**kleh**-tah
...by car	...de carro	deh **kah**-roo
How many kilometers to ___?	Quantos quilômetros para ___?	**kwahn**-toosh kee-**loo**-meh-troosh **pah**-rah
What's the... route to Lisbon?	Qual é a... estrada para Lisboa?	kwahl eh ah... ish-**trah**-dah **pah**-rah leezh-**boh**-ah
...most scenic	...mais bonito	mī sh boh-**nee**-too
...fastest	...mais rápida	mī sh **rah**-pee-dah
...most interesting	...mais interessante	mīsh een-teh-reh-**sahn**-teh
Point it out?	Aponte?	ah-**pohn**-teh
I'm lost.	Estou perdido[a].	ish-**toh** pehr-**dee**-doo
Where am I?	Onde é que estou?	**ohn**-deh eh keh ish-**toh**
Where is...?	Onde é que é...?	**ohn**-deh eh keh eh
The nearest...?	O próximo...?	oo **proh**-see-moo
Where is this address?	Onde é este endereço?	**ohn**-deh eh **ehsh**-teh ayn-deh-**ray**-soo

Route-Finding Words

city map	mapa da cidade	**mah**-pah dah see-**dah**-deh
road map	mapa da estrada	**mah**-pah dah ish-**trah**-dah
downtown	centro	**sayn**-troo
straight ahead	em frente	ayn **frayn**-teh
left	esquerda	ish-**kehr**-dah
right	direita	dee-**ray**-tah
first	primeira	pree-**may**-rah
next	próximo	**proh**-see-moo
intersection	cruzamento	kroo-zah-**mayn**-too
corner	esquina	ehsh-**kee**-nah
block	bloco	**bloh**-koo
roundabout	rotunda	roh-**toon**-dah
stoplight	sinal de luz	see-**nahl** deh loosh
square	praça	**prah**-sah
street	rua	**roo**-ah
bridge	ponte	**pohn**-teh
tunnel	túnel	**too**-nehl
highway, freeway	autoestrada	ow-too-ish-**trah**-dah

TRAVELING

north	norte	**nor**-teh
south	sul	sool
east	este	**ehsh**-teh
west	oeste	**wehsh**-teh

The Police

In any country, the flashing lights of a patrol car are a
sure sign that someone's in trouble. If it's you, try this
handy phrase: "*Desculpe, mas sou turista.*" (Sorry, I'm a
tourist.) Or, for the adventurous: "*Se não gostar da minha
condução, fique lá fora.*" (If you don't like how I drive, stay
off the sidewalk.)

I'm late for my tour.	Estou atrazado para o meu passeio turístico.	ish-**toh** ah-trah-**zah**-doo **pah**-rah oo **meh**-oo pah-**say**-oh too-**ree**-stee-koo
Can I buy your hat?	Posso comprar o seu chapeu?	**pos**-soo kohn-**prar** oo **seh**-oo chah-**pow**
What seems to be the problem?	Qual é o problema?	kwahl eh oo proo-**blay**-mah
Sorry, I'm a tourist.	Desculpe[a], mas sou turista.	dish-**kool**-peh mahsh **soh** too-**ree**-shtah

KEY PHRASES: DRIVING

car	carro	**kah**-roo
gas station	estação de gasolina	ish-tah-**sow** deh gah-zoo-**lee**-nah
parking lot	estaciona-mento	ish-tah-see-oo-nah-**mayn**-too
accident	acidente	ah-see-**dayn**-teh
left / right	esquerda / direita	ish-**kehr**-dah / dee-**ray**-tah
straight ahead	em frente	ayn **frayn**-teh
downtown	centro	**sayn**-troo
How do I get to ___?	Como vou para___?	**koh**-moo voh **pah**-rah
Where can I park?	Onde é que posso estacionar?	**ohn**-deh eh keh **pos**-soo ish-tah-see-oo-**nar**

TRAVELING

Reading Road Signs

abrandar	yield
baixa	center of town
construção na estrada	workers ahead
cuidado	caution
desvio	detour
devagar	slow
entrada	entrance
estacionamento proibido	no parking
obras	construction
outras as direçoes	other directions (out of town)
pare	stop
peões	pedestrians
próxima saída	next exit
saída	exit
sentido único	one-way street
todas as direçoes	all directions (out of town)

Other Signs You May See

aberto das... ás...	open from... to...
água não potável	undrinkable water
casa de banho, WC	toilet
cuidado	be careful
cuidado com o cão	mean dog
empurre / puxe	push / pull (but pronounced push!)
fechado para férias	closed for vacation
fechado para restauração	closed for restoration
homens / mulheres	men / women
ocupado	occupied
para alugar / venda	for rent / sale
perigo	danger
proibido	forbidden
proíbida a entrada	no entry
proibido fumar	no smoking
não há vagas	no vacancy
saída de emergência	emergency exit
Informação de Turismo	Tourist Information Office

TRAVELING

Standard Road Signs

STOP AND LEARN THESE ROAD SIGNS

Speed Limit (km/hr)

Yield

No Passing

End of No Passing Zone

One Way

Intersection

Main Road

Freeway

Danger

No Entry

No Entry for Cars

All Vehicles Prohibited

Parking

No Parking

Customs

Peace

TRAVELING

SLEEPING

Places to Stay

English	Portuguese	Pronunciation
hotel	*hotel*	oh-**tehl**
family-run hotel	*pensão, residência*	payn-**sow**, reh-zee-**dayn**-see-ah
fancy historic hotel	*pousada*	poh-**zah**-dah
room in private home	*quarto*	**kwar**-too
youth hostel	*pousada de juventude*	poh-**zah**-dah deh zhoo-vayn-**too**-deh
vacancy sign (literally "rooms")	*quartos*	**kwar**-toosh
no vacancy	*não há vagas*	no<u>w</u> ah **vah**-gahsh

Reserving a Room

I like to reserve rooms a few days in advance as I travel. But if my itinerary is set, I reserve before I leave home. To reserve from the U.S. by e-mail or fax, use the handy form in the appendix (online at www.ricksteves.com/reservation).

English	Portuguese	Pronunciation
Hello.	*Olá.*	oh-**lah**
Do you speak English?	*Fala inglês?*	**fah**-lah een-**glaysh**

51

Do you have a room for...?	Tem um quarto para...?	tay<u>n</u> oo<u>n</u> **kwar**-too **pah**-rah
...one person	...uma pessoa	**oo**-mah peh-**soh**-ah
...two people	...duas pessoas	**doo**-ahsh peh-**soh**-ahsh
...today / tomorrow	...hoje / amanhã	**oh**-zheh / ah-ming-**yah**
...the day after tomorrow	...depois de amanhã	day-**pwaysh** deh ah-ming-**yah**
...two nights	...duas noites	**doo**-ahsh **noy**-tehsh
...this Friday	...esta sexta-feira	**ehsh**-tah saysh-tah-**fay**-rah
...June 21	...vinte e um de Junho	**veen**-teh ee oo<u>n</u> deh **zhoon**-yoo
Yes or no?	Sim ou não?	seeng oh no<u>w</u>
I'd like...	Gostaria...	goosh-tah-**ree**-ah
...a private bathroom.	...uma casa de banho privada.	**oo**-mah **kah**-zah deh **bahn**-yoo pree-**vah**-dah
...your cheapest room.	...o quarto mais barato.	oo **kwar**-too mī sh bah-**rah**-too
...___ bed(s) for ___ person(s) in ___ room(s).	...___ cama(s) para ___ pessoa(s) no ___ quarto(s).	___ **kah**-mah(sh) **pah**-rah ___ peh-**soh**-ah(sh) noo ___ **kwar**-too(sh)
How much is it?	Quanto custa?	**kwahn**-too **koosh**-tah
Anything cheaper?	Nada mais barato?	**nah**-dah mī sh bah-**rah**-too
I'll take it.	Eu fico com este quarto.	**eh**-oo **fee**-koo koh<u>n</u> **ehsh**-teh **kwar**-too
My name is ___.	Chamo-me ___.	**shah**-moo-meh
I'll stay / We'll stay...	Fico / Ficamos...	**fee**-koo / fee-**kah**-moosh
...for ___ night(s).	...por ___ noite(s).	poor ___ **noy**-teh(sh)
I'll come / We'll come...	Venho / Vimos...	**vehn**-yoo / **vee**-moosh
...in the morning.	...de manhã.	deh ming-**yah**
...in the afternoon.	...de tarde.	deh **tar**-deh
...in the evening.	...ao anoitecer.	ow ah-noy-teh-**sehr**
...in one hour.	...dentro de uma hora.	**day<u>n</u>**-troo deh **oo**-mah **oh**-rah
...before 4:00 in the afternoon.	...antes das quatro da tarde.	**ahn**-tish dahsh **kwah**-troo dah **tar**-deh

| ...Friday before
6 p.m. | ...sexta-feira
antes das seis
horas da tarde. | saysh-tah-**fay**-rah
ahn-tish dahs saysh
oh-rahsh dah **tar**-deh |
| Thank you. | Obrigado[a]. | oh-bree-**gah**-doo |

O Alfabeto

If phoning, you can use the code alphabet below to spell out your name if necessary. Unless you're giving the hotelier your name as it appears on your credit card, consider using a shorter version of your name to make things easier.

A	ah	*Amélia*	ah-**mehl**-yah
B	bay	*Barco (boat)*	**bar**-koo
C	say	*Casa (house)*	**kah**-zah
D	day	*Dado (dice)*	**dah**-doo
E	eh	*Elefante*	ehl-eh-**fahn**-teh
F	ehf	*Faca (knife)*	**fah**-kah
G	**gee**-ah	*Girafa*	**zhee**-rah-fah
H	**eh**-gah	*Hora (hour)*	**oh**-rah
I	ee	*Inês*	ī-**nehz**
J	**zhot**-teh	*José*	zhoh-**zeh**
K	**kah**-pah	*Kapa*	**kah**-pah
L	ehl	*Lurdes*	**loor**-dehsh
M	ehm	*Maria*	mah-**ree**-ah
N	ehn	*Nadia*	**nah**-dee-ah
O	oh	*Orlando*	or-**lahn**-doo
P	pay	*Paulo*	**pow**-loo
Q	kay	*Quem (who)*	kayn
R	ehr	*Rui*	**roo**-ee
S	ehs	*Sonia*	**sohn**-yah
T	tay	*Tania*	**tahn**-yah
U	oo	*Uganda*	oo-**gahn**-dah
V	vay	*Victor*	**veek**-tor
W	**doob**-leh-vay	*William*	"William"
X	sheesh	*Xadres (chess)*	**zhah**-drehsh
Y	**eep**-soh-loo	*York*	"York"
Z	zay	*Zebra*	**zeh**-brah

Using a Credit Card

If you need to secure your reservation with a credit card, here's the lingo.

Is a deposit required?	*É preciso deixar depósito?*	eh preh-**see**-zoo day-**shar** day-**poh**-zee-too
Credit card O.K.?	*Cartão de crédito O.K.?*	kar-**tow** deh **kreh**-dee-too "O.K."
credit card	*cartão de crédito*	kar-**tow** deh **kreh**-dee-too
debit card	*cartão de debito*	kar-**tow** deh **deh**-bee-too
The name on the card is ___.	*O nome no cartão é ___.*	oo **noh**-meh noo kar-**tow** eh
The credit card number is...	*O numero do cartão é...*	oo **noo**-meh-roh doo kar-**tow** eh
0	*zero*	**zeh**-roo
1	*um*	oo<u>n</u>
2	*dois*	doysh
3	*três*	traysh
4	*quatro*	**kwah**-troo
5	*cinco*	**seeng**-koo
6	*seis*	saysh
7	*sete*	**seh**-teh
8	*oito*	**oy**-too
9	*nove*	**nah**-veh
Valid until...	*Válido até...*	**vah**-lee-doo ah-**teh**
January	*Janeiro*	zhah-**nay**-roo
February	*Fevereiro*	feh-veh-**ray**-roo
March	*Março*	**mar**-soo
April	*Abril*	ah-**breel**
May	*Maio*	**mah**-yoo
June	*Junho*	**zhoon**-yoo
July	*Julho*	**zhool**-yoo
August	*Agosto*	ah-**gohsh**-too
September	*Setembro*	seh-**tayn**-broo
October	*Outubro*	oh-**too**-broo
November	*Novembro*	noo-**vayn**-broo

SLEEPING

December	*Dezembro*	deh-**zayn**-broo
2003	*dois mil e três*	doysh meel ee traysh
2004	*dois mil e quatro*	doysh meel ee **kwah**-troo
2005	*dois mil e cinco*	doysh meel ee **seeng**-koo
2006	*dois mil e seis*	doysh meel ee saysh
2007	*dois mil e sete*	doysh meel ee **seh**-teh
2008	*dois mil e oito*	doysh meel ee **oy**-too
2009	*dois mil e nove*	doysh meel ee **nah**-veh
2010	*dois mil e dez*	doysh meel ee dehsh
Can I reserve with a credit card and pay in cash?	*Posso reservar com o cartão de crédito e depois pagar em dinheiro?*	**pos**-soo reh-zehr-**var** kohn oo kar-**tow** deh **kreh**-dee-too ee day-**pwaysh** pah-**gar** ayn deen-**yay**-roo
I have another card.	*Tenho outro cartão.*	**tayn**-yoo **oh**-troo kar-**tow**

If your *cartão de crédito* (credit card) is not approved, say "*Tenho outro cartão*" (I have another card)—if you do.

KEY PHRASES: SLEEPING

I want to make / confirm a reservation.	*Eu quero fazer / confirmar uma reserva.*	**eh**-oo **kay**-roo fah-**zehr** / kohn-feer-**mar** **oo**-mah reh-**zehr**-vah
I'd like a room (for two people), please.	*Queria um quarto (para duas pessoas), por favor.*	keh-**ree**-ah oon **kwar**-too (**pah**-rah **doo**-ahs peh-**soh**-ahs) poor fah-**vor**
...with / without / and	*...com / sem / e*	kohn / sayn / ee
...toilet	*...casa de banho*	**kah**-zah deh **bahn**-yoo
...shower	*...chuveiro*	shoo-**vay**-roo
Can I see the room?	*Posso ver o quarto?*	**pos**-soo vehr oo **kwar**-too
How much is it?	*Quanto custa?*	**kwahn**-too **koosh**-tah
Credit card O.K.?	*Cartão de crédito O.K.?*	kar-**tow** deh **kreh**-dee-too "O.K."

SLEEPING

Just the Fax, Ma'am

If you're booking a room by fax...

I want to send a fax.	*Quero mandar um fax.*	**kay**-roo mahn-**dar** oo<u>n</u> fahks
What is your fax number?	*Qual é o numero do seu fax?*	kwahl eh oo **noo**-meh-roh doo **seh**-oo fahks
Your fax number is not working.	*O seu fax não funciona.*	oo **seh**-oo fahks no<u>w</u> foon-see-**oh**-nah
Please turn on your fax machine.	*Por favor, ligue o seu fax.*	poor fah-**vor** lee-geh oo **seh**-oo fahks

Getting Specific

I'd like a room...	*Queria um quarto...*	keh-**ree**-ah oo<u>n</u> **kwar**-too
We'd like a room...	*Queriamos um quarto...*	keh-**ree**-ah-moosh oo<u>n</u> **kwar**-too
...with / without / and	*...com / sem / e*	koh<u>n</u> / say<u>n</u> / ee
...toilet	*...casa de banho*	**kah**-zah deh **bahn**-yoo
...shower	*...chuveiro*	shoo-**vay**-roo
...shower down the hall	*...chuveiro é no fundo do corredor*	shoo-**vay**-roo eh noo **foon**-doo doo koo-ray-**dor**
...bathtub	*...banheira*	bahn-**yay**-rah
...double bed	*...cama grande*	**kah**-mah **grahn**-deh
...twin beds	*...camas gémeas*	**kah**-mahsh **zheh**-may-ahsh
...balcony	*...varanda*	vah-**rahn**-dah
...view	*...vista*	**veesh**-tah
...with only a sink	*...só com um lavatório*	soh koh<u>n</u> oo<u>n</u> lah-vah-**tah**-ree-oo
...on the ground floor	*...no rés-do-chão*	noo **raysh**-doo-sho<u>w</u>
...television	*...televisão*	teh-leh-vee-**zo<u>w</u>**
...telephone	*...telefone*	teh-leh-**foh**-neh

SLEEPING

...air conditioning	...ar condicionado	ar kohn-dee-see-oh-**nah**-doo
...kitchenette	...kitchenete	"kitchenette"
Do you have...?	Tem...?	tayn
...an elevator	...um elevador	oon eh-leh-vah-**dor**
...a swimming pool	...uma piscina	**oo**-mah pee-**shee**-nah
I arrive Monday,	Chego	**shay**-goo
depart	segunda-feira, e	seh-goon-dah-**fay**-rah
Wednesday.	parto quarta-feira.	**par**-too kwar-tah-**fay**-rah
We arrive Monday,	Chegamos	shay-**gah**-moosh
depart	segunda-feira, e	seh-goon-dah-**fay**-rah ee
Wednesday.	partimos	par-**tee**-moosh
	quarta-feira.	kwar-tah-**fay**-rah
I am / We are	Estou / Estamos	ish-**toh** / ish-**tah**-moosh
desperate.	desesperado(s).	deh-zish-pehr-**ah**-doo(sh)
I will / We will	Dormo / Dormimos	**dor**-moo / dor-**mee**-mooz
sleep anywhere.	em qualquer lugar.	ayn kwahl-**kehr** loo-**gar**
I have a	Tenho um saco	**tayn**-yoo oon **sah**-koo
sleeping bag.	de dormir.	deh dor-**meer**
We have	Temos sacos	**tay**-moosh **sah**-koosh
sleeping bags.	de dormir.	deh dor-**meer**
Will you call	Pode contactar	**pod**-eh kohn-tahk-**tar**
another hotel	outro hotel	**oh**-troo oh-**tehl**
for me?	por mim?	poor meeng

Families

Do you have a...?	Tem um...?	tayn oon
...family room	...quarto para	**kwar**-too **pah**-rah
	familia	fah-**meel**-yah
...family rate	...preço para	**preh**-soo **pah**-rah
	familia	fah-**meel**-yah
...discount for	...disconto para	deesh-**kohn**-too **pah**-rah
children	crianças	kree-**ahn**-sahsh
I have / We have...	Tenho / Temos...	**tayn**-yoo / **tay**-moosh
...one child,	...uma criança	**oo**-mah kree-**ahn**-sah
age ___ months /	de ___ mêses /	deh ___ **may**-zish /
years.	anos.	**ah**-noosh

...two children, ages ___ and ___ years.	...duas crianças, de ___ e ___ anos.	**doo**-ahsh kree-**ahn**-sahsh deh ___ ee ___ **ah**-noosh
I'd like...	Gostaria...	goosh-tah-**ree**-ah
We'd like...	Gostaríamos...	goosh-tah-**ree**-ah-moosh
...a crib.	...um berço.	oon **behr**-soo
...a small extra bed.	...uma cama extra para crianças.	**oo**-mah **kah**-mah **ish**-trah **pah**-rah kree-**ahn**-sahsh
...bunk beds.	...beliches.	beh-**lee**-shehsh
babysitting service	serviços de ajuda com as crianças	sehr-**vee**-soosh deh ah-**zhoo**-dah koh<u>n</u> ahsh kree-**ahn**-sahsh
Is a... nearby?	Há um... perto?	ah oon... **pehr**-too
...park	...parque	**par**-keh
...playground	...parque de diversões	**par**-keh deh dee-vehr-**sowsh**
...swimming pool	...piscina	pee-**shee**-nah

The Portuguese call kids *miúdos* (little ones) or *marotos* (naughty ones).

Mobility Issues

Stairs are...	Escadas são...	ish-**kah**-dahsh so<u>w</u>
...impossible...	...impossíveis...	eem-poh-**see**-vaysh
...difficult...	...difíceis...	dee-**fee**-saysh
...for me / us.	...para mim / nós.	**pah**-rah meeng / nohsh
...for my husband / my wife.	...para meu marido / minha mulher.	**pah**-rah **meh**-oo mah-**ree**-doo / **meen**-yah mool-**yehr**
Do you have...?	Tem...?	tay<u>n</u>
...an elevator	...um elevador	oon eh-leh-vah-**dor**
...a ground floor room	...um quarto no rés-do-chão	oon **kwar**-too noo **raysh**-doo-sho<u>w</u>
...a wheelchair-accessible room	...uma cadeira de rodas-acesso ao quarto	**oo**-mah kah-**day**-rah deh **roh**-dahzh-ahsh-**seh**-soo ow **kwar**-too

SLEEPING

Confirming, Changing, and Canceling Reservations

You can use this template for your telephone call.

English	Portuguese	Pronunciation
I have / We have a reservation.	Tenho / Temos uma reserva.	**tayn**-yoo / **tay**-moosh **oo**-mah reh-**zehr**-vah
My name is ___.	Chamo-me ___.	**shah**-moo-meh
I want to... my reservation.	Quero... minha reserva.	**keh**-roo... **meen**-yah reh-**zehr**-vah
...confirm	...confirmar	kohn-feer-**mar**
...cancel	...cancelar	kahn-seh-**lar**
...change	...trocar	troh-**kar**
The reservation is / was for...	A reserva é / era para...	ah reh-**zehr**-vah eh / **eh**-rah **pah**-rah
...one person	...uma pessoa	**oo**-mah peh-**soh**-ah
...two people	...duas pessoas	**doo**-ahsh peh-**soh**-ahsh
...today / tomorrow	...hoje / amanhã	**oh**-zheh / ah-ming-**yah**
...August 13	...treze de Agosto	**tray**-zeh deh ah-**gohsh**-too
...one night / two nights	...uma noite / duas noites	**oo**-mah **noy**-teh / **doo**-ahsh **noy**-tehsh
Did you find my / our reservation?	Encontrou minha / nossa reserva?	ehn-**kohn**-troh **meen**-yah / **noh**-sah reh-**zehr**-vah
What is your cancellation policy?	Qual é a regra para cancelar?	kwahl eh ah **reh**-grah **pah**-rah kahn-seh-**lar**
Will I be billed for the first night if I can't make it?	Tenho que pagar se não chegar	**tayn**-yoo keh pah-**gar** seh no<u>w</u> shay-**gar**
I'd like to arrive instead on...	Em vez, gostaria de chegar...	ay<u>n</u> vaysh goosh-tah-**ree**-ah deh shay-**gar**
We'd like to arrive instead on...	Em vez, gostaríamos de chegar...	ay<u>n</u> vaysh goosh-tah-**ree**-ah-moosh deh shay-**gar**
Is everything O.K.?	Tudo bem?	**too**-doo bay<u>n</u>
Thank you.	Obrigado[a].	oh-bree-**gah**-doo
See you then.	Até á próxima.	ah-**teh** ah **proh**-see-mah
I'm sorry I need to cancel.	Desculpe eu tenho que cancelar.	dish-**kool**-peh **eh**-oo **tayn**-yoo keh kahn-seh-**lar**

SLEEPING

Nailing Down the Price

How much is...?	Quanto custa...?	**kwahn**-too **koosh**-tah
...a room	...um quarto	oon **kwar**-too
for ___ people	para ___ pessoas	**pah**-rah ___ peh-**soh**-ahsh
...your cheapest room	...o quarto mais barato	oo **kwar**-too mī sh bah-**rah**-too
Is breakfast included?	Pequeno almoço está incluido?	peh-**kay**-noo ahl-**moh**-soo ish-**tah** een-kloo-**ee**-doo
Is breakfast required?	É preciso pagar o pequeno almoço?	eh preh-**see**-zoo pah-**gar** oo peh-**kay**-noo ahl-**moh**-soo
How much without breakfast?	Quanto custa sem o pequeno almoço?	**kwahn**-too **koosh**-tah sayn oo peh-**kay**-noo ahl-**moh**-soo
Is half-pension required?	É preciso pagar as refeiçoes?	eh preh-**see**-zoo pah-**gar** ahsh reh-**fay**-soh-ish
Complete price?	Preço total?	**pray**-soo toh-**tahl**
Is it cheaper for three-night stays?	Há discontos para três noites?	ah deesh-**kohn**-toosh **pah**-rah traysh **noy**-tehsh
I will / We will stay three nights.	Vou / Vamos ficar três noites.	voh / **vah**-moosh fee-**kar** traysh **noy**-tehsh
Is it cheaper if I pay in cash?	Há algum disconto se eu pagar em dinheiro?	ah **ahl**-goon deesh-**kohn**-too seh **eh**-oo pah-**gar** ayn deen-**yay**-roo
What is the cost per week?	Quanto é por uma semana?	**kwahn**-too eh poor **oo**-mah seh-**mah**-nah

Choosing a Room

Can I see the room?	Posso ver o quarto?	**pos**-soo vehr oo **kwar**-too
Can we see the room?	Podemos ver o quarto?	poh-**day**-moosh vehr oo **kwar**-too
Show me / Show us another room?	Mostre-me / Mostre-nos outro quarto?	**mohsh**-treh-meh / **mohsh**-treh-nooz **oh**-troo **kwar**-too

Do you have a room that's...?	Tem um quarto...?	tayn oon **kwar**-too
...larger / smaller	...maior / pequeno	mī-**yor** / peh-**kay**-noo
...better / cheaper	...melhor / barato	mil-**yor** / bah-**rah**-too
...brighter	...mais claro	mī sh **klah**-roo
...in the back	...nas traseiras	nahsh trah-**zay**-rahsh
...quieter	...mais calmo	mī sh **kahl**-moo
Sorry, it's not right for me.	Desculpe, mas não para mim.	dish-**kool**-peh mahsh now **pah**-rah meeng
Sorry, it's not right for us.	Desculpe, mas não para nós.	dish-**kool**-peh mahsh now **pah**-rah nohsh
I'll take it	Eu fico com.	**eh**-oo **fee**-koo kohn
this room	este quarto.	**ehsh**-teh **kwar**-too
The key, please.	A chave, por favor.	ah **shah**-veh poor fah-**vor**
Sleep well.	Dorme bem.	**dor**-meh bayn
Good night.	Boa-noite.	boh-ah-**noy**-téh

Breakfast

Is breakfast included?	Pequeno almoço está incluido?	peh-**kay**-noo ahl-**moh**-soo ish-**tah** een-kloo-**ee**-doo
How much is breakfast?	Quanto custa o pequeno almoço?	**kwahn**-too **koosh**-tah oo peh-**kay**-noo ahl-**moh**-soo
When does breakfast start?	Quando começa o pequeno almoço?	**kwahn**-doo koh-**meh**-sah oo peh-**kay**-noo ahl-**moh**-soo
When does breakfast end?	Quando termina o pequeno almoço?	**kwahn**-doo tehr-**mee**-nah oo peh-**kay**-noo ahl-**moh**-soo
Where is breakfast served?	Quando servem o pequeno almoço?	**kwahn**-doo **sehr**-vayn oo peh-**kay**-noo ahl-**moh**-soo

Hotel Help

I'd like...	Gostaria...	goosh-tah-**ree**-ah
We'd like...	Gostaríamos...	goosh-tah-**ree**-ah-moosh

SLEEPING

English	Portuguese	Pronunciation
...a / another	...um / outro	oon / **oh**-troo
...different room.	...quarto diferente.	**kwar**-too dee-feh-**rehn**-teh
...towel.	...toalha.	too-**ahl**-yah
...clean towel(s).	...toalha(s) limpa(s) .	too-**ahl**-yah(sh) **leem**-pah(sh)
...pillow.	...almofada.	ahl-moh-**fah**-dah
...clean sheets.	...lençois limpos.	**layn**-soysh **leem**-poosh
...blanket.	...cobertor.	koo-behr-**tor**
...glass.	...copo.	**koh**-poo
...sink stopper.	...tampa para lava louça.	**tahn**-pah **pah**-rah **lah**-vah **loh**-sah
...soap.	...sabão.	sah-**bow**
...toilet paper.	...papel higiénico.	pah-**pehl** ee-zhee-**ehn**-ee-koo
...electrical adapter.	...tomada.	toh-**mah**-dah
...brighter light bulb.	...lâmpada mais forte.	**lahm**-pah-dah mīsh **for**-teh
...lamp.	...luz.	loosh
...chair.	...cadeira.	kah-**day**-rah
...table.	...mesa.	**meh**-zah
...modem.	...modem.	**moh**-dehm
...Internet access.	...acesso a Internet.	ahsh-**seh**-soo ah **een**-tehr-neht
...silence.	...silêncio.	see-**layn**-see-oo
...to speak to the manager.	...falar com o gerente.	fah-**lar** kohn oo zhehr-**ehn**-teh
I've fallen and I can't get up.	Eu caí e não posso levantar.	**eh**-oo kah-**ee** eh now **pos**-soo leh-vahn-**tar**
How can I make the room cooler / warmer?	Como posso por o quarto mais fresco / mais quente?	**koh**-moo **pos**-soo poor oo **kwar**-too mīsh **frehsh**-koo / mīsh **kayn**-teh
Where can I wash / hang my laundry?	Onde posso lavar / pendurar a minha roupa?	**ohn**-deh **pos**-soo lah-**var** / payn-doo-**rar** ah **meen**-yah **roh**-pah
Is a... laundry nearby?	Há uma... lavanderia por perto?	ah **oo**-mah... lah-vahn-dah-**ree**-ah poor **pehr**-too

...self-service	...self-service	"self-service"
...full service	...serviço completo	sehr-**vee**-soo kohn-**pleh**-too
I'd like to stay another night.	Gostaria de ficar outra noite.	goosh-tah-**ree**-ah deh fee-**kar** oh-trah **noy**-teh
We'd like to stay another night.	Gostaríamos de ficar outra noite.	goosh-tah-**ree**-ah-moosh deh fee-**kar** **oh**-trah **noy**-teh
Where can I park?	Onde é que` estaciono?	**ohn**-deh eh keh ish-tah-see-**oh**-noo
What time do you lock up?	A que horas fecha?	ah kee **oh**-rahsh **fay**-shah
Please wake me at 7:00.	Acorde-me ás sete da manhã, por favor.	ah-**kor**-deh-meh ahsh **seh**-teh dah ming-**yah** poor fah-**vor**
Where do you go for lunch / dinner / coffee?	Onde se pode ir almoçar / jantar / tomar um café?	**ohn**-deh seh **pod**-eh eer ahl-moh-**sar** / zhahn-**tar** / toh-**mar** oon kah-**feh**

Chill Out

Many hotel rooms in the Mediterranean part of Europe come with air-conditioning—often controlled with a stick (like a TV remote). Various sticks have the same basic features:

- fan icon (click to toggle through the wind power from light to gale)
- louver icon (click to choose: steady air flow or waves)
- snowflakes and sunshine icons (heat or cold, generally just one or the other is possible: cool air in summer, heat in winter)
- two clock settings (to determine how many hours the air-conditioning will stay on before turning off, or stay off before turning on).
- temperature control (20° or 21° is a comfortable temperature in Celsius–see the thermometer on page 187).

SLEEPING

Hotel Hassles

Come with me.	Venha comigo.	**vayn**-yah koo-**mee**-goo
I have / We have	Tenho / Temos	**tayn**-yoo / **tay**-moosh
a problem	um problema	oon proo-**blay**-mah
in the room.	no quarto.	noo **kwar**-too
It smells bad.	Cheira mal.	**shay**-rah mahl
bugs	insectos	een-**seh**-toosh
mice	ratos	**rah**-toosh
cockroaches	baratas	bah-**rah**-tahsh
prostitutes	prostitutas	proosh-tee-**too**-tahsh
I'm covered with	Estou todo	ish-**toh toh**-doo
bug bites.	picado.	pee-**kah**-doo
The bed is too	Esta cama	**ehsh**-tah **kah**-mah
soft / hard.	é muito	eh **mween**-too
	mole / dura.	**mah**-leh / **doo**-rah
I can't sleep.	Não consigo	now kohn-**see**-goo
	dormir.	dor-**meer**
The room is too...	O quarto é	oo **kwar**-too eh
	muito...	**mween**-too
...hot / cold.	...quente / frio.	**kayn**-teh / **free**-oo
...noisy / dirty.	...barulhento /	bah-rool-**yehn**-too /
	sujo.	**soo**-zhoo
I can't	Não posso	now **pos**-soo
open / shut...	abrir / fechar...	ah-**breer** / feh-**shar**
...the door /	...a porta /	ah **por**-tah /
the window.	a janela.	ah zhah-**neh**-lah
Air conditioner...	Ar condicio-	ar kohn-dee-see-oh-
	nado...	**nah**-doo
Lamp...	Candeeiro...	kahn-dee-**yay**-roo
Lightbulb...	Lâmpada...	**lahm**-pah-dah
Electrical outlet...	Tomada...	toh-**mah**-dah
Key...	Chave...	**shah**-veh
Lock...	Fechadura...	feh-shah-**doo**-rah
Window...	Janela...	zhah-**neh**-lah
Faucet...	Torneira...	tor-**nay**-rah

SLEEPING

Sink...	Lava louça...	**lah**-vah **loh**-sah
Toilet...	Lavatórios...	lah-vah-**tah**-ree-oosh
Shower...	Chuveiro...	shoo-**vay**-roo
...doesn't work.	...não funciona.	no<u>w</u> foon-see-**oh**-nah
There is no hot water.	Não há água quente.	no<u>w</u> ah **ah**-gwah **kayn**-teh
When is the water hot?	Quando há água quente?	**kwahn**-doo ah **ah**-gwah **kayn**-teh

Checking Out

When is check-out time?	A que horas é preciso pagar a conta e sair?	ah kee **oh**-rahsh eh preh-**see**-zoo pah-**gar** ah **kohn**-tah ee sah-**eer**
I'll leave...	Parto...	**par**-too
We'll leave...	Partimos...	par-**tee**-moosh
...today / tomorrow.	...hoje / amanhã.	**oh**-zheh / ah-ming-**yah**
...very early.	...muito cedo.	**mween**-too **say**-doo
Can I pay now?	Posso pagar agora?	**pos**-soo pah-**gar** ah-**gor**-ah
Can we pay now?	Podemos pagar agora?	poh-**day**-moosh pah-**gar** ah-**gor**-ah
The bill, please.	A conta, por favor.	ah **kohn**-tah poor fah-**vor**
Credit card O.K.?	Cartão de crédito O.K.?	kar-**tow** deh **kreh**-dee-too "O.K."
Everything was great.	Tudo foi óptimo.	**too**-doo foy **ot**-tee-moo
I slept like an angel.	Dormi como um anjo.	**dor**-mee **koh**-moo oo<u>n</u> **ahn**-zhoo
Will you call my next hotel...?	Pode telefonar para o meu próximo hotel...?	**pod**-eh teh-leh-foh-**nar** **pah**-rah oo **meh**-oo **proh**-see-moo oh-**tehl**
...for tonight	...para hoje a noite	**pah**-rah **oh**-zheh ah **noy**-teh
...to make a reservation	...para fazer uma reserva	**pah**-rah fah-**zehr oo**-mah reh-**zehr**-vah

SLEEPING

...to confirm a reservation	...para confirmar uma reserva.	**pah**-rah koh<u>n</u>-feer-**mar** **oo**-mah reh-**zehr**-vah
I will pay for the call.	Pago a chamada.	**pah**-goo ah shah-**mah**-dah
Can I / Can we...?	Posso / Podemos...?	**pos**-soo / poo-**day**-moosh
...leave baggage here until ___?	...deixar a bagagem aqui até ___?	day-**shar** ah bah-**gah**-zhay<u>n</u> ah-**kee** ah-**teh**

Camping

camping	campismo	kahm-**peesh**-moo
campsite	campismo	kahm-**peesh**-moo
tent	tenda	**tay<u>n</u>**-dah
The nearest campground?	O próximo parque de campismo?	oo **proh**-see-moo **par**-keh deh kahm-**peesh**-moo
Can I...?	Posso...?	**pos**-soo
Can we...?	Podemos...?	poo-**day**-moosh
...camp here for one night	...campar aqui por uma noite	kahm-**par** ah-**kee** poor **oo**-mah **noy**-teh
Are showers included?	Os chuveiros estam incluidos?	oosh shoo-**vay**-roosh ish-**tay<u>n</u>** een-kloo-**ee**-doosh

EATING

Restaurants

Types of Restaurants

Restaurant—Dining establishment with cuisine and service rated *de luxo* (luxury), *de primeira, de segunda,* or *de terceira classe* (first, second, or third class)

Adega tipica—Small restaurant serving local dishes (often with fado singing)

Casa de fados—Restaurant with fado singing

Churrasqueira—Barbeque and grill family-style restaurant

Comida a quilo—Lunch buffet restaurant (pay by weight)

Marisqueira—Seafood restaurant, sometimes expensive

Estalagem—Inn serving regional specialties

Casa de pasto—Informal, inexpensive eatery

Cervejaria—Pub or beer garden

Tasca—Small tavern

Finding a Restaurant

Where's a good...	*Onde há um bom...*	**ohn**-deh ah oo<u>n</u> boh<u>n</u>...
restaurant nearby?	*restaurante*	rish-toh-**rahn**-teh
	por perto?	poor **pehr**-too
...cheap	*...barato*	bah-**rah**-too

67

...local-style	...estilo regional	ish-**tee**-loo ray-zhee-oh-**nahl**
...untouristy	...não turistico	no<u>w</u> too-**reesh**-tee-koo
...vegetarian	...vegetariano	veh-zheh-tar-ree-**ah**-noo
...fast food	...comida rápida	koo-**mee**-dah rah-pee-dah
...self-service buffet	...bufete de auto-serviço	boo-**fay** deh ow-toh-sehr-**vee**-soo
...Chinese	...chinês	shee-**naysh**
fried chicken restaurant	churrasqueira	shoo-rahsh-**kway**-rah
beer garden	cervejaria	sehr-vay-zhah-**ree**-ah
with terrace	com esplanada	koh<u>n</u> ish-plah-**nah**-dah
with a salad bar	com bufete de saladas	koh<u>n</u> boo-**fay** deh sah-**lah**-dahsh
with candles	com velas	koh<u>n</u> **veh**-lahsh
romantic	romântico	roh-**mahn**-tee-koo
moderate price	preço razoável	**pray**-soo rah-**zwah**-vehl
a splurge	uma extravagância	**oo**-mah ish-trah-vah-**gahn**-see-ah
Is it better than McDonald's?	É melhor doque no McDonald's?	eh **mil**-yor **doh**-keh noo "McDonald's"

The Portuguese serve lunch from noon to 2 p.m. and dinner from 7:30 to 10:00 p.m. Save money by considering a *meia dose* (half portion) or a *prato do dia* (menu of the day).

Getting a Table

What time does this open / close?	A que horas é que abre / fecha?	ah kee **oh**-rahsh eh keh **ah**-breh / **fay**-shah
Are you open...?	Está aberto...?	ish-**tah** ah-**behr**-too
...today / tomorrow	...hoje / amanhã	**oh**-zheh / ah-ming-**yah**
...for lunch / dinner	...para o almoço / o jantar	**pah**-rah oo ahl-**moh**-soo / oo zhahn-**tar**
Are reservations recommended?	Recomenda fazer reserva?	reh-koh-**mehn**-dah fah-**zehr** reh-**zehr**-vah
I'd like...	Gostaria...	goosh-tah-**ree**-ah
We'd like...	Gostaríamos...	goosh-tah-**ree**-ah-moosh

...a table for one / two.	...uma mesa para uma / duas.	**oo**-mah **may**-zah **pah**-rah **oo**-mah / **doo**-ahsh
...to reserve a table for two people...	...de reservar uma mesa para duas pessoas...	deh reh-zehr-**var oo**-mah **may**-zah **pah**-rah **doo**-ahsh peh-**soh**-ahsh
...for today / tomorrow	...para hoje / amanhã	**pah**-rah oh-zheh / ah-ming-**yah**
...at 8:00 p.m.	...às oito.	ahz **oy**-too
My name is ___.	Chamo-me ___.	**shah**-moo-meh
I have a reservation for ___ people.	Tenho uma reserva para ___. pessoas	**teyn**-yoo **oo**-mah reh-**zehr**-vah **pah**-rah ___ peh-**soh**-ahsh
I'd like / We'd like to sit...	Gostaria / Gostaríamos de sentar...	goosh-tah-**ree**-ah / goosh-tah-**ree**-ah-moosh deh sayn-**tar**
...inside / outside.	...dentro / fora.	**dehn**-troo / **foh**-rah
...by the window.	...perto da janela.	**pehr**-too dah zhah-**neh**-lah
...with a view.	...com uma vista.	kohn **oo**-mah **veesh**-tah
...where it's quiet.	...onde é sossegado.	**ohn**-deh eh soh-seh-**gah**-doo
Non-smoking (if possible), please.	Não fumar [se for possível], por favor.	now foo-**mar** (seh for **pos**-see-vehl) poor fah-**vor**
Is this table free?	Esta mesa está livre?	**ehsh**-tah **meh**-zah ish-**tah lee**-vreh
Can I sit here?	Posso sentar-me aqui?	**pos**-soo sayn-**tar**-meh ah-**kee**
Can we sit here?	Podemos sentar-nos aqui?	poo-**day**-moosh sayn-**tar**-nooz ah-**kee**

The Menu

menu	ementa	eh-**mayn**-tah
special of the day	prato do dia	**prah**-too doo **dee**-ah
specialty of the house	especiali- dade da casa	ish-peh-see-ah-lee- **dah**-deh dah **kah**-zah
menu of the day	ementa do dia	eh-**mayn**-tah doo **dee**-ah
tourist menu	ementa turística	eh-**mayn**-tah too-**reesh**-tee-kah

EATING

combination plate	prato misto	**prah**-too **meesh**-too
breakfast	pequeno almoço	peh-**kay**-noo ahl-**moh**-soo
lunch	almoço	ahl-**moh**-soo
dinner	jantar	zhahn-**tar**
appetizers	entradas	ayn-**trah**-dahsh
sandwiches	sanduíches, sandes	sahnd-**weesh**-ish, **sahn**-dish
bread	pão	pow
salad	salada	sah-**lah**-dah
soup	sopa	**soh**-pah
first course	primeira refeição	pree-**may**-rah reh-fay-**sow**
main course	refeição principal	reh-fay-**sow** preen-see-**pahl**
side dishes	complementares	kohn-pleh-mayn-**tah**-rish
meat	carne	**kar**-neh
poultry	aves	**ah**-vish
fish	peixes	**pay**-sheesh
seafood, shellfish	marisco	mah-**reesh**-koo
children's plate	prato de criança	**prah**-too deh kree-**ahn**-sah
vegetables	legumes	lay-**goo**-mish
cheese	queijo	**kay**-zhoo
dessert	sobremesa	soo-breh-**may**-zah
munchies (tapas)	petiscos	peh-**teesh**-koosh
drink menu	ementa de bebidas	eh-**mayn**-tah deh beh-**bee**-dahsh
beverages	bebidas	beh-**bee**-dahsh
beer	cerveja	sehr-**vay**-zhah
wine	vinho	**veen**-yoo
cover charge	tixa aplicada	**tī**-shah ah-plee-**kah**-dah
service included	serviço incluído	sehr-**vee**-soo een-kloo-**ee**-doo
service not included	serviço não incluído	sehr-**vee**-soo now een-kloo-**ee**-doo
hot / cold	quente / frio	**kayn**-teh / **free**-oo
with / and / or / without	com / e / ou / sem	kohn / ee / oh / sayn

EATING

Sometimes the waiter will put appetizers on your table as a temptation before you even order. Just wave the food away if you don't want it. You'll pay (usually a per-person charge) if you consume even one olive.

Ordering

waiter	*empregado*	ehm-preh-**gah**-doo
waitress	*empregada*	ehm-preh-**gah**-dah
I'm / We're ready to order.	*Quero / Queremos pedir.*	**kay**-roo / keh-**ray**-moosh peh-**deer**
I'd like / We'd like...	*Queria / Queriamos...*	keh-**ree**-ah / keh-**ree**-ah-moosh
...just a drink.	*...só uma bebida.*	soh **oo**-mah beh-**bee**-dah
...a snack.	*...um petisco.*	oon peh-**teesh**-koo
...just a salad.	*...só uma salada.*	soh **oo**-mah sah-**lah**-dah
...a half portion.	*...meia dose.*	**may**-ah **doh**-zeh
...a tourist menu.	*...uma ementa turistica.*	**oo**-mah eh-**mayn**-tah too-**rees**-tee-kah
...to see the menu.	*...de ver a ementa.*	deh vehr ah eh-**mayn**-tah
...to order.	*...encomendar.*	ayn-koo-mayn-**dar**
...to eat.	*...de comer.*	deh koo-**mehr**
...to pay.	*...de pagar.*	deh pah-**gar**
...to throw up.	*...de vomitar.*	deh voh-mee-**tar**
Do you have...?	*Tem...?*	tayn
...an English menu	*...uma ementa em inglês*	**oo**-mah eh-**mayn**-tah ayn een-**glaysh**
...a lunch special	*...prato do dia*	**prah**-too doo **dee**-ah
What do you recommend?	*O que é que recomenda?*	oo keh eh keh ray-koo-**mayn**-dah
What's your favorite dish?	*Qual é seu prato preferido?*	kwahl eh **seh**-oo **prah**-too pray-feh-**ree**-doo
Is it...?	*Isto é...?*	**eesh**-too eh
...good	*...bom*	bohn
...expensive	*...caro*	**kah**-roo
...light	*...leve*	**leh**-veh

...filling	... enche	**ayn**-sheh
What is...?	O que é...?	oo keh eh
...that	...aquilo	ah-**kee**-loo
...local	...da região	dah rayzh-**yow**
...fresh	...fresco	**frehsh**-koo
...cheap and filling	...barato e enche	bah-**rah**-too ee **ayn**-sheh
...fast	...rápido	**rah**-pee-doo
Can we split this and have an extra plate?	Podemos dividir e ter outro prato?	poo-**day**-moosh dee-vee-**deer** ee tehr **oh**-troo **prah**-too
I've changed my mind.	Mudei de ideia.	**moo**-day deh ee-**day**-ah
Nothing with eyeballs.	Nada com olhos.	**nah**-dah kohn **ohl**-yoosh
Can I substitute (anything) for the ___?	Posso substituir (algo) por___?	**pos**-soo soob-shtee-too-**eer** (**ahl**-goo) poor ___
Can I / Can we get it "to go"?	Posso / Podemos levar esta comida?	**pos**-soo / poo-**day**-moosh leh-**var ehsh**-tah koo-**mee**-dah
"To go"? (for the road)	Para o caminho?	**pah**-rah oo kah-**meen**-yoo

This is the procedure at a restaurant: To summon a waiter, say, "*Por favor*" (Please). The waiter brings a menu and asks what you'd like to drink (*Quer tomar alguma coisa?*). When ready to take your order, the waiter says, "*Está pronto?*" After you've eaten, the waiter will ask if you're finished (*Terminou?*), if you'd like dessert (*Quer sobremesa?*), and if you want anything else (*Quer tomar mais alguma coisa?*). You ask for the bill: "*A conta, por favor.*"

Tableware and Condiments

plate	prato	**prah**-too
extra plate	outro prato	**oh**-troo **prah**-too
napkin	guardanapo	gwar-dah-**nah**-poo
silverware	talheres	tahl-**yehr**-ish

knife	faca	**fah**-kah
fork	garfo	**gar**-foo
spoon	colher	**kool**-yehr
cup	chávena	**shah**-veh-nah
glass	copo	**koh**-poo
carafe	jarro	**zhah**-roo
water	água	**ah**-gwah
bread	pão	po<u>w</u>
butter	manteiga	mahn-**tay**-gah
margarine	margarina	mar-gah-**ree**-nah
salt / pepper	sal / pimenta	sahl / pee-**may<u>n</u>**-tah
sugar	açúcar	ah-**soo**-kar
artificial sweetener	sacarina	sah-kah-**ree**-nah
honey	mel	mehl
mustard	mostarda	moosh-**tar**-dah
ketchup	ketchup	"ketchup"
mayonnaise	maionese	mah-yoh-**neh**-zeh
toothpick	palito	pah-**lee**-too

KEY PHRASES: RESTAURANTS

Where's a good restaurant nearby?	Onde há um bom restaurante por perto?	**ohn**-deh ah oo<u>n</u> boh<u>n</u> rish-toh-**rahn**-teh poor **pehr**-too
I'd like...	Gostaria...	goosh-tah-**ree**-ah
We'd like...	Gostaríamos...	goosh-tah-**ree**-ah-moosh
...a table for one / two.	...uma mesa para uma / duas.	**oo**-mah **may**-zah **pah**-rah **oo**-mah / **doo**-ahsh
Non-smoking (if possible).	Não fumar (se for possível).	No<u>w</u> foo-**mar** (seh for **pos**-see-vehl)
Is this table free?	Esta mesa está livre?	**ehsh**-tah **meh**-zah ish-**tah lee**-vreh
The menu (in English), please.	A ementa (em inglês), por favor.	ah eh-**may<u>n</u>**-tah (ay<u>n</u> een-**glaysh**) poor fah-**vor**
Bill, please.	Conta, por favor.	**koh<u>n</u>**-tah poor fah-**vor**
Credit card O.K.?	Cartão de crédito O.K.?	kar-**tow** deh **kreh**-dee-too "O.K."

EATING

The Food Arrives

Is this included with the meal?	Isto está incluído com a refeição?	eesh-too ish-tah een-kloo-ee-doo kohn ah reh-fay-sow
I did not order this.	Não pedi isto.	now peh-dee eesh-too
We did not order this.	Não pedimos isto.	now peh-dee-mooz eesh-too
Can you heat this up?	Pode aquecer a comida?	pod-eh ah-kay-sehr ah koo-mee-dah
A little.	Um pouco.	oon poh-koo
More. / Another.	Mais. / Outro.	mīsh / oh-troo
One more, please.	Mais um, por favor.	mīz oon poor fah-vor
The same.	O mesmo.	oo mehsh-moo
Enough.	Chega.	shay-gah
Finished.	Terminei.	tehr-mee-nay
I'm full.	Estou satisfeito[a].	ish-toh sah-teesh-fay-too

After bringing your meal, your server might wish you a cheery *"Bom-apetite!"* (pronounced boh<u>n</u>-ah-peh-tee-teh).

Complaints

This is...	Isto é...	eesh-too eh
...dirty.	...sujo.	soo-zhoo
...greasy.	...gorduroso.	gor-doo-roh-zoo
...salty.	...salgado.	sahl-gah-doo
...undercooked.	...malcozinhado.	mahl-koo-zeen-yah-doo
...overcooked.	...queimado.	kay-mah-doo
...inedible.	...não comestível.	now koo-mish-tee-vehl
...cold.	...frio.	free-oo
Do any of your customers return?	Os seus clientes voltam?	oosh seh-oosh klee-ayn-tish vohl-tohn
Yuck!	Porcaria!	poor-kah-ree-ah

Compliments to the Chef

Yummy!	Óptimo!	**ot**-tee-moo
Delicious!	Delicioso!	deh-lee-see-**oh**-zoo
Very tasty!	Muito gostoso!	**mween**-too goosh-**toh**-zoo
I love Portuguese / this food.	Adoro português / esta comida.	ah-**doh**-roo por-too-**gaysh** / **ehsh**-tah koo-**mee**-dah
Better than mom's cooking.	Melhor doque a comida da minha mãe.	mil-**yor doh**-keh ah koo-**mee**-dah dah **meen**-yah **mayn**-eh
My compliments to the chef!	Os meus parabéns ao chefe!	oosh **meh**-oosh pah-rah-**baynsh ah**-oo **sheh**-feh

Paying for Your Meal

The bill, please.	A conta, por favor.	ah **kohn**-tah poor fah-**vor**
Together.	Junta.	**zhoon**-tah
Separate checks.	Conta Separada.	**kohn**-tah seh-pah-**rah**-dah
Credit card O.K.?	Cartão de crédito O.K.?	kar-**tow** deh **kreh**-dee-too "O.K."
This is not correct.	Isto não está certo.	**eesh**-too no<u>w</u> ish-**tah sehr**-too
Can you explain this?	Pode-me explicar isto?	**pod**-eh-meh ish-plee-**kar eesh**-too
Can you explain / itemize the bill?	Pode explicar / descriminar esta conta?	**pod**-eh ish-plee-**kar** / dish-kree-mee-**nar ehsh**-tah **kohn**-tah
What if I wash the dishes?	E se eu lavar a loiça?	ee seh **eh**-oo lah-**var** ah **loy**-sah
Is tipping expected?	Esperam gorjeta?	ehsh-**pehr**-ay<u>n</u> gor-**zheh**-tah
What percent?	Qual é a porcentagem?	kwahl eh ah por-say<u>n</u>-**tah**-zhay<u>n</u>
tip	gorjeta	gor-**zheh**-tah

Keep the change.	*Fique com o troco.*	**fee**-keh koh<u>n</u> oo **troh**-koo
This is for you.	*Isto é para si.*	**eesh**-too eh **pah**-rah see
Could I have	*Posso ter o*	**pos**-soo tehr oo
a receipt, please?	recibo, por favor?	reh-**see**-boo poor fah-**vor**

In most restaurants, service is included—your menu typically will indicate this by noting *serviço incluído*. Still, if you like to tip and you're pleased with the service, it's customary to leave up to 5 percent. If service is not included (*serviço não incluído*), tip up to 10 percent. If you're uncertain whether to tip, ask another customer if tipping is expected (*Esperam gorjeta?*).

Special Concerns

In a Hurry

I'm / We're in	*Estou / Estamos*	ish-**toh** / ish-**tah**-moosh
a hurry.	com pressa.	koh<u>n</u> **preh**-sah
I need / We need...	*Preciso /*	preh-**see**-zoo /
	Precisamos...	preh-see-**zah**-moosh
...to be served	*...ser servidos*	sehr sehr-**vee**-doosh
quickly.	rápidamente.	rah-pee-dah-**mayn**-teh
Is that a problem?	*Há algum*	ah ahl-**goon**
	problema?	proo-**blay**-mah
I must / We must...	*Preciso /*	preh-**see**-zoo /
	Precisamos...	preh-see-**zah**-moosh
...leave in a	*...ir embora daqui*	eer ayn-**boh**-rah dah-**kee**
half hour /	em meia hora /	ayn **may**-ah oh-rah /
in one hour.	numa hora.	**noo**-mah oh-rah
When will the	*Quando é que a*	**kwahn**-doo eh keh ah
food be ready?	comida vai	koo-**mee**-dah vī
	estar pronta?	ish-**tar prohn**-tah

EATING

Dietary Restrictions

English	Portuguese	Pronunciation
I'm allergic to...	Sou alérgico[a] a...	soh ah-**lehr**-zhee-koo ah
I cannot eat...	Não posso comer...	no<u>w</u> **pos**-soo koh-**mehr**
He / She cannot eat...	Ele / Ela não pode comer...	**eh**-leh / **eh**-lah no<u>w</u> **pod**-eh koh-**mehr**
...dairy products.	...lacticínios.	lahk-tee-**see**-nee-oosh
...wheat	...trigo.	**tree**-goo
...meat / pork.	...carne / porco.	**kar**-neh / **por**-koo
...salt / sugar.	...sal / açúcar.	sahl / ah-**soo**-kar
...shellfish.	...mariscos.	mah-**reesh**-koosh
...spicy foods.	...comidas picantes.	koo-**mee**-dahsh pee-**kahn**-tish
...nuts.	...nozes.	**noh**-zish
I am diabetic.	Sou diabético[a].	soh dee-ah-**beh**-tee-koo
I'd / We'd like a...	Queria / Queríamos uma...	keh-**ree**-ah / keh-**ree**-ah-mooz **oo**-mah
...kosher meal.	...comida kosher.	koo-**mee**-dah **koh**-shehr
...low-fat meal.	...comida com pouca gordura.	koo-**mee**-dah koh<u>n</u> **poh**-kah gor-**doo**-rah
I eat only insects.	Só como insectos.	soh **koh**-moo een-**seh**-toosh
No salt.	Sem sal.	say<u>n</u> sahl
No sugar.	Sem açucar.	say<u>n</u> ah-**soo**-kar
No fat.	Sem gordura.	say<u>n</u> gor-**doo**-rah
Minimal fat.	Pouca gordura.	**poh**-kah gor-**doo**-rah
Low cholesterol.	Colesterol baixo.	koo-**lehsh**-teh-rohl **bī**-shoo
No caffeine.	Descaféinado.	dish-kah-feh-ee-**nah**-doo
No alcohol.	Sem alcool.	say<u>n</u> **ahl**-kahl
Organic.	Orgânico.	or-**gah**-nee-koo
I'm a...	Sou...	soh
...vegetarian.	...vegetariano[a].	veh-zheh-tar-ree-**ah**-noo
...strict vegetarian.	...rigorosamente vegetariano[a].	ree-goh-roh-zah-**mayn**-teh veh-zheh-tar-ree-**ah**-noo
...carnivore.	...carnivoro[a].	kar-nee-**voh**-roo
...big eater.	...comilão.	koo-mee-**low**

| Is any meat or animal fat used in this? | *Tem carne ou gordura animal nisso?* | tayn **kar**-neh oh gor-**doo**-rah ah-nee-**mahl** nee-soo |

Many Portuguese think "vegetarian" means "no red meat" or "not much meat." If you're a strict vegetarian, you'll have to make it very clear.

Children

Do you have...?	*Tem...?*	tayn
...a children's portion	*...uma refeição para criança*	**oo**-mah reh-fay-**sow** **pah**-rah kree-**ahn**-sah
...a half portion	*...uma meia dose*	**oo**-mah **may**-ah **doh**-zeh
...a high chair	*...uma cadeira alta*	**oo**-mah kah-**day**-rah **ahl**-tah
...a booster seat	*...um suporte para a cadeira*	oon soo-**por**-teh **pah**-rah ah kah-**day**-rah
plain noodles	*esparguete simples*	ish-par-**geh**-teh **seem**-plish
plain rice	*arroz simples*	ah-**rohzh seem**-plish
with butter	*com manteiga*	kohn mahn-**tay**-gah
no sauce	*sem molho*	sayn **mohl**-yoo
sauce or dressing on the side	*molho separado*	**mohl**-yoo seh-pah-**rah**-doo
pizza	*pizza*	**pee**-zah
...cheese only	*...só queijo*	soh **kay**-zhoo
...pepperoni and cheese	*...pepperoni e queijo*	peh-peh-**roh**-nee ee **kay**-zhoo
peanut butter and jelly sandwich	*sanduíche de manteiga de amendoim e geléia*	sahnd-**weesh**-eh deh mahn-**tay**-gah deh ah-mayn-**dweem** ee zheh-**lay**-ah
cheese sandwich...	*sanduíche de queijo...*	sahnd-**weesh**-eh deh **kay**-zhoo
...toasted	*...com pão torrado*	kohn pow too-**rah**-doo
hot dog	*cachrorro quente*	kahsh-**roh**-roh **kayn**-teh

English	Portuguese	Pronunciation
hamburger	hamburger	"hamburger"
cheeseburger	cheeseburger	"cheeseburger"
French fries	batatas fritas	bah-**tah**-tahsh **free**-tahsh
ketchup	ketchup	"ketchup"
crackers	bolaichas	boo-**lī**-shahsh
Nothing spicy.	Nada picante.	**nah**-dah pee-**kahn**-teh
Not too hot.	Não muito quente.	no̲w̲ **mween**-too **kayn**-teh
Please keep the food separate on the plate.	Por favor, deixe a comida separada no prato.	poor fah-**vor day**-sheh ah koo-**mee**-dah seh-pah-**rah**-dah noo **prah**-too
He / She will share....	Ele / Ela vai dividir...	**eh**-leh / **eh**-lah vī dee-vee-**deer**
They (m / f) will share...	Eles / Elas vão dividir...	**eh**-lish / **eh**-lahsh vo̲w̲ dee-vee-**deer**
...our meal.	...a nossa comida.	ah **noo**-sah koo-**mee**-dah
Please bring the food quickly.	Por favor, traga a comida rápidamente.	poor fah-**vor trah**-gah ah koo-**mee**-dah **rah**-pee-dah-may̲n̲-teh
I want / We want an extra...	Quero / Queremos... extra.	**kay**-roo / keh-**ray**-moosh... **ish**-trah
...plate.	...um prato.	oo̲n̲ **prah**-too
...cup.	...uma chávena.	**oo**-mah **shah**-veh-nah
...spoon / fork.	...uma colher / um garfo.	**oo**-mah **kool**-yehr / oo̲n̲ **gar**-foo
I want / We want two extra...	Quero / Queremos dois... extras.	**kay**-roo / keh-**ray**-moosh doysh... **ish**-trahsh
...plates.	...pratos .	**prah**-toosh
...cups.	...chávenas.	**shah**-veh-nahsh
...spoons / forks.	...colheres / garfos.	**kool**-yeh-rish / **gar**-foosh
Small milk (in a plastic cup).	Pouco leite (num copo plástico).	**poh**-koo **lay**-teh (noo̲m̲ **koh**-poo **plah**-shtee-koo)
straw(s).	palhinha(s).	pahl-**yeen**-yah(sh)
More napkins, please.	Mais guardanapos, por favor.	mī̲sh gwar-dah-**nah**-poosh poor fah-**vor**
Sorry for the mess.	Desculpe[a] a sujeira.	dish-**kool**-peh ah soo-**zhay**-rah

What's Cooking?

Breakfast

breakfast	pequeno almoço	peh-**kay**-noo ahl-**moh**-soo
bread	pão	pow
toast	torrada	too-**rah**-dah
roll	papo seco, pães	**pah**-poo **seh**-koo, paynsh
butter	manteiga	mahn-**tay**-gah
jelly	geléia	zheh-**lay**-ah
milk	leite	**lay**-teh
coffee / tea	café / chá	kah-**feh** / shah
Is breakfast included?	O pequeno almoço está incluido?	oo peh-**kay**-noo ahl-**moh**-soo ish-**tah** een-kloo-**ee**-doo

---

KEY PHRASES: WHAT'S COOKING

food	comida	koo-**mee**-dah
breakfast	pequeno almoço	peh-**kay**-noo ahl-**moh**-soo
lunch	almoço	ahl-**moh**-soo
dinner	jantar	zhahn-**tar**
bread	pão	pow
cheese	queijo	**kay**-zhoo
soup	sopa	**soh**-pah
salad	salada	sah-**lah**-dah
meat	carne	**kar**-neh
fish	peixe	**pay**-sheh
fruit	fruta	**froo**-tah
vegetables	legumes	lay-**goo**-mish
dessert	sobremesa	soo-breh-**may**-zah
Delicious!	Delicioso!	deh-lee-see-**oh**-zoo

EATING

What's Probably Not for Breakfast

omelet	omeleta	oh-meh-**leh**-tah
egg...	ovo...	**oh**-voo
...boiled /	...cozido / não	koo-**zee**-doo / no<u>w</u>
soft boiled /	muito cozido /	**mween**-too koo-**zee**-doo /
hard boiled	muito cozido	**mween**-too koo-**zee**-doo
eggs...	ovos...	**oh**-voosh
...fried	...estrelados	ish-treh-**lah**-doosh
...scrambled	...mexidos	mish-**ee**-doosh
ham	fiambre	fee-**ahm**-breh
cheese	queijo	**kay**-zhoo
yogurt	yogurte	yoo-**goor**-teh
cereal	cereal	seh-ree-**ahl**
pastry	pastel	pahsh-**tehl**
fruit juice	sumo de fruta	**soo**-moo deh **froo**-tah
orange juice	sumo de laranja	**soo**-moo deh lah-**rahn**-zhah
hot chocolate	leite com chocolate quente	**lay**-teh koh<u>n</u> shoo-koo-**lah**-teh **kayn**-teh

Appetizers and Snacks

acepipes, petiscos	ah-seh-**pee**-pish, peh-**teesh**-koosh	appetizers
amêijoas à Bulhão Pato	ah-**may**-zhoo-ahsh ah bool-**yow pah**-too	small clams in wine, garlic, and cilantro broth
camarão-carne ou peixe	kah-mah-**row**-kar-neh oh **pay**-sheh	fried pastry filled with meat or fish
camarãoes com piri piri	kah-mah-**rowsh** koh<u>n</u> **pee**-ree **pee**-ree	sautéed shrimp with garlic and hot pepper
chouriço assado	shoh-**ree**-soo ah-**sah**-doo	grilled smoked pork sausage flavored with garlic and paprika

crepe de galinha / legumes	**kreh**-peh deh gah-**leen**-yah / lay-**goo**-mish	fried, crispy crepe with chicken / vegetables
gambas fritas com alho	**gahm**-bahsh **free**-tahsh koh<u>n</u> **ahl**-yoo	sautéed garlic prawns
pasta de atum	**pahsh**-tah deh ah-**toon**	tuna paté
pasties / bolinhos de bacalhau	**pahsh**-tee-ish / boh-**leen**-yoosh deh bah-kahl-**yow**	cod fish cakes / balls
salgados	sahl-**gah**-doosh	savory pastries
santola recheada	sahn-**toh**-lah reh-shee-**ah**-dah	spider crab stuffed with its own meat

Sandwiches

I'd like a sandwich.	Gostaria uma sanduíche.	goosh-tah-**ree**-ah **oo**-mah sahnd-**weesh**-eh
We'd like two sandwiches.	Gostaríamos duas sanduíches.	goosh-tah-**ree**-ah-moosh **doo**-ahsh sahnd-**weesh**-ish
bread	pão	po<u>w</u>
toasted	torrada	too-**rah**-dah
toasted ham and cheese	tosta mista	**toosh**-tah **meesh**-tah
cheese	queijo	**kay**-zhoo
tuna	atum	ah-**toon**
fish	peixe	**pay**-sheh
chicken	frango	**frang**-goo
turkey	peru	peh-**roo**
ham	fiambre	fee-**ahm**-breh
salami	salame	sah-**lah**-meh
egg salad	salada de ovo	sah-**lah**-dah deh **oh**-voo
lettuce	alface	ahl-**fah**-seh
tomatoes	tomates	too-**mah**-tish
onions	cebolas	seh-**boh**-lahsh
mustard	mostarda	moosh-**tar**-dah

EATING

ketchup	ketchup	"ketchup"
mayonnaise	maionese	mah-yoh-**nay**-zeh
peanut butter	manteiga de amendoim	mahn-**tay**-gah deh ah-may<u>n</u>-**dweem**
jelly	geléia	zheh-**lay**-ah
pork sandwich	bifana no pão	bee-**fah**-nah noo po<u>w</u>
meat and fried egg on a roll	prego no pão	**preh**-goo noo po<u>w</u>
Does this come cold or warm?	É servido frio ou quente?	eh sehr-**vee**-doo **free**-oo oh **kay**<u>n</u>-teh
Heated, please.	Aquecido, por favor.	ah-keh-**see**-doo poor fah-**vor**

The Portuguese like pork sandwiches (*bifana no pão*) and meat and fried egg on a roll (*prego no pão*).

Say Cheese

cheese	queijo	**kay**-zhoo
sheep's cheese	queijo da serra	**kay**-zhoo dah **seh**-rah
fresh goat's cheese	queijo fresco	**kay**-zhoo **frehsh**-koo
ricotta-style cheese	requeijão	reh-kay-**zhow**
cheese plate	porção de queijo	por-**sow** deh **kay**-zhoo
Can I try a taste?	Posso provar?	**pos**-soo proh-**var**

Soups

soup...	sopa...	**soh**-pah
...of the day	...do dia	doo **dee**-ah
...vegetable	...de legumes	deh lay-**goo**-mish
broth...	canja...	**kay**<u>n</u>-zhah
...chicken	...de galinha	deh gah-**leen**-yah
...beef	...de bife	deh **bee**-feh
...fish	...de peixe	deh **pay**-sheh
...with noodles	...com massa	koh<u>n</u> **mah**-sah
...with rice	...com arroz	koh<u>n</u> ah-**rohsh**

EATING

84

Soup Specialties

caldo verde	**kahl**-doo **vehr**-deh	potato and kale soup with smoked sausage
creme de camarão	**kreh**-meh deh kah-mah-**row**	pureed, spicy shrimp soup
sopa de alentejana	**soh**-pah deh ah-**lehn**-teh-zhah-nah	soup with egg, bread, herbs and garlic
sopa de mariscos	**soh**-pah deh mah-**reesh**-koosh	shellfish soup
fish soup	**soh**-pah deh **pay**-sheh	*sopa de peixe*
sopa de pedra	**soh**-pah deh **pehd**-rah	vegetable soup with red beans and sausage
sopa de tomate com ovo	**soh**-pah deh too-**mah**-teh kohn **oh**-voo	tomato soup with poached egg

Salads

salad...	*salada...*	sah-**lah**-dah
...green / mixed	*...de alface / mista*	deh ahl-**fah**-seh / **meesh**-tah
...with octopus	*...de polvo*	deh **pohl**-voo
...with green peppers and grilled sardines	*...de pimento*	deh pee-**mayn**-too
...with tuna, potatoes, and egg	*...de atum*	deh ah-**toon**
...Russian (tuna with lots of mayo)	*...Russa*	**roo**-sah
...with ham and cheese	*...com fiambre e queijo*	kohn fee-**ahm**-breh ee **kay**-zhoo
...with egg	*...com ovo*	kohn **oh**-voo
lettuce	*alface*	ahl-**fah**-seh
tomato	*tomate*	too-**mah**-teh
onion	*cebola*	seh-**boh**-lah
cucumber	*pepino*	peh-**pee**-noo

EATING

oil / vinegar	óleo / vinagre	**ahl**-yoh / vee-**nah**-greh
dressing	molho	**mohl**-yoo
dressing on the side	molho separado	**mohl**-yoo seh-pah-**rah**-doo
What is in this salad?	O que tem na salada?	oo keh tayn nah sah-**lah**-dah

Seafood

seafood	marisco	mah-**reesh**-koo
assorted seafood	diversos mariscos	dee-**vehr**-soosh mah-**reesh**-koosh
fish	peixe	**pay**-sheh
fried white fish	filetes	feh-**leh**-tish
anchovies	anchovas	ahn-**shoh**-vahsh
barnacles	percebes	pehr-**sheh**-bish
bream (fish)	pargo	**par**-goo
clams	amêijoas	ah-**may**-zhoo-ahsh
cod	bacalhau	bah-kahl-**yow**
crab	caranguejo	kah-rahn-**gay**-zhoo
crayfish	lagostins	lah-**gohsh**-teengsh
cuttlefish	chocos	**shoh**-koosh
dungeness crab	sapateira	sah-pah-**tay**-rah
eel	enguia	ayn-**gwee**-ah
herring	arenque	ah-**rehn**-keh
lobster	lagosta	lah-**gohsh**-tah
mussels	mexilhões	meh-sheel-**yohnsh**
octopus	polvo	**pohl**-voo
oysters	ostras	**ohsh**-trahsh
prawns	gambas	**gahm**-bahsh
salmon	salmão	sahl-**mow**
sardines	sardinhas	sar-**deen**-yahsh
scad (like mackerel)	carapaus	kah-rah-**powsh**
scallops	escalopes	ish-kah-**loh**-pish
shrimp	camarão	kah-mah-**row**
sole	linguad	leen-goo-**ahd**
squid	lulas	**loo**-lahsh

EATING

swordfish	*espadarte*	ish-pah-**dar**-teh
tiger shrimp	*camarão tigre*	kah-mah-**ro<u>w</u> tee**-greh
trout	*truta*	**troo**-tah
tuna	*atum*	ah-**toon**
How much for	*Quanto para*	**kwahn**-too **pah**-rah
a portion?	*uma dose?*	**oo**-mah **doh**-zeh
What's fresh today?	*O que há de bem*	oo kee ah deh bay<u>n</u>
	fresco hoje?	**frehsh**-koo **oh**-zheh
Do you eat	*Come-se esta*	**koh**-meh-seh **ehsh**-tah
this part?	*parte?*	**par**-teh
Just the head,	*Só a cabeça,*	soh ah kah-**beh**-sah
please.	*por favor.*	poor fah-**vor**

In restaurants, seafood is sold by the "*KG*" (kilogram) or "*dose*" (portion). KG is dangerous. Ask, "*Quanto para uma dose?*" (How much for a portion?).

Seafood Specialties

arroz de	ah-**rohsh** deh	rich seafood rice dish,
marisco	mah-**reesh**-koo	similar to Spain's *paella*
arroz de	ah-**rohsh** deh	stew of octopus and rice
polvo	**pohl**-voo	
bacalhau	bah-kahl-**yow**	boiled cod with green
cozido	koh-**zee**-doo	beans and carrots
bife de	**bee**-feh deh	tuna steak often served
atum	ah-**toon**	with sautéed onions
caldeirada,	kahl-day-**rah**-dah,	bouillabaisse-like fish
açorda de	ah-**sor**-dah deh	stew thickened with
marisco	mah-**reesh**-koo	bread
cataplanas	kah-tah-**plah**-nahsh	hearty shellfish and
		ham stew
lulas	**loo**-lahsh	grilled squid
grelhadas	grehl-**yah**-dahsh	
percebes	pehr-**seh**-behsh	boiled barnacles
porco à	**por**-koo ah	clams and pork with
alentejana	ah-**lehn**-teh-zhah-nah	tomatoes and onion
sardinhas	sar-**deen**-yahz	broiled sardines
assadas	ah-**sah**-dash	

EATING

Percebes (boiled barnacles) are sold as munchies on the street, in bars, and sometimes in restaurants. To eat a barnacle, peel off and discard the outer skin, then wash it down with beer.

Poultry

poultry	aves	**ah**-vish
chicken	frango	**frang**-goo
stewing chicken	galinha	gah-**leen**-yah
duck	pato	**pah**-too
turkey	peru	peh-**roo**
partridge	perdiz	pehr-**deesh**
How long has this been dead?	À quanto tempo é que isto está morto?	ah **kwahn**-too **tayn**-poo eh keh **eesh**-too ish-**tah mor**-too

Meat

meat	carne	**kar**-neh
beef	carne de vaca	**kar**-neh deh **vah**-kah
beef steak	bife	**bee**-feh
ribsteak	costela	kohsh-**teh**-lah
bunny	coelho	**kwayl**-yoo
cutlet	costeleta	koosh-teh-**lay**-tah
a wee goat	cabrito	kah-**bree**-too
ham	fiambre	fee-**ahm**-breh
lamb	borrego, carneiro	bor-**reh**-goo, kah-**nay**-roo
pork	porco	**por**-koo
roast beef	carne assada	**kar**-neh ah-**sah**-dah
sausage	salsicha	sahl-**see**-shah
smoked ham	presunto	preh-**zoon**-too
suckling pig	leitão	lay-**tow**
veal	vitela	vee-**teh**-lah

AVOIDING MIS-STEAKS		
alive	*vivo*	**vee**-voo
raw	*crú*	kroo
very rare	*muito mal passado*	**mween**-too mahl pah-**sah**-doo
rare	*mal passado*	mahl pah-**sah**-doo
medium	*médio, no ponto*	**may**-dee-oo, noo **pohn**-too
well-done	*bem passado*	bay<u>n</u> pah-**sah**-doo
very well-done	*muito bem passado*	**mween**-too bay<u>n</u> pah-**sah**-doo
almost burnt	*quase queimada*	**kwah**-zeh kay-**mah**-dah

Meat, but...

These are the cheapest items on a menu for good reason.

brains	*mioleira*	mee-oh-**lay**-rah
kidney	*rim*	reeng
liver	*fígado*	**fee**-gah-doo
snails	*caracóis*	kah-rah-**koysh**
tongue	*lingua*	**leeng**-gwah
tripe	*tripas*	**tree**-pahsh

Main Course Specialties

coelho à caçador	**kwayl**-yoo ah kah-sah-**dor**	rabbit with carrots and potatoes
costeletas de porco à alentejana	kohsh-teh-**leh**-tahsh deh **por**-koo ah ah-**lehn**-teh-zhah-nah	pork chops with tomatoes and onions
cozida à portuguesa	koo-**zee**-dah ah por-too-**gay**-zah	boiled dinner with different meats, sausages, vegetables, rice, and beans
feijoada	**fay**-zhoh-ah-dah	pork and sausage with beans

EATING

frango no churrasco	**frang**-goo noo shoo-**rahsh**-koo	roasted chicken with hot and spicy piri-piri sauce
leitão assado	lay-**tow** ah-**sah**-doo	roast suckling pig
perna de cabrito	**pehr**-nah deh kah-**bree**-too	roasted leg of baby goat
rojões	roh-**zhohnsh**	crispy, fried pork

How It's Prepared

assorted	diversos	dee-**vehr**-soosh
baked	no forno	noo **for**-noo
boiled	cozido	koo-**zee**-doo
braised	flamejado	flah-meh-**zhah**-doo
broiled	grelhado	grehl-**yah**-doo
cold	frio	**free**-oo
cooked	cozinhado	koo-zeen-**yah**-doo
deep fried	frito	**free**-too
fillet	filete	fee-**leh**-teh
fresh	fresco	**frehsh**-koo
fried	frito	**free**-too
grilled	grelhado	grehl-**yah**-doo
homemade	caseiro	kah-**zay**-roo
hot	quente	**kayn**-teh
in cream sauce	com natas	kohn **nah**-tahsh
medium	meio passado	**may**-oo pah-**sah**-doo
microwave	microondas	mee-kroo-**ohn**-dahsh
mild	médio	**meh**-dee-oo
mixed	mista	**meesh**-tah
poached	escalfado	ish-kahl-**fah**-doo
rare	mal passado	mahl pah-**sah**-doo
raw	crú	kroo
roasted	assado	ah-**sah**-doo
sautéed	sautée	sow-**teh**
smoked	fumado	foo-**mah**-doo
sour	amargo	ah-**mar**-goo
Spanish-style (peppers and tomatoes)	Espanhola	ish-pahn-**yoh**-lah

spicy hot	*picante*	pee-**kahn**-teh
steamed	*cozido ao vapor*	koo-**zee**-doo ow vah-**por**
stuffed	*recheado*	reh-shee-**ah**-doo
sweet	*doce*	**doh**-seh
well-done	*bem passado*	bay<u>n</u> pah-**sah**-doo
with rice	*com arroz*	koh<u>n</u> ah-**rohsh**

Veggies

vegetables	*legumes*	lay-**goo**-mish
mixed veggies	*verduras*	vehr-**doo**-rahsh
	sortidas	sor-**tee**-dahsh
artichoke	*alcachofra*	ahl-kah-**shoh**-frah
asparagus	*espargos*	ish-**par**-goosh
beans	*feijões*	fay-**zhohnsh**
beets	*beterraba*	beh-teh-**rah**-bah
broccoli	*brócolo*	**broh**-koo-loo
cabbage	*couve*	**koh**-veh
carrots	*cenoura*	seh-**noh**-rah
cauliflower	*couve-flor*	**koh**-veh-flor
corn	*milho*	**meel**-yoo
cucumbers	*pepinos*	peh-**pee**-noosh
eggplant	*berinjela*	beh-reen-**zheh**-lah
French fries	*batatas fritas*	bah-**tah**-tahsh **free**-tahsh
garlic	*alho*	**ahl**-yoo
green beans	*feijões verdes*	fay-**zhohnsh vehr**-dish
lentils	*lentilhas*	lehn-**teel**-yahsh
mushrooms	*cogumelos*	koo-goo-**meh**-loosh
olives	*azeitonas*	ah-zay-**toh**-nahsh
onions	*cebolas*	seh-**boh**-lahsh
peas	*ervilhas*	ehr-**veel**-yahsh
pepper...	*pimento...*	pee-**mayn**-too
...green / hot / red	*...verde / picante / vermelho*	**vehr**-deh / pee-**kahn**-teh / vehr-**mehl**-yoo
pickle	*pepino de conserva*	peh-**pee**-noo deh koh<u>n</u>-**sehr**-vah
potatoes	*batatas*	bah-**tah**-tahsh

rice	arroz	ah-**rohsh**
spaghetti	esparguete	ish-par-**geh**-teh
spinach	espinafre	ish-pee-**nah**-freh
tomatoes	tomates	too-**mah**-tish
truffle	trufa	**troo**-fah
zucchini	courgette	koor-**zheh**-teh

You can usually get green beans and carrots (*feijões verdes e cenoura*) instead of the standard French fries by just asking. Another healthy vegetable side dish is *favas com azeite* (fava beans with olive oil).

Fruits

apple	maçã	mah-**sah**
apricot	damasco	dah-**mahsh**-koo
banana	banana	bah-**nah**-nah
berries	bagas	**bah**-gahsh
cantaloupe	meloa	meh-**low**-ah
cherry	cereja	seh-**ray**-zhah
date	fruto seco	**froo**-too **say**-koo
fig	figo	**fee**-goo
fruit	fruta	**froo**-tah
grapefruit	toranja	toh-**rahn**-zhah
grapes	uvas	**oo**-vahsh
honeydew melon	melão	meh-**low**
lemon	limão	lee-**mow**
orange	laranja	lah-**rahn**-zhah
peach	pêssego	**pay**-seh-goo
pear	pêra	**pay**-rah
pineapple	ananás	ah-nah-**nahsh**
plum	ameixa	ah-**may**-shah
prune	ameixa seca	ah-**may**-shah **say**-kah
raspberry	framboesa	frahm-**bway**-zah
strawberry	morango	moo-**rang**-goo
tangerine	tangerina	tahn-zheh-**ree**-nah
watermelon	melancia	meh-**lahn**-see-ah

Nuts to You

almond	*amêndoa*	ah-**mayn**-dwah
chestnut	*castanha*	kahsh-**tahn**-yah
coconut	*coco*	**koh**-koo
hazelnut	*avelã*	ah-veh-**lah**
peanut	*amendoim*	ah-mayn-**dweem**
pistachio	*pistácio*	peesh-**tah**-see-oo
walnut	*noz*	nohsh

Just Desserts

dessert	*sobremesa*	soo-breh-**may**-zah
cake	*bolo*	**boh**-loo
ice cream...	*gelado...*	zheh-**lah**-doo
...cone	*...numa cone*	**noo**-mah **koh**-neh
...cup	*...numa chávena*	**noo**-mah **shah**-veh-nah
scoop of ice cream	*uma colher de gelado*	**kool**-yehr deh zheh-**lah**-doo
vanilla	*baunilha*	bow-**neel**-yah
chocolate	*chocolate*	shoo-koo-**lah**-teh
strawberry	*morango*	moo-**rang**-goo
fruit cup	*salada de fruta*	sah-**lah**-dah deh **froo**-tah
tart	*tarte*	**tar**-teh
whipped cream	*chântily*	**shahn**-tee-lee
chocolate mousse	*mousse de chocolate*	**moo**-seh deh shoo-koo-**lah**-teh
pudding	*pudim*	**poo**-deem
pastry	*pastelaria*	pahsh-teh-lah-**ree**-ah
cookies	*bolos*	**boh**-loosh
candy	*rebuçados*	ray-boo-**sah**-doosh
low calorie	*poucas calorias*	**poh**-kahsh kah-loo-**ree**-ahsh
homemade	*caseiro*	kah-**zay**-roo
We'll split one.	*Vamos dividir um.*	**vah**-moosh dee-vee-**deer** oon
Two forks / Two spoons, please.	*Dois garfos / Duas colheres, por favor.*	doysh **gar**-foosh / **doo**-ahsh **kool**-yeh-rish poor fah-**vor**

English	Portuguese	Pronunciation
I shouldn't, but...	*Não devia, mas...*	no<u>w</u> deh-**vee**-ah mahsh
Exquisite!	*Requintado!*	ray-keen-**tah**-doo
It's heavenly!	*É divinal!*	eh dee-vee-**nahl**
Death by chocolate.	*Morro por chocolate.*	**moh**-roo poor shoo-koo-**lah**-teh
Better than sex.	*Melhor que sexo.*	mil-**yor** keh **sehk**-soo
A moment on the lips, forever on the hips.	*Um momento nos lábios, para sempre nos quadris.*	oo<u>n</u> moh-**mehn**-too noosh **lah**-bee-oosh **pah**-rah **sayn**-preh noosh kwah-**dreesh**

Dessert Specialties

Portuguese	Pronunciation	English
arroz doce	ah-**rohsh doh**-seh	rice pudding
bolo podre	**boh**-loo **poh**-dreh	honey and cinnamon cake
fios de ovos	**fee**-oosh deh **oh**-voosh	sweet egg pudding
flan, pudim flan	flah<u>n</u>, **poo**-deem flah<u>n</u>	caramel custard
leite creme	**lay**-teh **kreh**-meh	cream custard
pastel de nata, pastel de Belém	**pahsh**-tehl deh **nah**-tah, **pahsh**-tehl deh beh-**layn**	cream custard tarts, called pastel de Belém in Belém and Lisbon, otherwise pastel de nata
queijadas	kay-**zhah**-dahsh	cheesecake
sonhos	**sohn**-yoosh	fried sweet dough, sprinkled with cinnamon and sugar
travesseiros	trah-veh-**say**-roosh	almond pastries
trouxas de ovos	**troo**-shahsh deh **oh**-voosh	sweet egg rolls

EATING

Drinking

Water, Milk, and Juice

English	Portuguese	Pronunciation
mineral water...	*água mineral...*	**ah**-gwah mee-neh-**rahl**
...with / without gas	*...com / sem gás*	koh<u>n</u> / say<u>n</u> gahsh
tap water	*água da torneira*	**ah**-gwah dah tor-**nay**-rah
whole milk	*leite gordo*	**lay**-teh **gor**-doo
skim milk	*leite magro*	**lay**-teh **mah**-groo
fresh milk	*leite fresco*	**lay**-teh **frehsh**-koo
hot chocolate	*leite com chocolate quente*	**lay**-teh koh<u>n</u> shoo-koo-**lah**-teh **kayn**-teh
fruit juice	*sumo de fruta*	**soo**-moo deh **froo**-tah
100% juice	*cem por cento sumo*	say<u>n</u> pehr **sayn**-too **soo**-moo
orange juice (pure)	*sumo de laranja (puro)*	**soo**-moo deh lah-**rahn**-zhah (**poo**-roo)
apple juice	*sumo de maçã*	**soo**-moo deh mah-**sah**
lemonade	*limonada*	lee-moh-**nah**-dah
with / without...	*com / sem...*	koh<u>n</u> / say<u>n</u>
...sugar	*...açúcar*	ah-**soo**-kar
...ice	*...gelo*	**zhay**-loo
glass / cup	*copo / chávena*	**koh**-poo / **shah**-veh-nah
small / large	*pequena / grande*	peh-**kay**-nah / **grahn**-deh
bottle	*garrafa*	gah-**rah**-fah
Is this water safe to drink?	*Posso beber esta água?*	**pos**-soo beh-**behr** **ehsh**-tah **ah**-gwah

Tap water is free at restaurants—ask for *água da torneira*. If you like mineral water, your big decision is *com* or *sem gás* (with or without carbonation). *Com gás* is a taste well worth acquiring. The light, sturdy plastic water bottles are great to pack along and re-use as you travel.

EATING

KEY PHRASES: DRINKING		
drink	*bebida*	beh-**bee**-dah
(mineral) water	*água (mineral)*	**ah**-gwah (mee-neh-**rahl**)
tap water	*água da torneira*	**ah**-gwah dah tor-**nay**-rah
milk	*leite*	**lay**-teh
juice	*sumo*	**soo**-moo
coffee	*café*	kah-**feh**
tea	*chá*	shah
wine	*vinho*	**veen**-yoo
beer	*cerveja*	sehr-**vay**-zhah
Cheers!	*Saúde!*	sah-**oo**-deh

Coffee and Tea

coffee...	*café...*	kah-**feh**
...black	*...prêto*	**pray**-too
...with milk	*...com leite*	koh<u>n</u> **lay**-teh
...with sugar	*...com açucar*	koh<u>n</u> ah-**soo**-kar
...American-style	*...estilo Americano*	ish-**tee**-loo ah-meh-ree-**kah**-noo
milk with a dash of coffee	*galão*	gah-**low**
coffee latte	*meia de leite*	**may**-ah deh **lay**-teh
espresso	*bica*	**bee**-kah
espresso with a touch of milk	*pingo*	**peen**-goo
espresso with milk	*garoto*	gah-**roh**-too
espresso with a touch of brandy	*uma bica com uma pinga*	**oo**-mah **bee**-kah koh<u>n</u> **oo**-mah **peen**-gah
decaffeinated	*descaféinado*	dish-kah-fay-**nah**-doo
instant coffee	*Néscafe*	**nehsh**-kah-feh
sugar	*açúcar*	ah-**soo**-kar
hot water	*água quente*	**ah**-gwah **kayn**-teh
tea / lemon	*chá / limão*	shah / lee-**mow**
tea bag	*saquinho de chá*	sah-**keen**-yoo deh shah

EATING

herbal tea	*chá de ervas*	shah deh **ehr**-vahsh
fruit tea	*chá de frutas*	shah deh **froo**-tahsh
small / large	*pequeno / grande*	peh-**kay**-noo / **grahn**-deh
Another cup.	*Outra chávena.*	**oh**-trah **shah**-veh-nah
Same price if I	*É o mesmo*	eh oo **mehsh**-moo
sit or stand?	*preço se me*	**preh**-soo seh meh
	sentar ou se	sehn-**tar** oh seh
	estiver de pé?	ish-tee-**vehr** deh pay

Only tourists take milk with their coffee throughout the day. The Portuguese add milk only at breakfast.

Wine

I would like...	*Gostaria...*	goosh-tah-**ree**-ah
We would like...	*Gostaríamos...*	goosh-tah-**ree**-ah-moosh
...a glass...	*...um copo...*	oon **koh**-poo
...a carafe...	*...um jarro...*	oon **zhah**-roo
...a bottle...	*...uma garrafa...*	**oo**-mah gah-**rah**-fah
...a 5-liter jug...	*...um garrafão...*	oon gah-rah-**fow**
...a barrel...	*...um barril...*	oon bah-**reel**
...a vat...	*...uma pipa...*	**oo**-mah **pee**-pah
...of red wine	*...de vinho tinto*	deh **veen**-yoo **teen**-too
...of white wine	*...de vinho branco*	deh **veen**-yoo **brang**-koo
...of the region.	*...da região.*	dah rayzh-**yow**
...the wine list.	*...a lista de*	ah **leesh**-tah deh
	vinhos.	**veen**-yoosh

Wine Words

wine	*vinho*	**veen**-yoo
select wine	*vinho reserva*	**veen**-yoo reh-**zehr**-vah
(good year)		
table wine	*vinho de mesa*	**veen**-yoo deh **may**-zah
cheap house wine	*vinho da casa*	**veen**-yoo dah **kah**-zah
local	*local*	loo-**kahl**
of the region	*da região*	dah rayzh-**yow**
red	*tinto*	**teen**-too
white	*branco*	**brang**-koo

EATING

rosé	*rosé*	roh-**zay**
sparkling	*espumante*	ish-poo-**mahn**-teh
light	*leve*	**leh**-veh
fruity	*sabor a frutas*	sah-**bor** ah **froo**-tahsh
sweet	*doce*	**doh**-seh
medium	*médio*	**meh**-dee-oo
semi-dry	*meio seco*	**may**-oo **say**-koo
dry	*seco*	**say**-koo
very dry	*muito seco*	**mween**-too **say**-koo
full-bodied	*bem encorporado*	bayn ayn-kor-por-**ah**-doo
mature	*maduro*	mah-**doo**-roo
cork	*rolha*	**rohl**-yah
corkscrew	*saca-rolhas*	sah-kah-**rohl**-yahsh
vineyard	*vendimas*	vehn-**dee**-mahsh
wine-tasting	*provas de vinho*	**proh**-vahsh deh **veen**-yoo
What is a good year (vintage)?	*Qual foi um bom ano?*	kwahl foy oon bohn **ah**-noo
What do you recommend?	*O que é que recomenda?*	oo keh eh keh ray-koo-**mayn**-dah

Portugal produces 55 percent of the world's cork. Cork oak grows well all over the country, especially on the Alentejo plains. The trees must be 25 years old before the first bark can be cut. After that, the trees are stripped every nine years and will produce for approximately one hundred years. Portuguese cork is valued for its lightness. Although cork can sometimes contaminate wine bottles, plastic substitutes still aren't serious competition for the natural plugs.

Wine Labels

These are the terms usually found on a Portuguese wine label.

DOC (denominação de origem controlada)	a wine that meets country-wide laws defining how and where quality wine is made
IPR (indicação de proveniência regulamentada)	a wine that meets quality control standards for regional wine

EATING

reserva	reserve or higher-quality wine, aged longer
casta	grape variety
Quinta	vineyard and wine producing estate
engarrafado na origem / Quinta	estate bottled
engarrafado por...	bottled by...
produzido por...	produced by...

For good, cheap wine, it's **vinho de casa** (house wine). A
northern Portuguese specialty is **vinho verde** (green wine).
This effervescent young wine, which goes well with shell-
fish, comes in red or white; while many argue that both
are bad, the white is clearly better. From the island of
Madeira comes a sweet, white, fortified wine called
Madeira, better used for cooking than drinking. The same
island produces a semi-sweet **verdelho** and a dry aperitif
version called **sercial**. **Moscatel**, a sweet white from the
Setubal region, is best with dessert or as an aperitif.
Portugal also produces more rosé wine than other countries—the best known is **Mateus**, a sweet, bubbly wine. If
you're looking for a drier, full-bodied red, try the wines
from the Dão and Colares regions.

Beer

beer	cerveja	sehr-**vay**-zhah
from the tap	a copo	ah **koh**-poo
bottle	garrafa	gah-**rah**-fah
light / dark	leve / escura	**leh**-veh / ish-**koo**-rah
local / imported	local / importada	loo-**kahl** / ayn-poor-**tah**-dah
small / large	pequena / grande	peh-**kay**-nah / **grahn**-deh
small mug of draft beer (20 cl)	imperial	ayn-peh-ree-**ahl**
medium mug of draft beer (33 cl)	principe	**preen**-see-peh
large mug of draft beer (50 cl)	caneca	kah-**neh**-kah

EATING

one liter draft beer	girafe	zhee-**rah**-feh
thin glass of draft beer with no foam	fino	**fee**-noo
low-calorie	poucas calorias	**poh**-kahsh kah-loo-**ree**-ahsh
alcohol-free	sem alcool	sayn **ahl**-kahl
cold	fresca	**frehsh**-kah
colder	mais fresca	mīsh **frehsh**-kah
beer garden	cervejaria	sehr-vay-zhah-**ree**-ah

Portuguese beer is stronger than its Spanish cousin—
Cuidado (Be careful)! Sagres, Super Bock, and Cristal are
the most popular lagers. For a meal with your beer, look
for a *cervejaria* (beer garden).

Bar Talk

Want to go out for a drink?	Vamos tomar una bebida?	**vah**-moosh toh-**mar** **oo**-mah beh-**bee**-dah
I'll buy you a drink.	Pago a sua bebida.	**pah**-goo ah **soo**-ah beh-**bee**-dah
It's on me.	É por minha conta.	eh poor **meen**-yah **kohn**-tah
What would you like?	O que é que gostaria?	oo keh eh keh goosh-tah-**ree**-ah
I'd like a...	Queria...	keh-**ree**-ah
I don't drink alcohol.	Não bebo alcool.	now beh-boo **ahl**-kahl
alcohol-free	sem alcool	sayn **ahl**-kahl
What is the local specialty?	Qual é a especialidade local?	kwahl eh ah ish-peh-see-ah-lee-**dah**-deh loo-**kahl**
What's a good drink for a man / woman?	O que bebem os homens / as mulheres?	oo keh **beh**-bayn oosh **ah**-maynsh / ahsh mool-**yeh**-rish
Straight.	Puro.	**poo**-roo
With / Without...	Com / Sem...	kohn / sayn

...alcohol.	*...alcool.*	**ahl**-kahl
...ice.	*...gelo.*	**zhay**-loo
One more.	*Mais uma.*	mĩ sh **oo**-mah
Cheers!	*Saúde!*	sah-**oo**-deh
Long live Portugal!	*Vida longa*	**vee**-dah **lohn**-gah
	Portugal!	poor-too-**gahl**
I'm...	*Estou...*	ish-**toh**
...tipsy.	*...tonto[a].*	**tohn**-too
...drunk.	*...bêbado[a].*	**bay**-bah-doo
...hungover.	*...com uma*	koh<u>n</u> **oo**-mah
	ressaca.	reh-**sah**-kah

In Lisbon, hole-in-the-wall bars sell *ginjinha* (zheen-**zheen**-yah), a sweet liqueur of cherry-like ginja berries, sugar, and schnapps.

Standard aperitifs are *martini com cerveja* (a type of vermouth topped with beer), *um branco seco* (a glass of dry white wine), and *água ardente* (firewater made from grape seeds). Favorite after-dinner drinks include *amêndoa amarga* (local amaretto), *armarguinha* (another sweet almond liqueur), *licor beirdo* (made from aromatic plants), and *bagaço* (firewater from grape husks).

Porto (port) is the famous fortified wine in a category of its own. Produced in northern Portugal, port takes its name from the city of Porto. The sweetest and cheapest versions are the red and ruby blends (from several different harvests); these young fortified wines are aged just three years. Tawny ports are semi-sweet red blends named after the color of the oak barrels they're aged in. Vintage port, the most valued, comes from a single high-quality harvest and is aged up to 20 years.

Picnicking

At the Market

English	Portuguese	Pronunciation
Self-service?	Self-service?	"self-service"
Ripe for today?	Está maduro?	ish-**tah** mah-**doo**-roo
Does it need to be cooked?	Isto precisa de ser cozinhado?	**eesh**-too preh-**see**-zah deh sehr koo-zeen-**yah**-doo
A little taste?	Um pouco de sabor?	oon **poh**-koo deh sah-**bor**
Fifty grams.	Cinquenta gramas.	seeng-**kwayn**-tah **grah**-mahsh
One hundred grams.	Cem gramas.	sayn **grah**-mahsh
More. / Less.	Mais. / Menos.	mī sh / **may**-noosh
A piece.	Um pedaço.	oon peh-**dah**-soo
A slice.	Uma fatia.	**oo**-mah fah-**tee**-ah
Four slices.	Quatro fatias.	**kwah**-troo fah-**tee**-ahsh
Sliced (fine).	Cortadas (em fatias finas).	kor-**tah**-dahsh (ayn fah-**tee**-ahsh **fee**-nahsh)
Half.	Metade.	meh-**tah**-deh
A small bag.	Um saco pequeno.	oon **sah**-koo peh-**kay**-noo
A bag, please.	Um saco, por favor.	oon **sah**-koo poor fah-**vor**
Will you make... for me / us?	Pode fazer... para mim / nós?	**pod**-eh fah-**zehr**... **pah**-rah meeng / nohsh
...a sandwich	...uma sanduíche	**oo**-mah sahnd-**weesh**-eh
...two sandwiches	...duas sanduíches	**doo**-ahsh sahnd-**weesh**-ish
To take out.	Levar para fora.	leh-**var pah**-rah **for**-ah
Can I / Can we use the...?	Posso / Podemos usar o...?	**pos**-soo / poo-**day**-moosh oo-**zar** oo
...microwave	...microndas	mee-kroo-**ohn**-dahsh
May I borrow a...?	Pode-me emprestar um...?	**pod**-eh-meh ayn-preh-**star** oon
Do you have a...?	Tem um...?	tayn oon
Where can I buy / find a...?	A onde posso compra / encontrar um...?	ah **ohn**-deh **pos**-soo kohn-**prar** / ayn-kohn-**trar** oon

...corkscrew	...saca-rolhas	sah-kah-**rohl**-yahsh
...can opener	...abre-latas	ah-breh-**lah**-tahsh
Is there a park nearby?	Há algum parque perto?	ah **ahl**-goon **par**-keh **pehr**-too
Where is a good place to picnic?	Onde há um bom lugar para um piquenique?	**ohn**-deh ah oon bohn loo-**gar pah**-rah oon **peek**-neek
Is picnicking allowed here?	É permitido fazer piquenique aqui?	eh pehr-mee-**tee**-doo fah-**zehr peek**-neek ah-**kee**

Picnic Prose

open air market	mercado municipal	mehr-**kah**-doo moo-nee-see-**pahl**
grocery store	mercearia	mehr-see-ah-**ree**-ah
supermarket	supermercado	soo-pehr-mehr-**kah**-doo
delicatessen	charcutaria	shehr-koo-teh-**ree**-ah
bakery	padaria	pah-dah-**ree**-ah
pastry shop	pastelaria	pahsh-teh-lah-**ree**-ah
sweets shop	confeitaria	kohn-fay-tah-**ree**-ah
picnic	piquenique	**peek**-neek
sandwich	sanduíche, sande	sahnd-**weesh**-eh, **sahn**-deh
bread (whole wheat)	pão (de trigo)	**pow** (deh **tree**-goo)
roll	papo seco, pães	**pah**-poo **seh**-koo, pay<u>n</u>sh
ham	fiambre	fee-**ahm**-breh
sausage	salsicha	sahl-**see**-shah
cheese	queijo	**kay**-zhoo
mustard...	mostarda...	moosh-**tar**-dah
mayonnaise...	maionese...	mah-yoh-**neh**-zeh
...in a tube	...num tubo	noom **too**-boo
yogurt	yogurte	yoo-**goor**-teh
fruit	fruta	**froo**-tah
box of juice	pacote de sumo	pah-**koh**-teh deh **soo**-moo

EATING

cold drinks	bebidas frias	beh-**bee**-dahsh **free**-ahsh
spoon / fork...	colher / garfo...	**kool**-yehr / **gar**-foo
...made of plastic	...plástico	**plahsh**-tee-koo
cup / plate...	chávena / prato...	**shah**-veh-nah / **prah**-too
...made of paper	...de papel	deh pah-**pehl**

You can shop at a *supermercado,* but smaller shops are more fun. Get bread for your *sanduíche* at a *padaria* and order meat and cheese by the gram at a *mercearia.* For a meal on the run on a bun, try a *prego no pão* (meat and egg roll) or a *tosta mista* (toasted cheese and ham sandwich).

MENU
DECODER

Portuguese/English

This won't contain every word on your menu, but it'll help you get *mesilhões* (mussels) instead of *mioleira* (brains). An English/Portuguese Decoder follows.

a copo	from the tap
acepipes	appetizers
açorda	chowder
açúcar	sugar
água	water
água ardente	firewater
água da torneira	tap water
água mineral	mineral water
alcachofra	artichoke
alcool	alcohol
alentejana	with tomatoes and onions
alface	lettuce
alho	garlic
almoço	lunch
amargo	sour
amêijoas	clams

amêijoas à Bulhão Pato	small clams in wine, garlic, and cilantro broth
ameixa	plum
ameixa seca	prune
amêndoa	almond
amendoim	peanut
ananás	pineapple
anchovas	anchovies
aquecido	heated
arenque	herring
arroz	rice
arroz de marisco	seafood rice dish (paella)
arroz de polvo	octopus, rice stew
arroz doce	rice pudding
assado	roasted, broiled
atum	tuna
avelã	hazelnut
aves	poultry
azeitonas	olives
bacalhau	cod
bacalhau cozido	boiled cod with green beans and carrots
bagas	berries
banana	banana
batata	potato
batatas fritas	French fries
baunilha	vanilla
bebida	beverage
bem encorporado	full-bodied (wine)
bem passado	well-done (meat)
berinjela	eggplant
beterraba	beets
bica	espresso
bifana no pão	pork sandwich
bife	beef steak
bife de atum	tuna steak with onions
bola	scoop
bolaichas	crackers

bolo	cake
bolo podre	honey and cinnamon cake
bolos	cookies
borrego	lamb
branco	white
brócolos	broccoli
cabrito	baby goat
cachorro (quente)	hot dog
café	coffee
café com açucar	coffee with sugar
café com leite	coffee with milk
café estilo Americano	American-style coffee
café prêto	black coffee
caldeirada	fish stew
caldo verde	soup with potato, kale, and sausage
camarão	shrimp
camarão tigre	tiger shrimp
camarão-carne	fried pastry filled with meat
camarãoes com piri piri	sautéed shrimp with garlic and hot peppers
camarão-peixe	fried pastry filled with fish
caneca	large draft beer (50 cl)
canja	broth
caracóis	snails
caranguejo	crab
carapaus	scad (like mackerel)
carne	meat
carneiro	lamb
casa	house
caseiro	homemade
casta	grape variety
castanha	chestnut
cataplanas	shellfish and ham stew
cebola	onion
cenoura	carrots
cereja	cherry
cerveja	beer
chá	tea

chá de ervas	herbal tea
chá de frutas	fruit tea
chá gelado	iced tea
chântily	whipped cream
chávena	cup
chinês	Chinese
choco	cuttlefish
chouriço	smoked pork sausage
chouriço assado	grilled smoked pork sausage
coco	coconut
coelho	bunny
coelho à caçador	rabbit with carrots and potatoes
cogumelos	mushrooms
colher	spoon; scoop (ice cream)
com	with
comida	food
compota	jam
cone	cone
copo	glass
cortada	sliced
costela	ribsteak
costeleta	cutlet
costeletas de porco à alentejana	pork chops with tomatoes and onions
courgette	zucchini
couve	cabbage
couve-flor	cauliflower
cozida à portuguesa	Portuguese boiled dinner with meats and vegetables
cozido	boiled
cozido ao vapor	steamed
cozinhado	cooked
creme de camarão	pureed spicy shrimp soup
crepe de galinha / legumes	chicken / vegetable crepe
crú	raw
da região	of the region
damasco	apricot
de	of

descaféinado	decaffeinated
diversos	assorted
doce	sweet
dose	portion
e	and
ementa	menu
ementa do dia	menu of the day
ementa turistica	tourist menu
enguia	eel
entradas	appetizers
ervas	herbs
ervilhas	peas
escalfado	poached
escalopes	scallops
espadarte	swordfish
Espanhola	with peppers and tomatoes
espargos	asparagus
esparguete	spaghetti
especialidade	specialty
especialidade da casa	specialty of the house
espinafre	spinach
espumante	sparkling (wine)
estilo	style
estrelados	fried
faca	knife
factura	receipt
fatia	slice
feijoada	beans with pork and sausage
feijões	beans
feijões verdes	green beans
fiambre	ham
fígado	liver
figo	fig
filete	fillet
filetes	fried white fish
fino	thin glass of draft beer
fios de ovos	sweet egg pudding
flamejado	braised

flan	caramel custard
forno	baked
framboesa	raspberry
frango	chicken
frango no churrasco	roasted chicken with piri-piri sauce
fresco	fresh
frio	cold
frito	fried or deep-fried
fruta	fruit
fruto seco	date
fumado	smoked
galão	milk with a dash of coffee
galinha	stewing chicken
gambas	prawns
gambas fritas com alho	sautéed garlic prawns
garfo	fork
garoto	espresso with milk
garrafa	bottle
gelado	ice cream, iced
geléia	jelly
gelo	ice
girafe	one-liter draft beer
gordura	fat
gostoso	tasty
grande	large
grelhado	grilled, broiled
guardanapo	napkin
imperial	small draft beer (20 cl)
importada	imported
incluido	included
jantar	dinner
jarro	carafe
lagosta	lobster
lagostins	crayfish
laranja	orange
legumes	vegetables
leitão	suckling pig
leitão assado	roast suckling pig

leite	milk
leite com chocolate quente	hot chocolate
leite creme	cream custard
leite fresco	fresh milk
leite gordo	whole milk
leite magro	skim milk
lentilhas	lentils
leve	light (wine)
limão	lemon
lingua	tongue
linguad	sole
lista	list
lulas	squid
lulas grelhadas	grilled squid
maçã	apple
maduro	mature (wine)
maionese	mayonnaise
mal passado	rare (meat)
manteiga	butter
manteiga de amendoim	peanut butter
margarina	margarine
marisco	seafood, shellfish
massa	pasta
médio	mild; medium (meat or wine)
meia de leite	coffee with equal portions milk
meia dose	half portion
meio seco	semi-dry (wine)
mel	honey
melancia	watermelon
melão	honeydew melon
meloa	cantaloupe
mesa	table
mexidos	scrambled
mexilhões	mussels
microondas	microwave
milho	corn
mioleira	brains
mista	mixed
molho	sauce, dressing

morango	strawberry
mostarda	mustard
mousse	chocolate mousse
muito	very
muito bem passado	very well-done (meat)
muito mal passado	very rare (meat)
muito seco	very dry (wine)
não	not
Néscafe	instant coffee
no forno	baked
no ponto	medium (meat)
noz	walnut
óleo	oil
omeleta	omelet
orgânico	organic
ostras	oysters
ou	or
ovo	egg
ovo cozido	boiled egg
ovo muito cozido	hard-boiled egg
ovo não muito cozido	soft-boiled egg
ovos estrelados	fried eggs
ovos mexidos	scrambled eggs
pães	roll
palhinha	straw
palito	toothpick
pão	bread
pão de trigo	whole wheat bread
papo seco	roll
para levar	"to go"
pargo	bream (fish)
pasta de atum	tuna paté
pastas	bread with sardine spread
pastel de Belém	cream custard tarts
pastel de nata	cream cake
pastelaria	pastry
pasties de bacalhau	cod fish cakes
pato	duck
pedaço	piece

peixe	fish
pepinos	cucumbers
pepinos de conserva	pickles
pequeno	small
pequeno almoço	breakfast
pêra	pear
percebes	barnacles
perdiz	partridge
perna de cabrito	roasted leg of baby goat
peru	turkey
pêssego	peach
petiscos	munchies (tapas)
picante	spicy hot
pimenta	pepper (seasoning)
pimento	bell pepper
pimento picante	hot pepper
pimento verde	green pepper
pimento vermelho	red pepper
pingo	espresso with a touch of milk
pistácio	pistachio
polvo	octopus
porção	portion
porco	pork
porco à alentejana	clams and pork with tomatoes
porto	port (fortified wine)
poucas calorias	low calorie
prato	plate
prato do dia	special of the day
prato misto	combination plate
prego no pão	meat and fried egg roll
presunto	smoked ham
principe	medium draft beer (33 cl)
pudim	pudding
pudim flan	caramel custard
puro	pure
queijadas	cheesecake
queijo	cheese
queijo di serra	sheep cheese
queijo fresco	fresh goat cheese

quente	hot (temperature)
Quinta	vineyard
rebuçados	candy
recheado	stuffed
recibo	receipt
refeição	meal
região	local
requeijão	ricotta-style cheese
rim	kidney
rojões	crispy-fried pork
rolha	cork
rosé	rosé (wine)
sacarina	artificial sweetener
saca-rolhas	corkscrew
sal	salt
salada	salad
salada de alface	green salad
salada de atum	salad with tuna, potatoes, and egg
salada de ovo	egg salad
salada de pimento	salad with green peppers and grilled sardines
salada de polvo	salad with octopus
salada mista	mixed salad
salada Russa	Russian salad (tuna and mayo)
salame	salami
salgados	savory pastries
salmão	salmon
salsicha	sausage
sande	sandwich
sanduíche	sandwich
santola recheada	stuffed spider crab
sapateira	Dungeness crab
saquinho de chá	tea bag
sardinhas	sardines
sardinhas assadas	broiled sardines
seco	dry (wine)
sem	without
separado	on the side
sobremesa	dessert

sonhos	fried sweet dough, sprinkled with cinnamon and sugar
sopa	soup
sopa de alentejana	soup with egg, bread, and herbs
sopa de mariscos	shellfish soup
sopa de pedra	vegetable soup with sausage
sopa de peixe	fish soup
sopa de tomate com ovo	tomato soup with poached egg
sumo	juice
talheres	silverware
tangerina	tangerine
tarte	tart
tinto	red
tixa aplicada	cover charge
tomate	tomato
toranja	grapefruit
torrada	toast
torrado	toasted
tosta mista	toasted ham and cheese sandwich
toucinho	bacon
travesseiros	almond pastries
trigo	wheat
tripas	tripe
trouxas de ovos	sweet egg rolls
trufa	truffle
truta	trout
uvas	grapes
vaca	beef
vapor	steamed
vendimas	vineyard
verde	green
vinagre	vinegar
vinho	wine
vinho da casa	cheap house wine
vinho de mesa	table wine
vinho reserva	select wine (good year)
vitela	veal
yogurte	yogurt

English/Portuguese

alcohol	alcool
almond	amendoa
anchovies	anchovas
and	e
appetizers	entradas, petiscos, acepipes
apple	maçã
apricot	damasco
artichoke	alcachofra
artificial sweetener	sacarina
asparagus	espargos
assorted	diversos
bacon	toucinho
baked	(no) forno
banana	banana
barnacles	percebes
beans	feijões
beans, green	feijões verdes
beef	vaca
beef steak	bife
beer	cerveja
beer, draft, large (50 cl)	caneca
beer, draft, medium (33 cl)	principe
beer, draft, one liter	girafe
beer, draft, small (20 cl)	imperial
beer, draft, thin glass	fino
beer, from the tap	a copo
beets	beterraba
bell pepper	pimento
berries	bagas
beverage	bebida
boiled	cozido
boiled egg	ovo cozido
bottle	garrafa
brains	mioleira
braised	flamejado

bread	pão
bread, whole wheat	pão de trigo
breakfast	pequeno almoço
bream (fish)	pargo
broccoli	brócolos
broiled	grelhado
broth	canja
butter	manteiga
cabbage	couve
cake	bolo
candy	rebuçados
cantaloupe	meloa
carafe	jarro
caramel custard	(pudim) flan
carrots	cenoura
cauliflower	couve-flor
cheese	queijo
cheese, goat	queijo fresco
cheese, ricotta-style	requeijão
cheese, sheep	queijo di serra
cheeseburger	cheeseburger
cheesecake	queijadas
cherry	cereja
chestnut	castanha
chicken	frango
chicken, stewing	galinha
Chinese	chines
chocolate mousse	mousse
chocolate, hot	leite com chocolate quente
chowder	açorda
clams	ameijoas
coconut	coco
cod	bacalhau
coffee	café
coffee with equal portions milk	meia de leite
coffee with lots of milk	galão
coffee with milk	café com leite

coffee with sugar	café com açucar
coffee, American-style	café estilo Americano
coffee, black	café preto
coffee, espresso	bica
coffee, espresso with a touch of milk	pingo
coffee, espresso with milk	garoto
coffee, instant	Néscafe
cold	frio
combination plate	prato misto
cone	cone
cooked	cozinhado
cookies	bolos
cork	rolha
corkscrew	saca-rolhas
corn	milho
cover charge	tixa aplicada
crab	caranguejo
crab, Dungeness	sapateira
crackers	bolaichas
crayfish	lagostins
cream custard	leite creme
cream custard tarts	pastel de nata; pastel de Belém (in Belém and Lisbon)
cream, whipped	chantily
cucumbers	pepinos
cup	chávena
custard, caramel	flan, pudim flan
custard, cream	leite creme
cutlet	costeleta
cuttlefish	choco
date	fruto seco
decaffeinated	descaféinado
dessert	sobremesa
dinner	jantar
dressing	molho
dry (wine)	seco
duck	pato

Dungeness crab	sapateira
eel	enguia
egg	ovo
egg salad	salada de ovo
egg, boiled	ovo cozido
egg, hard-boiled	ovo muito cozido
egg, soft-boiled	ovo não muito cozido
eggplant	berinjela
eggs, fried	ovos estrelados
eggs, scrambled	ovos mexidos
espresso	bica
espresso with a touch of milk	pingo
espresso with milk	garoto
fat	gordura
fig	figo
fillet	filete
firewater	água ardente
fish	peixe
food	comida
fork	garfo
French fries	batatas fritas
fresh	fresco
fried	frito; estrelado (eggs)
fried eggs	ovos estrelados
fried white fish	filetes
from the tap	a copo
fruit	fruta
fruit tea	chá de frutas
full-bodied (wine)	bem encorporado
garlic	alho
glass	copo
goat (baby)	cabrito
goat cheese	queijo fresco
grapefruit	toranja
grapes	uvas
green	verde
green beans	feijões verdes
green pepper	pimento verde

green salad	salada de alface
grilled	grelhado
half portion	meia dose
ham	fiambre
ham, smoked	presunto
hamburger	hamburger
hard-boiled egg	ovo muito cozido
hazelnut	avelã
heated	aquecido
herbal tea	chá de ervas
herbs	ervas
herring	arenque
homemade	caseiro
honey	mel
honeydew melon	melão
hot (temperature)	quente
hot (spicy)	picante
hot chocolate	leite com chocolate quente
hot dog	cachorro (quente)
hot pepper	pimento picante
house	casa
house wine	vinho da casa
ice	gelo
ice cream	gelado
iced	gelado
iced tea	chá gelado
imported	importada
included	incluido
instant coffee	Néscafe
jam	compota
jelly	geléia
juice	sumo
kidney	rim
knife	faca
lamb	borrego, carneiro
large	grande
lemon	limão
lentils	lentilhas

lettuce	alface
light (wine)	leve
list	lista
liver	fígado
lobster	lagosta
local	local, (da) região
low calorie	poucas calorias
lunch	almoço
margarine	margarina
mature (wine)	maduro
mayonnaise	maionese
meal	refeição
meat	carne
meat, medium	médio, no ponto
meat, rare	mal passado
meat, raw	crú
meat, very rare	muito mal passado
meat, very well-done	muito bem passado
meat, well-done	bem passado
medium (meat)	médio, no ponto
medium (wine)	médio
melon, honeydew	melão
menu	ementa
menu of the day	ementa do dia
menu, tourist	ementa turistica
microwave	microondas
mild	médio
milk	leite
milk, fresh	leite fresco
milk, skim	leite magro
milk, whole	leite gordo
mineral water	água mineral
mixed	mista
mixed salad	salada mista
mousse, chocolate	mousse
munchies (tapas)	petiscos
mushrooms	cogumelos
mussels	mexilhões

mustard	mostarda
napkin	guardanapo
not	não
octopus	polvo
of	de
oil	óleo
olives	azeitonas
omelet	omeleta
on the side	separado
onion	cebola
or	ou
orange	laranja
organic	organico
oysters	ostras
partridge	perdiz
pasta	massa
pastry	pastelaria
peach	pessego
peanut	amendoim
peanut butter	manteiga de amendoim
pear	pera
peas	ervilhas
pepper (seasoning)	pimenta
pepper, bell	pimento
pepper, green	pimento verde
pepper, hot	pimento picante
pepper, red	pimento vermelho
pickles	pepinos de conserva
piece	pedaço
pig, suckling	leitão
pineapple	ananás
pistachio	pistácio
plate	prato
plum	ameixa
poached	escalfado
pork	porco
pork sandwich	bifana no pão
port (fortified wine)	porto

portion	dose, porção
potato	batata
poultry	aves
prawns	gambas
prune	ameixa seca
pudding	pudim
pudding, rice	arroz doce
pure	puro
rabbit	coelho
rare (meat)	mal passado
raspberry	framboesa
raw	crú
receipt	recibo, factura
red (wine)	tinto
red pepper	pimento vermelho
ribsteak	costela
rice	arroz
rice pudding	arroz doce
roasted	assado
roll	papo seco, pães
rosé (wine)	rosé
salad	salada
salad, egg	salada de ovo
salad, green	salada de alface
salad, mixed	salada mista
salad, Russian (tuna and mayo)	salada Russa
salami	salame
salmon	salmão
salt	sal
sandwich	sanduíche, sande
sandwich, pork	bifana no pão
sardines	sardinhas
sauce	molho
sausage	salsicha
scad (like mackerel)	carapaus
scallops	escalopes
scoop	bola

scoop (ice cream)	colher
scrambled	mexidos
scrambled eggs	ovos mexidos
seafood	marisco
semi-dry (wine)	meio seco
sheep cheese	queijo di serra
shellfish	marisco
shrimp	camarão
shrimp, tiger	camarão tigre
side, on the	separado
silverware	talheres
skim milk	leite magro
slice	fatia
sliced	cortada
small	pequeno
smoked	fumado
smoked ham	presunto
snails	caracóis
soft-boiled egg	ovo não muito cozido
sole	linguad
soup	sopa
sour	amargo
spaghetti	esparguete
sparkling (wine)	espumante
special of the day	prato do dia
specialty	especialidade
specialty of the house	especialidade da casa
spicy hot	picante
spinach	espinafre
spoon	colher
squid	lulas
steak, beef	bife
steak, tuna	bife de atum
steamed	(cozido ao) vapor
stew, fish	caldeirada
straw	palhinha
strawberry	morango
stuffed	recheado

style	estilo
suckling pig	leitão
sugar	açúcar
sweet	doce
sweetener, artificial	sacarina
swordfish	espadarte
table	mesa
table wine	vinho de mesa
tangerine	tangerina
tap water	água da torneira
tap, from the	a copo
tart	tarte
tasty	gostoso
tea	chá
tea bag	saquinho de chá
tea, herbal	chá de ervas
tea, iced	chá gelado
tiger shrimp	camarão tigre
"to go"	para levar
toast	torrada
toasted	torrado
tomato	tomate
tongue	lingua
toothpick	palito
tripe	tripas
trout	truta
truffle	trufa
tuna	atum
turkey	peru
vanilla	baunilha
veal	vitela
vegetable	legumes
very	muito
very dry (wine)	muito seco
very rare (meat)	muito mal passado
very well-done (meat)	muito bem passado
vinegar	vinagre
vineyard	vendimas, Quinta

walnut	noz
water	água
water, mineral	água mineral
water, tap	água da torneira
watermelon	melancia
well-done (meat)	bem passado
wheat	trigo
whipped cream	chantily
white	branco
whole milk	leite gordo
wine	vinho
wine, dry	seco
wine, fortified (port)	porto
wine, full-bodied	bem encorporado
wine, house	vinho da casa
wine, light	leve
wine, mature	maduro
wine, medium	médio
wine, red	tinto
wine, rosé	rosé
wine, select (good year)	vinho reserva
wine, semi-dry	meio seco
wine, sparkling	espumante
wine, table	vinho de mesa
wine, very dry	muito seco
wine, white	branco
with	com
without	sem
yogurt	yogurte
zucchini	courgette

ACTIVITIES

Sightseeing

Where?

Where is...?	Onde é...?	**ohn**-deh eh
...the best view	...a melhor vista	ah mil-**yor veesh**-tah
...the main square	...a praça principal	ah **prah**-sah preen-see-**pahl**
...the old town center	...a parte da cidade velha	ah **par**-teh dah see-**dah**-deh **vehl**-yah
...the museum	...o museu	oo moo-**zeh**-oo
...the castle	...o castelo	oo kahsh-**teh**-loo
...the ruins	...as ruínas	ahsh roo-**ee**-nahsh
...an amusement park	...o parque de diversões	oo **par**-keh deh dee-vehr-**sowsh**
...the tourist information office	...a informação turistica	ah een-for-mah-**sow** too-**reesh**-tee-kah
...the toilet	...a casa de banho	ah **kah**-zah deh **bahn**-yoo
...the entrance / exit	...a entrada / saída	ah ayn-**trah**-dah / sah-**ee**-dah
Is there a festival nearby?	Há um festival aqui perto?	ah oon fehsh-tee-**vahl** ah-**kee pehr**-too

At the Sight

Do you have...?	Tem...?	tayn
...information	...informações	een-for-mah-**sowsh**
...a guidebook	...um guia	oon **gee**-ah
...in English	...em inglês	ayn een-**glaysh**
Is it free?	É grátis?	eh **grah**-teesh
How much is it?	Quanto custa?	**kwahn**-too **koosh**-tah
Is the ticket good all day?	O bilhete é bom para o dia inteiro?	oo beel-**yeh**-teh eh bohn **pah**-rah oo **dee**-ah een-**tay**-roo
Can I get back in?	Posso reentrar?	**pos**-soo reh-ayn-**trar**
What time does this open / close?	A que horas é que abre / fecha?	ah kee **oh**-rahsh eh keh **ah**-breh / **fay**-shah
What time is the last entry?	A que horas é a última entrada?	ah kee **oh**-rahsh eh ah **ool**-tee-mah ayn-**trah**-dah

Please

PLEASE let me in.	POR FAVOR deixe-me entrar.	poor fah-**vor** **day**-sheh-meh ayn-**trar**
PLEASE let us in.	POR FAVOR, deixe-nos entrar.	poor fah-**vor** **day**-sheh-nooz ayn-**trar**
I've traveled all the way from ___.	Estou a viajar de muito longe ___.	ish-**toh** ah vee-ah-**zhar** deh **mween**-too **lohn**-zheh
We've traveled all the way from ___.	Nós estamos a viajar de muito longe ___.	nohsh ish-**tah**-moosh ah vee-ah-**zhar** deh **mween**-too **lohn**-zheh
I must leave tomorrow.	Tenho que partir amanhã.	**tayn**-yoo keh par-**teer** ah-ming-**yah**
We must leave tomorrow.	Temos que partir amanhã.	**tay**-moosh keh par-**teer** ah-ming-**yah**
I promise I'll be fast.	Prometo que sou rápido[a].	proo-**may**-too keh soh **rah**-pee-doo
We promise we'll be fast.	Prometemos que seremos rápidos.	proo-meh-**teh**-moosh keh seh-**reh**-moosh **rah**-pee-doosh

It was my mother's dying wish that I see this.	Era o ultimo desejo da minha mãe, que eu visse isto.	**eh**-rah oo **ool**-tee-moo deh-**zeh**-zhoo dah **meen**-yah **mayn**-eh keh **eh**-oo **vee**-seh **eesh**-too
I've always wanted to see this.	Eu sempre quiz ver isto.	**eh**-oo **sehm**-preh keesh vehr **eesh**-too
We've always wanted to see this.	Nós sempre quizemos ver isto.	nohsh **sehm**-preh kee-**zeh**-moosh vehr **eesh**-too

Tours

Do you have...?	Tem...?	tayn
...an audioguide...	...um audio guia...	oon **ow**-dee-oo **gee**-ah
...a guided tour...	...uma visita guiada...	**oo**-mah vee-**zee**-tah gee-**ah**-dah
...a city walking tour...	...passeio a pé pela cidade...	pah-**say**-oo ah peh **peh**-lah see-**dah**-deh
...in English	...em inglês	ayn een-**glaysh**
When is the next tour in English?	Quando é a próxima visita guiada em inglês?	**kwahn**-doo eh ah **proh**-see-mah vee-**zee**-tah gee-**ah**-dah ayn een-**glaysh**
Is it free?	É grátis?	eh **grah**-teesh
How much is it?	Quanto custa?	**kwahn**-too **koosh**-tah
How long does it last?	Quanto tempo leva?	**kwahn**-too **tayn**-poo **leh**-vah
Can I join a tour in progress?	Posso juntar-me ao grupo em processo?	**pos**-soo zhoon-**tar**-meh ow **groo**-poo ayn proh-**say**-soo
Can we join a tour in progress?	Podemos juntar-nos ao grupo em processo?	poo-**day**-moosh zhoon-**tar**-nooz ow **groo**-poo ayn proh-**say**-soo

To help you decipher entrance signs, *adultos* is the price an adult pays, an *obra* is an exhibit, a *visita guiada* is a guided tour, and the words "*Você está aqui*" on a map mean "You are here."

Discounts

You may be eligible for discounts at tourist sites, hotels, or on buses and trains—ask.

Is there a discount for...?	Tem desconto para...?	tay<u>n</u> dish-**koh<u>n</u>**-too **pah**-rah
...youths	...jovens	**zhah**-vay<u>n</u>sh
...students	...estudantes	ish-too-**dahn**-tish
...families	...familias	fah-**meel**-yahsh
...seniors	...idosos	id-**oh**-zoosh
...groups	...grupos	**groo**-poosh
I am...	Tenho...	**tayn**-yoo
He / She is...	Ele / Ela tem...	**eh**-leh / **eh**-lah tay<u>n</u>
... ___ years old.	... ___ anos.	___ **ah**-noosh
I am	Sou...	soh
He / She is...	Ele / Ela é...	**eh**-leh / **eh**-lah eh
...extremely old.	...velhinho.	vehl-**yeen**-hoo

In the Museum

Where is...?	Onde é...?	**ohn**-deh eh
I'd like to see...	Gostaria de ver...	goosh-tah-**ree**-ah deh vehr
We'd like to see...	Gostaríamos de ver...	goosh-tah-**ree**-ah-moosh deh vehr
Photo / Video O.K?	Foto / Vídeo O.K.?	**foh**-too / **vee**-day-oo "O.K."
No flash / tripod.	Não flash / tripé.	no<u>w</u> flahsh / tree-**peh**
I like it.	Eu gosto.	**eh**-oo **gohsh**-too
It's so...	É tão...	eh to<u>w</u>
...beautiful.	...lindo.	**leen**-doo
...ugly.	...feio.	**fay**-oo
...strange.	...estranho.	ish-**trahn**-yoo
...boring.	...aborrecido.	ah-boh-reh-**see**-doo
...interesting.	...interessante.	een-teh-reh-**sahn**-teh
...thought-provoking.	...provocante.	proh-voh-**kahn**-teh
...B.S.	...porcaria.	por-kah-**ree**-ah
I don't get it.	Não percebo.	no<u>w</u> pehr-**seh**-boo

Is it upside down?	Está aõ contrario?	ish-**tah** ow kohn-**trah**-ree-oo
Who did this?	Quem fez isto?	ka<u>y</u>n fehz **eesh**-too
How old is this?	Quantos anos tem isto?	**kwahn**-toosh ah-noosh tay<u>n</u> **eesh**-too
Wow!	Fiche!	**fee**-sheh
My feet hurt!	Os meus pés estão cansados!	oosh **meh**-oosh pehsh ish-**tow** kah<u>n</u>-**sah**-doosh
I'm exhausted!	Estou estoirado[a]!	ish-**toh** ish-toy-**rah**-doo
We're exhausted! (m / f)	Estamos estoirados[as]!	ish-**tah**-moosh ish-toy-**rah**-doosh

Art and Architecture

art	arte	**ar**-teh
artist	artista	ar-**teesh**-tah
painting	pintura	peeng-**too**-rah
self portrait	auto-retrato	ow-too-reh-**trah**-too
sculptor	escultor[a]	ish-kool-**tor**
sculpture	escultura	ish-kool-**too**-rah
architect	arquiteto	ar-kee-**teh**-too
architecture	arquitetura	ar-kee-teh-**too**-rah
original	original	oo-ree-zhee-**nahl**
restored	restaurado	rish-too-**rah**-doo
B.C.	A.C.	ah say
A.D.	D.C.	day say
century	secúlo	seh-**koo**-loo
style	estilo	ish-**tee**-loo
copy by ___	copiado por__	koo-pee-**ah**-doo poor
after the style of ___	como o estilo de___	**koh**-moo oo ish-**tee**-loo deh
from the school of ___	da escola de___	dah ish-**koh**-lah deh
abstract	abstrato	ahb-**shtrah**-too
ancient	antigo	ahn-**tee**-goo
Art Nouveau	arte nova	**ar**-teh **noh**-vah
Baroque	barroco	bah-**roh**-koo
classical	clássico	**klah**-see-koo
Gothic	gótico	**got**-ee-koo

Impressionist	impressionista	eem-preh-see-oo-**neesh**-tah
medieval	mediaval	meh-dee-ah-**vahl**
Modern art	arte moderna	**ar**-teh moh-**dehr**-nah
Moorish	mouro	**moh**-roo
Renaissance	renascimento	reh-nahsh-see-**mayn**-too
Romanesque	românico	roo-**mah**-nee-koo
Romantic	romântico	roo-**mahn**-tee-koo
Manueline	Manuelino	mah-neh-weh-**lee**-noo

Portugal's golden age of trade and exploration gave birth to a lavish, flamboyant Gothic style called "Manueline," named after King Manuel of the early 16th century.

Castles and Palaces

castle	castelo	kahsh-**teh**-loo
palace	palâcio	pah-**lah**-see-oo
kitchen	cozinha	koh-**zeen**-yah
cellar	celeiro	seh-**lay**-roo
dungeon	masmorra	mahsh-**moh**-rah
moat	fosso	**foh**-soo
fortified walls	fortificação	for-tee-fee-kah-**sow**
tower	torre	**tor**-reh
fountain	fonte	**fohn**-teh
garden	jardim	zhar-**deeng**
king	rei	ray
queen	raínha	rah-**een**-yah
knights	cavaleiros	kah-vah-**lay**-roosh

Religious Words

cathedral	catedral	kah-teh-**drahl**
church	igreija	ee-**gray**-zhah
monastery	monestério	moo-nish-**teh**-ree-oo
mosque	mesquita	mehsh-**kee**-tah
synagogue	sinagoga	see-nah-**goh**-gah
chapel	capela	kah-**peh**-lah

ACTIVITIES

altar	*altar*	ahl-**tar**
bells	*sinos*	**see**-noosh
choir	*coral*	koo-**rahl**
cloister	*mosteiro*	moo-**shtay**-roo
cross	*cruz*	kroosh
crypt	*caixão*	kī-**show**
dome	*cúpula*	**koo**-poo-lah
organ	*orgão*	or-**gow**
pulpit	*púlpito*	**pool**-pee-too
relic	*rélica*	**reh**-lee-kah
treasury	*tesoraria*	teh-zoh-**rah**-ree-ah
saint	*santo[a]*	**sahn**-too
God	*Deus*	**deh**-oosh
Christian	*Cristão*	kreesh-**tow**
Protestant	*Protestante*	proh-tish-**tayn**-teh
Catholic	*Católico[a]*	kah-**tal**-ee-koo
Jewish	*Judeu*	**zhoo**-deh-oo
Muslim	*Muçulmano[a]*	moo-sool-**mah**-noo
agnostic	*agnóstico[a]*	ahg-**nash**-tee-koo
atheist	*ateu*	ah-**teh**-oo
When is the mass / service?	*Quando é a missa / serviço?*	**kwahn**-doo eh ah **mee**-sah / sehr-**vee**-soo
Are there concerts in the church?	*Dão concertos na igreija?*	dow kohn-**sehr**-toosh nah ee-**gray**-zhah

---

KEY PHRASES: SIGHTSEEING

Where is...?	*Onde é...?*	**ohn**-deh eh
How much is it?	*Quanto custa?*	**kwahn**-too **koosh**-tah
What time does this open / close?	*A que horas é que abre / fecha?*	ah kee **oh**-rahsh eh keh **ah**-breh / **fay**-shah
Do you have a guided tour?	*Tem uma visita guiada?*	tayn **oo**-mah vee-**zee**-tah gee-**ah**-dah
When is the next tour in English?	*Quando é a próxima visita guiada em inglês?*	**kwahn**-doo eh ah **proh**-see-mah vee-**zee**-tah gee-**ah**-dah ayn een-**glaysh**

Shopping

Portuguese Shops

Where is a...?	Onde é um...?	**ohn**-deh eh oo<u>n</u>
antique shop	antiquário	ahn-tee-**kwah**-ree-oo
art gallery	galeria de arte	gah-leh-**ree**-ah deh **ar**-teh
bakery	padaria	pah-dah-**ree**-ah
barber shop	barbeiro	bar-**bay**-roo
beauty salon	cabelareiro	kah-beh-lah-**ray**-roo
book shop	livraria	leev-rah-**ree**-ah
camera shop	loja fotográfica	**lah**-zhah foh-toh-**grah**-fee-kah
cell phone shop	loja de telemóveis	**lah**-zhah deh teh-leh-**mow**-veh-eesh
clothing boutique	loja de roupa	**lah**-zhah deh **roh**-pah
coffee shop	café	kah-**feh**
delicatessen	charcutaria	shehr-koo-teh-**ree**-ah
department store	grande armazen	**grahn**-deh ar-mah-**zayn**
flea market	feira	**fay**-rah
flower market	mercado de flores	mehr-**kah**-doo deh **floh**-rish
grocery store	mercearia	mehr-see-ah-**ree**-ah
hardware store	casa de ferragens	**kah**-zah deh feh-rah-**zhayn**
Internet café	café Internet	kah-**feh een**-tehr-neht
jewelry shop	joalheria	zhoo-ahl-yeh-**ree**-ah
launderette	lavandaria	lah-vahn-dah-**ree**-ah
newsstand	quiosque	kee-**ahsh**-keh
office supplies	papelaria	pah-peh-lah-**ree**-ah
open air market	mercado municipal	mehr-**kah**-doo moo-nee-see-**pahl**
optician	oculista	ok-oo-**leesh**-tah
pastry shop	pastelaria	pahsh-teh-lah-**ree**-ah
pharmacy	farmácia	far-**mah**-see-ah

photocopy shop	*casa de fotocopias*	**kah**-zah deh foo-too-koh-**pee**-ahsh
shopping mall	*centro comercial*	**sayn**-troo koo-mehr-see-**ahl**
souvenir shop	*loja de lembranças*	**lah**-zhah deh layn-**brang**-sahsh
supermarket	*supermercado*	soo-pehr-mehr-**kah**-doo
sweets shop	*confeitaria*	kohn-fay-tah-**ree**-ah
toy store	*loja de brinquedos*	**lah**-zhah deh breeng-**kay**-doosh
travel agency	*agência de viagens*	ah-**zhayn**-see-ah deh vee-**ah**-zhaynsh
used bookstore	*loja de livros usados*	**lah**-zhah deh **leev**-rooz oo-**zah**-doosh
...with books in English	*...com livros em ingles*	kohn **leev**-rooz ayn een-**glaysh**
wine shop	*loja de vinhos*	**lah**-zhah deh **veen**-yoosh

In Portugal, most shops close for lunch from about 13:00 till 15:00, and all day on Sundays.

Shop Till You Drop

opening hours	*horário*	oh-**rah**-ree-oo
sale	*saldo*	**sahl**-doo
Where can I buy...?	*Onde compro...?*	**ohn**-deh **kohn**-proo
Where can we buy...?	*Onde compramos...?*	**ohn**-deh kohn-**prah**-moosh
How much is it?	*Quanto custa?*	**kwahn**-too **koosh**-tah
I'm / We're...	*Estou / Estamos...*	ish-**toh** / ish-**tah**-moosh
...just browsing.	*...só a olhar.*	soh ah ohl-**yar**
I'd like...	*Gostaria...*	goosh-tah-**ree**-ah
Do you have...?	*Tem...?*	tayn
...more	*...mais*	mīsh
...something cheaper	*...alguma coisa mais barato*	ahl-**goo**-mah **koy**-zah mīsh bah-**rah**-too
Better quality, please.	*Melhor qualidade, por favor.*	mil-**yor** kwah-lee-**dah**-deh poor fah-**vor**

English	Portuguese	Pronunciation
genuine / imitation	genuino / imitação	zheh-noo-**ee**-noo / eem-mee-tah-**sow**
Can I / Can we see more?	Posso / Podemos ver mais?	**pos**-soo / poo-**day**-moosh vehr mĩ sh
This one.	Este aqui.	**ehsh**-teh ah-**kee**
Can I try it on?	Posso exprimentar?	**pos**-soo ish-pree-mayn-**tar**
Do you have a mirror?	Tem um espelho?	tayn oon ish-**payl**-yoo
Too...	Muito...	**mween**-too
...big.	...grande.	**grahn**-deh
...small.	...pequeno.	peh-**kay**-noo
...expensive.	...caro.	**kah**-roo
It's too...	É muito...	eh **mween**-too
...short / long.	...curto / longo.	**koor**-too / **lon**-goo
...tight / loose.	...apertado / largo.	ah-pehr-**tah**-doo / **lar**-goo
...dark / light.	...escuro / claro.	ehsh-**koo**-roo / **klah**-roo
What is this made of?	Isto é feito de quê?	**eesh**-too eh **fay**-too deh kay
Is it machine washable?	Posso lavar á máquina?	**pos**-soo lah-**var** ah **mah**-kee-nah
Will it shrink?	Vai encolher?	vĩ ayn-kohl-**yehr**
Will it fade in the wash?	A côr sai na lavagem?	ah kor sĩ nah lah-**vah**-zhayn
Credit card O.K.?	Cartão de crédito O.K.?	kar-**tow** deh **kreh**-dee-too "O.K."
Can you ship this?	Pode enviar isto?	**pod**-eh ayn-vee-**ar** **eesh**-too
Tax-free?	Livre de impostos?	**lee**-vreh deh eem-**pohsh**-toosh
I'll think about it.	Vou pensar.	voh payn-**sar**
What time do you close?	A que horas é que fecha?	ah kee **oh**-rahsh eh keh **fay**-shah
What time do you open tomorrow?	A que horas é que abre amanhã?	ah kee **oh**-rahsh eh keh **ah**-breh ah-ming-**yah**

Street Markets

Did you make this?	*Foi você que fez isto?*	foy voh-**say** keh fehz **eesh**-too
Is that your best price?	*É o seu melhor preço?*	eh oo **seh**-oo mil-**yor** **pray**-soo
Cheaper?	*Mais barato?*	m?sh bah-**rah**-too
My last offer.	*A minha última oferta.*	ah **meen**-yah **ool**-tee-mah oo-**fehr**-tah
Good price.	*Bom preço.*	boh<u>n</u> **pray**-soo
I'll take it.	*Eu levo.*	**eh**-oo **leh**-voo
We'll take it.	*Nós levamos.*	nohsh leh-**vah**-moosh
I'm nearly broke.	*Estou quase sem dinheiro.*	ish-**toh kwah**-zeh say<u>n</u> deen-**yay**-roo
We're nearly broke.	*Estamos quase sem dinheiro.*	ish-**tah**-moosh **kwah**-zeh say<u>n</u> deen-**yay**-roo
My male friend...	*O meu amigo...*	oo **meh**-oo ah-**mee**-goo
My female friend...	*A minha amiga...*	ah **meen**-yah ah-**mee**-gah
My husband...	*O meu marido...*	oo **meh**-oo mah-**ree**-doo
My wife...	*A minha mulher...*	ah **meen**-yah mool-**yehr**
...has the money.	*...tem o dinheiro.*	tay<u>n</u> oo deen-**yay**-roo

At street markets, it's common to bargain.

KEY PHRASES: SHOPPING

Where can I buy...?	*Onde compro...?*	**ohn**-deh **kohn**-proo
Where is a...?	*Onde é um...?*	**ohn**-deh eh oo<u>n</u>
...grocery store	*...mercearia*	mehr-see-ah-**ree**-ah
...department store	*...grande armazen*	**grahn**-deh ar-mah-**zayn**
...Internet café	*...café Internet*	kah-**feh een**-tehr-neht
...launderette	*...lavandaria*	lah-vahn-dah-**ree**-ah
...pharmacy	*...farmácia*	far-**mah**-see-ah
How much is it?	*Quanto custa?*	**kwahn**-too **koosh**-tah
I'm just browsing.	*Estou só a olhar.*	ish-**toh** sah ah ohl-**yar**

Clothes

For...	Para...	**pah**-rah
...a male / female baby.	...um menino / uma menina bebé.	oon meh-**nee**-noo / **oo**-mah meh-**nee**-nah bay-**bay**
...a child (m /f)	...um menino / uma menina.	oon meh-**nee**-noo / **oo**-mah meh-**nee**-nah
...a teenager (m /f)	...um rapaz / uma rapariga.	oon rah-**pahsh** / **oo**-mah rah-pah-**ree**-gah
...a man.	...um homen.	oon **oh**-mayn
...a woman.	...uma senhora.	**oo**-mah sehn-**yoh**-rah
bathrobe	robe	**roh**-beh
bib	babete	bah-**beh**-teh
belt	cinto	**seen**-too
bra	soutien	**soo**-tee-ayn
clothing	roupas	**roh**-pahsh
dress	vestido	vehsh-**tee**-doo
flip-flops	sandálias de dedo	sahn-**dah**-lee-ahsh deh **deh**-doo
gloves	luvas	**loo**-vahsh
hat	chapéu	chah-**pow**
jacket	casaco	kah-**zah**-koo
jeans	ganga	**gahn**-gah
nightgown	camisa de dormir	kah-**mee**-zah deh dor-**meer**
nylons	meia de vidro, collants	**may**-ah deh **veed**-roo, koh-**lahnts**
pajamas	pijamas	pee-**zhah**-mahsh
pants	calças	**kahl**-sahsh
raincoat	capa de chuva	**kah**-pah deh **shoo**-vah
sandals	sandálias	sahn-**dah**-lee-ahsh
scarf	lenço	**lehn**-soo
shirt...	camisa...	kah-**mee**-zah
...long-sleeved	...manga-longa	mayn-gah-**lohn**-gah
...short-sleeved	...manga-curta	mayn-gah-**koor**-tah
...sleeveless	...sem mangas	sayn **mayn**-gahsh

shoelaces	cordão de sapatos	kor-**dow** deh sah-**pah**-toosh
shoes	sapatos	sah-**pah**-toosh
shorts	calções	kahl-**sowsh**
skirt	saia	**sah**-ee-ah
sleeper (for baby)	pijama	pee-**zhah**-mah
slip	combinação	kohn-bee-nah-**sow**
slippers	chinélos	shee-**neh**-loosh
socks	meias	**meh**-ee-ahsh
sweater	camisolas	kah-**mee**-zoh-lahsh
swimsuit	fato de banho	**fah**-too deh **bahn**-yoo
tennis shoes	tenis	**teh**-nees
T-shirt	T-shirt	"T-shirt"
underwear	roupas de interior	**roh**-pahsh deh in-teh-ree-**oor**
vest	colete	koh-**leh**-teh

Colors

black	prêto	**pray**-too
blue	azul	**ah**-zool
brown	castanho	kah-**shtayn**-yoo
gray	cinzento	seen-**zehn**-too
green	verde	**vehr**-deh
orange	laranja	lah-**rayn**-zhah
pink	rosa	**roh**-zah
purple	roxo	**roh**-shoh
red	vermelho, encarnado	vehr-**mehl**-yoo, ehn-kar-**nah**-doo
white	branco	**brang**-koo
yellow	amarelo	ah-mah-**reh**-loo
dark / light	escuro / claro	ehsh-**koo**-roo / **klah**-roo
Lighter...	Mais claro...	mīsh **klah**-roo
Brighter...	Mais brilhante...	mīsh breel-**yahn**-teh
Darker...	Mais escuro...	mīsh ehsh-**koo**-roo
...shade.	...tonalidade.	toh-nah-lee-**dah**-deh

Materials

brass	*latão*	lah-**tow**
bronze	*bronze*	**brohn**-zeh
ceramic	*ceramica*	seh-**rah**-mee-kah
copper	*cobre*	**koh**-breh
cotton	*algodão*	ahl-goh-**dow**
glass	*vidro*	**veed**-roo
gold	*ouro*	**oh**-roo
lace	*renda*	**rehn**-dah
leather	*pele*	**peh**-leh
linen	*linho*	**leen**-yoh
marble	*mármore*	**mar**-mor-eh
metal	*metal*	meh-**tahl**
nylon	*nylon*	**nī**-lohn
paper	*papel*	pah-**pehl**
pewter	*estanho*	ehsh-**tahn**-yoo
plastic	*plástico*	**plahsh**-tee-koo
polyester	*poliester*	poh-lee-**ehsh**-tehr
porcelain	*porcelana*	por-seh-**lah**-nah
silk	*seda*	**seh**-dah
silver	*prata*	**prah**-tah
velvet	*veludo*	veh-**loo**-doo
wood	*madeira*	mah-**day**-rah
wool	*lã*	lahn

Jewelry

bracelet	*bracelete*	brah-seh-**leh**-teh
brooch	*broche*	**broh**-sheh
earrings	*brincos*	**breen**-koosh
jewelry	*jóias*	**zhoh**-ee-ahsh
necklace	*côlar*	**koh**-lar
ring	*anel*	**ah**-nehl
Is this...?	*Isto é...?*	**eesh**-too eh
...sterling silver	*...de prata*	deh **prah**-tah
...real gold	*...de ouro*	deh **oh**-roo
...stolen	*...roubado*	roh-**bah**-doo

Sports

Bicycling

English	Portuguese	Pronunciation
bicycle	bicicleta	bee-see-**kleh**-tah
mountain bike	bicicleta de montanha	bee-see-**kleh**-tah deh mohn-**tahn**-yah
I'd like to rent a bicycle.	Gostaria de alugar uma bicicleta.	goosh-tah-**ree**-ah deh ah-loo-**gar oo**-mah bee-see-**kleh**-tah
We'd like to rent two bicycles.	Gostaríamos de alugar duas bicicletas.	goosh-tah-**ree**-ah-moosh deh ah-loo-**gar doo**-ahsh bee-see-**kleh**-tahsh
How much per...?	Quanto é por...?	**kwahn**-too eh poor
...hour	...hora	**oh**-rah
...half day	...meio-dia	may-oo-**dee**-ah
...day	...dia	**dee**-ah
Is a deposit required?	É preciso depósito impresindível?	eh preh-**see**-zoo deh-**poh**-zee-too eem-preh-seen-**dee**-vehl
deposit	depósito	deh-**poh**-zee-too
helmet	capacete	kah-pah-**seh**-teh
lock	aluquete	ah-loo-**keh**-teh
air / no air	ar / não há ar	ar / no<u>w</u> ah ar
tire	pneu	**pehn**-yoo
pump	bomba	**bohm**-bah
map	mapa	**mah**-pah
How many gears?	Quantas mudanças?	**kwahn**-tahsh **moo**-dahn-sahsh
What is a...	O que é uma...	oo keh eh **oo**-mah...
route of about ___ kilometers?	rota de cerca de ___ kilómetros?	**roo**-tah deh **sehr**-kah deh ___ kee-**loo**-meh-troosh
...good	...bom	boh<u>n</u>
...scenic	...bonita	boh-**nee**-tah
...interesting	...interessante	een-teh-reh-**sahn**-teh
...easy	...fácil	**fah**-seel

How many minutes / hours by bicycle?	Quantos minutos / horas de bicicleta?	kwahn-toosh mee-noo-toosh / oh-rahsh deh bee-see-kleh-tah
I (don't) like hills.	Eu (não) gosto de subídas.	eh-oo (now) gohsh-too deh soo-bee-dahsh
I brake for bakeries.	Paro em todas as padarias.	pah-roo ayn toh-dahsh ahsh pah-dah-ree-ahsh

For more on route-finding, see page 47 in the Traveling chapter.

Swimming and Boating

Where can I / can we rent a...?	Onde posso / podemos alugar um...?	ohn-deh pos-soo / poh-day-moosh ah-loo-gar oon
...paddleboat	...gaivota	gī-voh-tah
...rowboat	...barco a rêmo	bar-koo ah ray-moo
...boat	...barco	bar-koo
...sailboat	...veleiro	veh-lay-roo
How much per...?	Quanto é por...?	kwahn-too eh poor
...hour	...hora	oh-rah
...half day	...meio-dia	may-oo-dee-ah
...day	...dia	dee-ah
beach	praia	prī-ah
nude beach	praia de nudismo	prī-ah deh noo-deezh-moo
Where's a good beach?	Onde fica uma boa praia?	ohn-deh fee-kah oo-mah boh-ah prī-ah
Is it safe for swimming?	É seguro nadar?	eh seh-goo-roo nah-dar
flip-flops	sandálias	sahn-dah-lee-ahsh
pool	piscina	pee-shee-nah
snorkel and mask	tubo e máscara para mergulho	too-boo ee mahsh-kah-rah pah-rah mehr-gool-yoo
sunglasses	óculos de sol	oh-koo-loosh deh sool
sunscreen	crème proteção solar	kreh-meh proh-teh-sow soh-lar

surfboard	prancha	**prayn**-shah
surfer	surfista	**soor**-fee-shtah
swimsuit	fato de banho	**fah**-too deh **bahn**-yoo
towel	toalha	too-**ahl**-yah
waterskiing	esqui aquático	ish-**kee** ah-**kwah**-tee-koo
windsurfing	windsurfing	"windsurfing"

In Portugal, nearly any beach is topless. For a nude beach, keep your eyes peeled for a *praia de nudismo.*

Sports Talk

sports	desporto	dish-**por**-too
game	jogo	**zhoh**-goo
championship	campeonato	kahm-peh-oo-**nah**-too
soccer	futebol	foo-teh-**bohl**
basketball	basquetebol	bash-keht-**bohl**
hockey	hóquei	**oh**-kay
American football	futebol americano	foo-teh-**bohl** ah-meh-ree-**kah**-noo
baseball	basebol	bayz-**bohl**
tennis	ténis	**teh**-neesh
golf	golfe	"golf"
skiing	esquiar	ish-kee-**ar**
gymnastics	ginastica	zheen-**ahsh**-tee-kah
jogging	correr	koh-**rehr**
Olympics	Olímpicos	oh-**leem**-pee-koosh
medal...	medalha...	meh-**dahl**-yah
...gold / silver / bronze	...de ouro / de prata / de bronze	deh **oh**-roo / deh **prah**-tah / deh **brohn**-zeh
What is your favorite sport / athlete / team?	Qual é o seu desporto / atleta / equipe favorito?	kwahl eh oo **seh**-oo dish-**por**-too / aht-**leh**-tah / eh-**kee**-peh fah-voh-**ree**-too
Where can I see a game?	Onde posso ver um jogo?	**ohn**-deh **pos**-soo vehr oon **zhoh**-goo
Where's a good place to jog?	A onde há um bom sitio para correr?	ah **ohn**-deh ah oon bohn **see**-tee-oo **pah**-rah koh-**rer**

Entertainment

What's happening tonight?	O que se passa esta noite?	oo keh seh **pah**-sah **ehsh**-tah **noy**-teh
What do you recommend?	O que é que recomenda?	oo keh eh keh ray-koo-**mayn**-dah
Where is it?	Onde é?	**ohn**-deh eh
How do I / do we get there?	Como chego / chegamos lá?	**koh**-moo **shay**-goo / shay-**gah**-moosh lah
Is it free?	É gratis?	eh **grah**-teesh
Are there seats available?	Hà mais assentos?	ah mīz ah-**sehn**-toosh
Where can I buy a ticket?	Onde posso comprar um bilhete?	**ohn**-deh **pos**-soo kohn-**prar** oon beel-**yeh**-teh
Do you have tickets for today / tonight?	Há bilhetes para hoje / hoje a noite?	ah beel-**yeh**-tish **pah**-rah **oh**-zheh / **oh**-zheh ah **noy**-teh
When does it start?	Quando começa?	**kwahn**-doo koh-**meh**-sah
When does it end?	Quando termina?	**kwahn**-doo tehr-**mee**-nah
Where's the best place to dance nearby?	Onde é o melhor lugar para dançar por aqui?	**ohn**-deh eh oo mil-**yor** loo-**gar pah**-rah dah<u>n</u>-**sar** poor ah-**kee**
Where do people stroll?	Onde se pode passear?	**ohn**-deh seh **pod**-eh pah-seh-**ar**

Fado is Portugal's mournful style of folk singing. An evening absorbed in these fishermen's "blues" can leave you with sorrow creases. A good show is powerful stuff.

Entertaining Words

movie...	filme...	**feel**-meh
...original version	...versão original	vehr-**sow** oo-ree-zhee-**nahl**
...in English	...em inglês	ay<u>n</u> een-**glaysh**

...with subtitles	...com legendas	kohn leh-**zhayn**-dahsh
...dubbed	...dobrado	doo-**brah**-doo
music...	música...	**moo**-zee-kah
...live	...ao vivo	ow **vee**-voo
...classical	...clássico	**klah**-see-koo
...folk	...folclore	fool-**klah**-reh
...opera	...ópera	**oh**-peh-rah
...symphony	...simfonia	seeng-foh-**nee**-ah
...choir	...coral	koo-**rahl**
rock / jazz / blues	rock / jazz / blues	"rock" / zhahz / bloosh
singer	cantor[a]	kahn-**tor**
concert	concerto	kohn-**sehr**-too
show	espetáculo	ish-peh-**tah**-koo-loo
(folk) dancing	dança (folclórica)	**dahn**-sah (fool-**klah**-ree-kah)
cockfight	briga de galo	**bree**-gah deh **gah**-loo
disco	disco	**deesh**-koo
bar with live music	bar com música ao vivo	bar kohn **moo**-zee-kah ow **vee**-voo
nightclub	nightclub, bar	"nightclub," bar
(no) cover charge	(não) entrada	(now) ayn-**trah**-dah
sold out	vendido	vehn-**dee**-doo

CONNECT

Phoning

I'd like to buy a...	*Quero compar um...*	**kay**-roo kohn-**prar** oon
...telephone card.	*...cartão telefónico.*	kar-**tow** teh-leh-**foh**-nee-koo
...cheap	*...cartão telefónico*	kar-**tow** teh-leh-**foh**-nee-koo
international	*económico*	eh-koo-**noh**-mee-koo
telephone card.	*para chamadas*	**pah**-rah shah-**mah**-dahsh
	internacionais.	een-tehr-nah-see-oh-**nīsh**
Where is the	*Onde é o próximo*	**ohn**-deh eh oo **proh**-see-moo
nearest phone?	*telefone?*	teh-leh-**foh**-neh
It doesn't work.	*Não funciona.*	no<u>w</u> foon-see-**oh**-nah
May I use your	*Posso utilizar*	**pos**-soo oo-tee-lee-**zar**
phone?	*o seu telefone?*	oo **seh**-oo teh-leh-**foh**-neh
Can you talk for me?	*Pode falar por mim?*	**pod**-eh fah-**lar** poor meeng
It's busy.	*Está ocupado.*	ish-**tah** oo-koo-**pah**-doo
Will you try again?	*Pode tentar*	**pod**-eh tayn-**tar**
	novamente?	noo-vah-**mayn**-teh
Hello. (answering	*Está.*	ish-**tah**
the phone)		
My name is ___.	*Chamo-me ___.*	**shah**-moo-meh
Sorry, I speak	*Desculpe, eu so*	dish-**kool**-peh, **eh**-oo soh
only a little	*falo um pouquinho*	**fah**-loo oo<u>n</u> poh-**keen**-yoo
Portuguese.	*português.*	poor-too-**gaysh**

145

| Speak slowly and clearly. | *Fale devagar e claramente.* | **fah**-leh deh-vah-**gar** eh klah-rah-**mayn**-teh |
| Wait a moment. | *Espere um momento.* | ehsh-**peh**-reh oo<u>n</u> moo-**mayn**-too |

In this book, you'll find the phrases you need to reserve a hotel room (page 51) or a table at a restaurant (page 68). To spell your name over the phone, use the code alphabet on page 53.

Make your calls using a handy phone card. These are sold at post offices, train stations, *quiosques* (newsstands), *tabacarias* (tobacco shops), and machines near phone booths. There are two kinds of phone cards:

1) an insertable card (*cartão telefónico*) that you slide into a phone in a phone booth, and...

2) a cheaper-per-minute international phone card (with a scratch-off PIN code) that you can use from any phone, usually even from your hotel room. To get a PIN card, ask for a *cartão telefónico económico para chamadas internacionais*.

At phone booths, you'll encounter these words on the phone: *introduzir o cartão* (insert the card), *marque o numero* (dial your number), and *importancia restante* (the amount of money left on your card). At any time while you're dialing, you may hear a brusque recording: "*Esse numero não existe*" (The number you're dialing does not work). You can also make phone calls from easy to use metered phones in post offices, telephone offices. For more tips, see "Let's Talk Telephones" on page 258 in the Appendix.

Telephone Words

telephone	*telefone*	teh-leh-**foh**-neh
telephone card	*cartão telefónico*	kar-**tow** teh-leh-**foh**-nee-koo
cheap telephone card with a PIN code	*cartão telefónico económico para chamadas internacionais*	kar-**tow** teh-leh-**foh**-nee-koo eh-koo-**noh**-mee-koo **pah**-rah shah-**mah**-dahsh een-tehr-nah-see-oh-**nīsh**

CONNECT

PIN code	código pessoal	**koh**-dee-goo peh-soh-**ahl**
phone booth	telefone publico	teh-leh-**foh**-neh **poob**-lee-koo
out of service	desligado	dish-lee-**gah**-doo
metered phone	telefone com contador	teh-leh-**foh**-neh koh<u>n</u> koh<u>n</u>-tah-**dor**
post office	correios	koo-**ray**-oosh
phone office	puesto telefónico	**pway**-shtoo teh-leh-**foh**-nee-koo
operator	telefonista	teh-leh-foh-**neesh**-tah
international assistance	assistência internacional	ah-seesh-**tayn**-see-ah een-tehr-nah-see-oo-**nahl**
international call	chamada internacional	shah-**mah**-dah een-tehr-nah-see-oo-**nahl**
collect call	chamada para pagar	shah-**mah**-dah pah-rah pah-**gar**
credit card call	chamada com cartão de crédito	shah-**mah**-dah koh<u>n</u> kar-**tow** deh **kreh**-dee-too
toll-free call	chamada taxa grátis	shah-**mah**-dah **tah**-shah **grah**-teesh
fax	fax	fahks
country code	código do país	**kod**-ee-goo doo pah-**eesh**
area code	código da área	**kod**-ee-goo dah **ah**-ray-ah
extension	extenção	ish-tehn-**sow**
telephone book	lista telefónica	**leesh**-tah teh-leh-**foh**-nee-kah
yellow pages	páginas amarelas	**pah**-zhee-nahsh ah-mah-**reh**-lahsh

CONNECT

Cell Phones

Where is a cell phone shop?	Onde é a loja que vende telemoveis?	**ohn**-deh eh ah **lah**-zhah keh **vehn**-deh teh-leh-**moh**-veh-ish
I'd like / We'd like...	Queria / Queriamos...	keh-**ree**-ah / keh-**ree**-ah-moosh
...a cell phone.	...um telemóvel.	oo<u>n</u> teh-leh-**moh**-vehl

...a chip.	...um cartão.	oon kar-**tow**
...to buy more time.	...carregar o cartão.	kah-reh-**gar** oo kar-**tow**
How do you...?	Como se...?	**koh**-moo seh
...make calls	...faz uma chamada	fahz **oo**-mah shah-**mah**-dah
...receive calls	...receber chamadas	reh-seh-**behr** shah-**mah**-dahs
Will this work outside this country?	Posso usar fôra do país?	**pos**-soo oo-**zar** **foh**-rah doo pah-**eesh**
Where can I buy a chip for this service / phone?	Onde posso comprar um cartão para este serviço / telefone?	**ohn**-deh **pos**-soo kohn-**prar** oon kar-**tow** **pah**-rah **ehsh**-teh sehr-**vee**-soo / teh-leh-**foh**-neh

Many travelers now buy cell phones in Europe to make both local and international calls. You'll pay under $100 for a "locked" phone that works only in the country you buy it in (includes about $20 worth of calls). You can buy additional time at a newsstand or cell phone shop. An "unlocked" phone is more expensive (over $100), but it works all over Europe: when you cross a border, buy a SIM card at a cell phone shop and insert the pop-out chip, which comes with a new phone number. Pricier tri-band phones (*telefone de linha tripula*) also work in North America.

E-Mail and the Web

E-Mail

My e-mail address is ___.	Meu endereço eletrônico é ___.	**meh**-oo ay<u>n</u>-deh-**ray**-soo eh-leh-**troh**-nee-koo eh
What's your e-mail address?	Qual é o seu endereço eletrônico?	kwahl eh oo **seh**-oo ay<u>n</u>-deh-**ray**-soo eh-leh-**troh**-nee-koo
Can I use this computer to check my e-mail?	Posso usar este computador para verificar o meu e-mail?	**pos**-soo oo-**zar ehsh**-teh kohm-poo-tah-**dor pah**-rah veh-ree-fee-**kar** oo **meh**-oo **ee**-mayl
Where can I / can we access the Internet?	Onde posso / podemos usar a Internet?	**oh<u>n</u>**-deh **pos**-soo / poh-**day**-mooz oo-**zar** ah **een**-tehr-neht
Where is an Internet cafe?	A onde é o café Internet?	ah **oh<u>n</u>**-deh eh oo kah-**feh een**-tehr-neht
How much for... minutes?	Quanto é por... minutos?	**kwahn**-too eh poor mee-**noo**-toosh
...10	...dez	dehsh
...15	...quinze	**keen**-zeh
...30	...trinta	**treen**-tah
...60	...sessenta	seh-**sayn**-tah
Help me, please.	Por favor ajude-me.	poor **fah**-vor ah-**zhoo**-deh-meh
How do I...?	Como...?	**koh**-moo
...start this	...ligo	**lee**-goo
...send a file	...mando uma página	**mahn**-doo **oo**-mah **pah**-zhee-nah
...print out a file	...emprimo uma página	ay<u>n</u>-**pree**-moo **oo**-mah **pah**-zhee-nah

...make this symbol	...faço este símbolo	**fah**-soo **ehsh**-teh **seeng**-boh-loo
...type @	...escrevo arrôba	ish-**kreh**-voo ah-**roh**-bah
This isn't working.	Isto está avariado.	**eesh**-too ish-**tah** ah-vah-ree-**ah**-doo

Web Words

e-mail	e-mail	**ee**-mayl
e-mail address	endereço eletrônico	ayn-deh-**ray**-soo eh-leh-**troh**-nee-koo
Web site	local da Web	loh-**kahl** dah wehb
Internet	Internet	**een**-tehr-neht
surf the Web	navegar a Web	nah-veh-**gar** ah wehb
download	transferência	traynsh-feh-**rayn**-see-ah
@ sign	arrôba	ah-**roh**-bah
dot	ponto	**pohn**-too
hyphen (-)	hífen	**hee**-fehn
underscore (_)	sublinhar	soob-leen-**yar**
modem	modem	**moh**-dehm

On Screen

abrir	open	**guardar**	save
eliminar	delete	**imprimir**	print
enviar	send	**escrever**	write
escrever	write	**mensagem**	message
ficheiro	file	**voltar**	reply

KEY PHRASES: E-MAIL AND THE WEB

e-mail	e-mail	**ee**-mayl
Internet	Internet	**een**-tehr-neht
Where is the nearest Internet café?	A onde é o próximo café Internet?	ah **ohn**-deh eh oo **proh**-see-moo kah-**feh een**-tehr-neht
I'd like to check my e-mail.	Gostaria ver o meu e-mail.	goosh-tah-**ree**-ah vehr oo **meh**-oo **ee**-mayl

CONNECT

Mailing

Where is the post office?	Onde é os correios?	oh<u>n</u>-deh eh oosh koo-**ray**-oosh
Which window for...?	Que janela para...?	keh zhah-**neh**-lah **pah**-rah
Is this the line for...?	Esta é a fila para...?	**ehsh**-tah eh ah **fee**-lah **pah**-rah
...stamps	...selos	**say**-loosh
...packages	...embrulhos	ay<u>n</u>-**brool**-yoosh
To the United States...	Para os Estados Unidos...	**pah**-rah ooz ish-**tah**-doosh oo-**nee**-doosh
...by air mail.	...por avião.	poor ahv-**yow**
...by surface mail.	...de barco.	deh **bar**-koo
...slow and cheap.	...sem pressa e barato.	say<u>n</u> **preh**-sah eh bah-**rah**-too
How much is it?	Quanto custa?	**kwahn**-too **koosh**-tah
How much to send a letter / postcard to...?	Quanto custa para mundar uma carta / um cartão postal para...?	**kwahn**-too **koosh**-tah **pah**-rah moon-**dar** **oo**-mah **kar**-tah / oo<u>n</u> kar-**tow** poosh-**tahl** **pah**-rah
I need stamps for ___ postcards to...	Preciso de selos para ___ cartões postais para...	preh-**see**-zoo deh **say**-loosh **pah**-rah ___ kar-**towsh** poosh-**tïsh pah**-rah
...America	...América	ah-**meh**-ree-kah
...Canada	...Canadá	kah-nah-**dah**
Pretty stamps, please.	Selos bonitos, por favor.	**say**-loosh boh-**nee**-toosh, poor fah-**vor**
I always choose the slowest line.	Eu sempre escolho a bicha mais lenta.	**eh**-oo **sehm**-preh ehsh-**kohl**-yoh ah **bee**-shah mïsh **lehn**-tah
How many days will it take?	Quantos dias é que demora?	**kwahn**-toosh **dee**-ahsh eh keh deh-**moh**-rah

Handy Postal Words

post office	correios	koo-**ray**-oosh
stamp	selo	**say**-loo
postcard	cartão postal	kar-**tow** poosh-**tahl**
letter	carta	**kar**-tah
envelope	envelope	ay<u>n</u>-veh-**loh**-peh
package	embrulho	ay<u>n</u>-**brool**-yoo
box...	caixa...	**kī**-shah
...cardboard	...cartolina	kar-toh-**lee**-nah
string	fio	**fee**-oo
tape	adesivo	ah-deh-**zee**-voo
mailbox	caixa postal	**kī**-shah poosh-**tahl**
air mail	por avião	poor ahv-**yow**
express	expresso	ish-**preh**-soo
surface mail	de barco	deh **bar**-koo
slow and cheap	sem pressa e barato	say<u>n</u> **preh**-sah eh bah-**rah**-too
book rate	o livro da tabela de preços	oo **leev**-roo dah tah-**beh**-lah deh **preh**-soosh
weight limit	limite de peso	lee-**mee**-teh deh **pay**-zoo
registered	registrado	ray-zheesh-**trah**-doo
insured	seguro	say-**goo**-roo
fragile	frágil	**frah**-zheel
contents	conteúdo	koh<u>n</u>-teh-**oo**-doo
customs	alfândega	ahl-**fahn**-deh-gah
sender	remetente	reh-meh-**tayn**-teh
destination	destino	dish-**tee**-noo
to / from	para / de	**pah**-rah / deh
address	endereço	ay<u>n</u>-deh-**ray**-soo
zip code	código postal	**kod**-ee-goo poosh-**tahl**
general delivery	Despacho Geral	dehsh-**pah**-shoo zheh-**rahl**

In Portugal, you can often get stamps at a *quiosque* (news-stand) or *tabacaria* (tobacco shop). As long as you know which stamps you need, this is a great convenience.

HELP!

Help!	*Socorro!*	soo-**koh**-roo
Help me!	*Ajude-me!*	ah-**zhoo**-deh-meh
Call a doctor!	*Chame um doutor!*	**shah**-meh oo<u>n</u> doh-**tor**
Call...	*Chame...*	**shah**-meh
...the police.	*...a polícia.*	ah poo-**lee**-see-ah
...an ambulance.	*...a ambulância.*	ah ay<u>n</u>-boo-**lahn**-see-ah
...the fire department.	*...os bombeiros.*	oosh boh<u>n</u>-**bay**-roosh
I'm lost.	*Estou perdido[a].*	ish-**toh** pehr-**dee**-doo
We're lost.	*Estamos perdidos[as].*	ish-**tah**-moosh pehr-**dee**-doosh
Thank you for your help.	*Obrigado[a] por a sua ajuda.*	oh-bree-**gah**-doo poor ah **soo**-ah ah-**zhoo**-dah
You are very kind.	*Você é muito gentil.*	voh-**say** eh **mween**-too zhay<u>n</u>-**teel**

KEY PHRASES: HELP!

accident	*acidente*	ah-see-**dayn**-teh
emergency	*emergência*	ee-mehr-**zhayn**-see-ah
police	*polícia*	poo-**lee**-see-ah
Help!	*Socorro!*	soo-**koh**-roo
Call a doctor / the police!	*Chame um doutor / a polícia!*	**shah**-meh oo<u>n</u> doh-**tor** / ah poo-**lee**-see-ah
Stop, thief!	*Pare, ladrão!*	**pah**-reh lah-**drow**

153

Theft and Loss

Stop, thief!	*Pare, ladrão!*	**pah**-reh lah-**drow**
I have been robbed.	*Fui roubado[a].*	fwee roh-**bah**-doo
We have been robbed.	*Fomos roubados[as].*	**foh**-moosh roh-**bah**-doosh
A thief took...	*Um ladrão levou...*	oo<u>n</u> lah-**drow** leh-**voh**
Thieves took...	*Ladrões levaram...*	lah-**drowsh** leh-**vah**-ray<u>n</u>
I've lost my...	*Perdi o meu...*	**pehr**-dee oo **meh**-oo
...money.	*...dinheiro.*	deen-**yay**-roo
...passport.	*...passaporte.*	pah-sah-**por**-teh
...ticket.	*...bilhete.*	beel-**yeh**-teh
...baggage.	*...bagagem.*	bah-**gah**-zhay<u>n</u>
I've lost my...	*Perdi a minha...*	**pehr**-dee ah **meen**-yah
...purse.	*...bolsa.*	**bohl**-sah
...wallet.	*...carteira.*	kar-**tay**-rah
...faith in humankind.	*...fé na humanidade.*	feh nah oo-mah-nee-**dah**-deh
We've lost...	*Perdemos...*	pehr-**deh**-moosh
...our money.	*...o nosso dinheiro.*	oo **noh**-soo deen-**yay**-roo
...our passports.	*...nossos passaportes.*	**noh**-soosh pah-sah-**por**-tish
...our tickets.	*...nossos bilhetes.*	**noh**-soosh beel-**yeh**-tish
...our baggage.	*...nossa bagagem.*	**noh**-sah bah-**gah**-zhay<u>n</u>
I want to contact my embassy.	*Quero contactar a minha embaixada.*	**kay**-roo koh<u>n</u>-tahk-**tar** ah **meen**-yah ay<u>n</u>-bī-**shah**-dah
I need to file a police report for my insurance.	*Quero fazer uma ocorrência na policia para o meu seguro.*	**kay**-roo fah-**zehr** oo-mah oh-koh-**rayn**-see-ah nah poo-**lee**-see-ah **pah**-rah oo **meh**-oo seh-**goo**-roo

See page 260 in the Appendix for information on the U.S. Embassy in Portugal.

Helpful Words

ambulance	*ambulância*	ay<u>n</u>-boo-**lahn**-see-ah
accident	*acidente*	ah-see-**dayn**-teh
injured	*ferido*	feh-**ree**-doo
emergency	*emergência*	ee-mehr-**zhayn**-see-ah
emergency room	*sala de emergência*	**sah**-lah deh ee-mehr-**zhayn**-see-ah
fire	*fogo*	**foh**-goo
police	*polícia*	poo-**lee**-see-ah
smoke	*fumo*	**foo**-moo
thief	*ladrão*	lah-**drow**
pickpocket	*carteirista*	kar-tay-**rish**-tah

Help for Women

Leave me alone.	*Deixe-me em paz.*	**day**-sheh-meh ay<u>n</u> pahsh
I want to be alone.	*Quero estar só.*	**keh**-roo ish-**tar** soh
I'm not interested.	*Não estou interessada.*	no<u>w</u> ish-**toh** een-teh-reh-**sah**-dah
I'm married.	*Sou casada.*	soh kah-**zah**-dah
I'm a lesbian.	*Sou lésbia.*	soh **lehzh**-bee-ah
I have a contagious disease.	*Tenho uma doença contagiosa.*	**tayn**-yoo **oo**-mah doo-**ayn**-sah koh<u>n</u>-tah-zhee-**oh**-zah
You are bothering me.	*Você está a incomodar-me.*	voh-**say** ish-**tah** ah een-koh-moh-**dar**-meh
This man is bothering me.	*Este senhore está a incomodar-me.*	**ehsh**-teh sin-**yoh**-reh ish-**tah** ah een-koh-moh-**dar**-meh
You are intrusive.	*Você é curioso.*	voh-**say** eh koo-ree-**oh**-zoh
Don't touch me.	*Não me toque.*	no<u>w</u> meh **toh**-keh
You're disgusting.	*Tu dás-me nojo.*	too **dahsh**-meh **noh**-zhoo
Stop following me.	*Pare de me seguir.*	**pah**-reh deh meh seh-**geer**

Stop it!	*Pare com isso!*	**pah**-reh koh<u>n</u> **ee**-soo
Enough!	*Chega!*	**shay**-gah
Go away.	*Vá-se embora.*	**vah**-seh ay<u>n</u>-**boh**-rah
Get lost!	*Desapareça!*	day-zah-pah-**ray**-sah
Drop dead!	*Quero que morra!*	**keh**-roo keh **moh**-rah
I'll call the police!	*Vou chamar a polícia!*	voh shah-**mar** ah poo-**lee**-see-ah

SERVICES

Laundry

English	Portuguese	Pronunciation
Is a... laundry nearby?	Há uma... lavanderia por perto?	ah **oo**-mah... lah-vahn-dah-**ree**-ah poor **pehr**-too
...self-service	...self-service	"self-service"
...full-service	...serviço completo	sehr-**vee**-soo koh<u>n</u>-**pleh**-too
Help me, please.	Por favor ajude-me.	poor fah-**vor** ah-**zhoo**-dah-meh
How does this work?	Como funciona?	**koh**-moo foon-see-**oh**-nah
Where is the soap?	Onde está o sabão?	**oh<u>n</u>**-deh ish-**tah** oo sah-**bow**
Are these yours?	São seus?	sow **seh**-oosh
This stinks.	Cheira muito mal.	**shay**-rah **mween**-too mahl
Smells like...	Cheira como...	**shay**-rah **koh**-moo
...spring time.	...primavera.	pree-mah-**veh**-rah
...a locker room.	...um gabinet.	oo<u>n</u> gah-bee-**neht**
...cheese.	...queijo.	**kay**-zhoo
I need change.	Preciso de troco.	pray-**see**-zoo deh **troh**-koo

Same-day service?	*No mesmo dia?*	noo **mehsh**-moo **dee**-ah
By when do I need to drop off my clothes?	*Quando é que tenho de deixar as minhas roupas?*	**kwahn**-doo eh keh **tayn**-yoo deh day-**shar** ahsh **meen**-yahsh **roh**-pahsh
When will my clothes be ready?	*Quando é que as minhas roupas estão prontas?*	**kwahn**-doo eh keh ahsh **meen**-yahsh **roh**-pahsh ish-**tow prohn**-tahsh
Dried?	*Secas?*	**say**-kahsh
Folded?	*Dobradas?*	doo-**brah**-dahsh
Hey there, what's spinning?	*O que está a rodar?*	oo keh ish-**tah** ah roh-**dar**

Clean words

full-service laundry	*serviço completo lavandaria*	sehr-**vee**-soo kohn-**pleh**-too lah-vahn-dah-**ree**-ah
self-service laundry	*self-service lavandaria*	"self-service" lah-vahn-dah-**ree**-ah
wash / dry	*lavar / secar*	lah-**var** / say-**kar**
washer / dryer	*máquina de lavar roupa / secador*	**mah**-kee-nah deh lah-**var roh**-pah / **seh**-kah-dor
detergent	*detergente*	deh-tehr-**zhayn**-teh
token	*ficha*	**fee**-shah
whites	*roupa branca*	**roh**-pah **brahng**-kah
colors	*roupa de cor*	**roh**-pah deh kor
delicates	*roupa delicada*	**roh**-pah deh-lee-**kah**-dah
handwash	*lavar à mão*	lah-**var** ah mow

Haircuts

Where is a barber / hair salon?	*Onde é o barbeiro / cabelereiro?*	**ohn**-deh eh oo bar-**bay**-roo / kah-beh-lah-**ray**-roo
I'd like...	*Eu queria...*	**eh**-oo keh-**ree**-ah
...a haircut.	*...um cortar o cabelo.*	oon kor-**tar** oo kah-**beh**-loo
...a permanent.	*...uma permanente.*	**oo**-mah pehr-mah-**nayn**-teh

...just a trim.	...cortar só as pontas.	kor-**tar** soh ahsh **pohn**-tahsh
Cut about this much off.	Corte este tanto.	**kor**-teh **ehsh**-teh **tayn**-too
Cut my bangs here.	Cortar a minha franja.	kor-**tar** ah **meen**-yah **frayn**-zhah
Longer / Shorter here.	Mais longo / Mais curto aqui.	mī sh **lon**-goo / mī sh **koor**-too ah-**kee**
I'd like my hair...	Eu gosto do meu cabelo...	eh-oo **gohsh**-too doo **meh**-oo kah-**beh**-loo
...short.	...curto.	**koor**-too
...colored.	...tingido.	teen-**zhee**-doo
...shampooed.	...lavado.	lah-**vah**-doo
...blow dried.	...seco.	**seh**-koo
It looks good.	Está bom.	ish-**tah** boh<u>n</u>

Repair

These handy lines can apply to any repair, whether it's a ripped rucksack, bad haircut, or crabby camera.

This is broken.	Isto está avariado.	**eesh**-too ish-**tah** ah-vah-ree-**ah**-doo
Can you fix it?	Pode reparar isto?	**pod**-eh reh-pah-**rar** **eesh**-too
Just do the essentials.	Faça só o que for preciso.	**fah**-sah soh oo keh for preh-**see**-zoo
How much will it cost?	Quanto vai custar?	**kwahn**-too vī koosh-tar
When will it be ready?	Quando é que vai estar pronto?	**kwahn**-doo eh keh vī ish-**tar** proh<u>n</u>-too
I need it by ___.	Preciso até ___.	preh-**see**-zoo ah-**teh**
We need it by ___.	Precisamos até ___.	preh-see-**zah**-moosh ah-**teh**
Without it, I'm...	Sem isto eu estou...	say<u>n</u> **eesh**-too **eh**-oo ish-**toh**
...lost.	...perdido[a].	pehr-**dee**-doo
...stuck.	...aflito[a].	ah-**flee**-too
...toast.	...frito.	**free**-too

SERVICES

Filling out Forms

Sr. / Sra. / Menina	Mr. / Mrs. / Miss
nome	first name
apelido	last name
endereço	address
rua	street
cidade	city
estado	state
pais	country
nacionalidade	nationality
origem / destino	origin / destination
idade	age
dia de nascimento	date of birth
lugar de nascimento	place of birth
sexo	sex
masculino	male
feminino	female
casado / casada	married man / married woman
solteiro / solteira	single man / single woman
profissão	profession
adulto	adult
criança / rapaz / rapariga	child / boy / girl
crianças	children
familia	family
assinatura	signature
data	date

When filling out dates, do it European-style: day/month/year.

HEALTH

I am sick.	*Estou doente.*	ish-**toh** doo-**ayn**-teh
I feel (very) sick.	*Sinto-me*	**seeng**-too-meh
	(muito) mal.	(**mween**-too) mahl
My husband /	*Meu marido /*	**meh**-oo mah-**ree**-doo /
My wife...	*Minha mulher...*	**meen**-yah mool-**yehr**
My son /	*Meu filho /*	**meh**-oo **feel**-yoo /
My daughter...	*Minha filha...*	**meen**-yah **feel**-yah
My male friend /	*Meu amigo /*	**meh**-oo ah-**mee**-goo /
My female friend...	*Minha amiga...*	**meen**-yah ah-**mee**-gah
...feels (very) sick.	*...sente-se*	**sehn**-teh-seh
	(muito) mal.	(**mween**-too) mahl
It's urgent.	*É urgente.*	eh oor-**zhayn**-teh
I need / We need	*Eu preciso /*	**eh**-oo preh-**see**-zoo /
to see a doctor...	*Nós precisamos*	nohsh preh-see-**zah**-moosh
	ver um doutor...	vehr oon doh-**tor**
...who speaks	*...que fale inglês.*	keh **fah**-leh een-**glaysh**
English.		
Please call a doctor.	*Por favor telefone*	poor fah-**vor** teh-leh-**foh**-neh
	ão doutor.	o<u>w</u> doh-**tor**
Could a doctor	*Um doutor pode*	oo<u>n</u> doh-**tor pod**-eh
come here?	*vir cá?*	veer kah
I am...	*Sou...*	soh
He / She is...	*Ele / Ela é...*	**eh**-leh / **eh**-lah eh

161

...allergic to penicillin / sulfa.	...alérgico[a] a pinicilina / sulfa.	ah-**lehr**-zhee-koo ah pee-nee-see-**lee**-nah / **sool**-fah
I am diabetic.	Sou diabético[a].	soh dee-ah-**beh**-tee-koo
I have cancer.	Eu tenho cancer.	**eh**-oo **tayn**-yoo **kan**-sehr
I had a heart attack __ years ago.	Tive um ataque do coração á ___ anos átraz.	**tee**-veh oon ah-**tah**-keh doo koo-rah-**sow** ah ___ **ah**-nooz **ah**-trahsh
It hurts here.	Dói aqui.	doy ah-**kee**
I feel faint.	Sinto-me tonta.	**seeng**-too-meh **tohn**-tah
It hurts to urinate.	Dói a urinar.	doy ah oo-ree-**nar**
I have body odor.	Tenho cheiro corporal.	**tayn**-yoo **shay**-roo kor-poo-**rahl**
I'm going bald.	Estou a ficar caréca.	ish-**toh** ah fee-**kar** kah-**reh**-kah
Is it serious?	É grave?	eh **grah**-veh
Is it contagious?	É contagioso?	eh kohn-tah-zhee-**oh**-zoo
Aging sucks.	Envelhecer é muito chato.	ehn-vehl-yeh-**sehr** eh **mween**-too **shah**-too
Take one pill every __ hours for __ days before / with meals.	Tome um comprimido a cada ___ horas por ___ dias antes / com as refeições.	**toh**-meh oon kohn-pree-**mee**-doo ah **kah**-dah ___ **oh**-rahsh poor ___ **dee**-ahsh **ahn**-tish / kohn ahsh reh-fay-**sowsh**
I need a receipt for my insurance.	Preciso do recibo para o meu seguro.	preh-**see**-zoo doo reh-**see**-boo **pah**-rah oo **meh**-oo seh-**goo**-roo

Ailments

I have...	Tenho...	**tayn**-yoo
He / She has...	Ele / Ela tem...	**eh**-leh / **eh**-lah tayn
I / We need medication for...	Preciso / Precisamos de medicamentos para...	preh-**see**-zoo / preh-see-**zah**-moosh deh meh-dee-kah-**mayn**-toosh **pah**-rah

HEALTH

...arthritis.	...artrite.	**art**-ree-teh
...asthma.	...asma.	**ahzh**-mah
...athlete's foot (fungus).	...pé de atleta (fungo).	peh deh aht-**leh**-tah (**foong**-goo)
...bad breath.	...mau halito.	mow ah-**lee**-too
...blisters.	...bolhas.	**bohl**-yahsh
...bug bites.	...picadelas de insectos.	pee-kah-**deh**-lahsh deh een-**sehk**-toosh
...a burn.	...uma queimadura.	**oo**-mah kay-mah-**doo**-rah
...chest pains.	...uma dor no peito.	**oo**-mah dor noo **pay**-too
...chills.	...arrepios.	ah-reh-**pee**-oosh
...a cold.	...uma constipação.	**oo**-mah kohnsh-tee-pah-**sow**
...congestion.	...congestão.	kohn-zhish-**tow**
...constipation.	...prisão de ventre.	pree-**zow** deh **vayn**-treh
...a cough.	...uma tosse.	**oo**-mah **tos**-seh
...cramps.	...dor, cãibra.	dor, **kayn**-brah
...diabetes.	...diabetes.	dee-ah-**beh**-tish
...diarrhea.	...diarréia.	dee-ah-**ray**-ah
...dizziness.	...tonturas.	tohn-**too**-rahsh
...earache.	...dor de ouvido.	dor deh **oh**-vee-doo
...epilepsy.	...epilepcia.	eh-pee-**lehp**-see-ah
...a fever.	...febre.	**feh**-breh
...the flu.	...uma gripe.	**oo**-mah **gree**-peh
...food poisoning.	...envenanamento alimentar.	ayn-vehn-ahn-ah-**mayn**-too ah-lee-mayn-**tar**
...the giggles.	...gargalhadas.	gar-gahl-**yah**-dahsh
...hay fever.	...febre dos fenos.	**feh**-breh doosh **feh**-noosh
...a headache.	...uma dor de cabeça.	**oo**-mah dor deh kah-**beh**-sah
...a heart condition.	...problema no coração.	proo-**blay**-mah noo koo-rah-**sow**
...hemorrhoids.	...hemorróidas.	eh-moh-**rah**-dahsh
...high blood pressure.	...tensão alta.	tayn-**sow ahl**-tah
...indigestion.	...uma indigestão.	**oo**-mah een-dee-zhish-**tow**
...an infection.	...uma infecção.	**oo**-mah een-fehk-**sow**

HEALTH

English	Portuguese	Pronunciation
...inflammation.	...inflamação.	een-flah-mah-**sow**
...a migraine.	...uma enxaqueca.	**oo**-mah ayn-shah-**keh**-kah
...nausea.	...náusea.	**now**-zeh-ah
...pneumonia.	...pneumonia.	pehn-yoo-moh-**nee**-ah
...a rash.	...uma erupção.	**oo**-mah ee-roop-**sow**
...sinus problems.	...sinosite.	see-noh-**zee**-teh
...a sore throat.	...uma dor de garganta.	**oo**-mah dor deh gar-**gahn**-tah
...a stomach ache.	...uma dor de estômago.	**oo**-mah dor deh ish-**toh**-mah-goo
...sunburn.	...queimadura solar.	kay-mah-**doo**-rah soh-**lar**
...a swelling.	...um inchado.	oon een-**shah**-doo
...a toothache.	...uma dor de dente.	**oo**-mah dor deh **dayn**-teh
...a urinary infection.	...uma infecção urinaria.	**oo**-mah een-fehk-**sow** oo-ree-**nah**-ree-ah
...a venereal disease.	...uma doença venéria.	**oo**-mah doo-**ayn**-sah veh-**neh**-ree-ah
...vicious sunburn.	...queimadura solar grave.	kay-mah-**doo**-rah soh-**lar grah**-veh
...vomiting.	...vómitos.	**vah**-mee-toosh
...worms.	...vermes.	**vehr**-mish

Women's Health

English	Portuguese	Pronunciation
menstruation	menstruação	mayn-shtroo-ah-**sow**
menstrual cramps	cólicas	**kol**-ee-kahsh
period	menstruação, período	mehn-shtroo-ah-**sow**, peh-**ree**-oh-doo
pregnancy (test)	(teste de) gravidez	(**tehsh**-teh deh) grah-vee-**dehsh**
miscarriage	abôrto natural	ah-**bor**-too nah-too-**rahl**
abortion	abôrto	ah-**bor**-too
birth control pills	pilula anti-concepcional	peel-**oo**-lah ahn-tee-kohn-sehp-see-oh-**nahl**
diaphragm	diafragma	dee-ah-**frahg**-mah
I'd like to see a female...	Eu quero ver uma...	**eh**-oo **kay**-roo vehr **oo**-mah

...doctor.	...doutora.	doh-**toh**-rah
...gynecologist.	...enicologista.	eh-nee-koh-loh-**zhee**-stah
I've missed	Faltou o meu	**fahl**-toh oo **meh**-oo
a period.	período.	peh-**ree**-oh-doo
My last period	O meu ultimo	oo **meh**-oo **ool**-tee-moo
started on ___.	período	peh-**ree**-oh-doo
	começou em ___.	kohn-meh-**soh** ayn
I am / She is...	Eu estou / Ela	**eh**-oo ish-**toh** / **eh**-lah
pregnant.	está gravida...	ish-**stah grah**-vee-dah
...___ months	...de ___ mesês.	deh ___ **meh**-zaysh

Parts of the Body

ankle	tornozelo	tor-noo-**zeh**-loo
arm	braço	**brah**-soo
back	costas	**kosh**-tahsh
bladder	bexiga	beh-**shee**-gah
breast	mama	**mah**-mah
buttocks	traseiro	trah-**zay**-roo
chest	peito	**pay**-too
ear	ouvido	**oh**-vee-doo
elbow	cotôvelo	koo-**toh**-veh-loo
eye	olho	**ohl**-yoo
face	rosto	**rohsh**-too
finger	dedo	**deh**-doo
foot	pé	peh
hair	cabelo	kah-**beh**-loo
hand	mão	mow
head	cabeça	kah-**beh**-sah
heart	coração	koo-rah-**sow**
intestines	intestino	een-tish-**tee**-noo
knee	joelho	zhoo-**ehl**-yoo
leg	perna	**pehr**-nah
lung	pulmão	pool-**mow**
mouth	boca	**boh**-kah
navel	umbigo	oon-**bee**-goo
neck	pescoço	pehsh-**koh**-soh

HEALTH

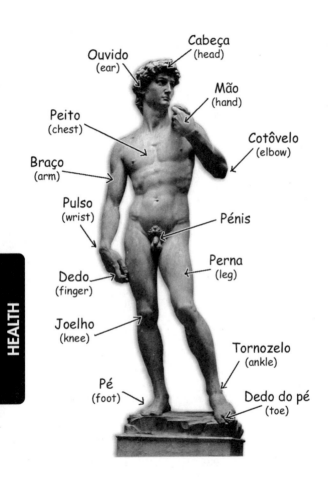

Cabeça (head)
Ouvido (ear)
Mão (hand)
Peito (chest)
Cotôvelo (elbow)
Braço (arm)
Pulso (wrist)
Pénis
Dedo (finger)
Perna (leg)
Joelho (knee)
Tornozelo (ankle)
Pé (foot)
Dedo do pé (toe)

HEALTH

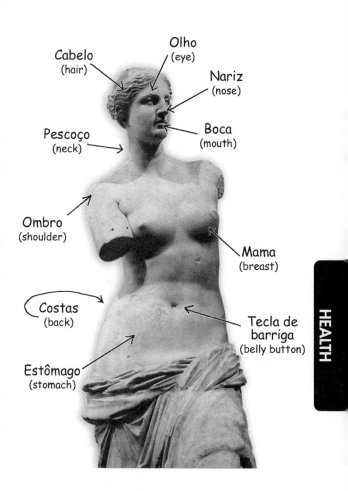

Cabelo
(hair)

Olho
(eye)

Nariz
(nose)

Boca
(mouth)

Pescoço
(neck)

Ombro
(shoulder)

Mama
(breast)

Costas
(back)

Tecla de
barriga
(belly button)

Estômago
(stomach)

HEALTH

nose	nariz	**nah**-reesh
penis	pénis	**peh**-neesh
rectum	recto	**rehk**-too
shoulder	ombro	**ohn**-broo
stomach	estômago	ish-**toh**-mah-goo
teeth	dentes	**dehn**-tish
testicles	testículos	tish-**tee**-koo-loosh
throat	garganta	gar-**gahn**-tah
toe	dedo do pé	**deh**-doo doo peh
urethra	uretra	oo-**reht**-rah
uterus	útero	**oo**-teh-roo
vagina	vagina	vah-**zhee**-nah
waist	cintura	seen-**too**-rah
wrist	pulso	**pool**-soo

Healthy Words

24-hour pharmacy	farmácia aberta vinte e quatro horas	far-**mah**-see-ah ah-**behr**-tah **veen**-teh ee **kwah**-troo **oh**-rahsh
bleeding	sangrar	sang-**grar**
blood	sangue	**sang**-geh
contraceptives	contracepçaõ	kohn-trah-sehp-**sow**
dentist	dentista	dayn-**teesh**-tah
doctor	doutor[a], médico[a]	doh-**tor**, **may**-dee-koo
health insurance	seguro de saúde	say-**goo**-roo deh sah-**oo**-deh
hospital	hospital	ohsh-pee-**tahl**
medical clinic	clinica médica	**klee**-nee-kah **may**-dee-kah
medicine	medicina	meh-dee-**zee**-nah
nurse	enfermeira	ayn-fehr-**may**-rah
pain	dor	dor
pharmacy	farmácia	far-**mah**-see-ah
pill	comprimido	kohn-pree-**mee**-doo
prescription	receita médica	reh-**say**-tah **may**-dee-kah
refill	encher	ayn-**shehr**
unconscious	inconciente	een-kohn-see-**ehn**-teh
x-ray	raio X	**ray**-oo sheesh

First-Aid Kit

antacid	*remédio*	reh-**meh**-dee-oo
	para azia	**pah**-rah ah-**zee**-ah
antibiotic	*antibiótico*	ahn-tee-bee-**oh**-tee-koo
aspirin	*aspirina*	ahsh-pee-**ree**-nah
non-aspirin	*substituto*	soob-shtee-**too**-too
substitute	*para aspirina*	**pah**-rah ahsh-pee-**ree**-nah
bandage	*gaze*	**gah**-zeh
band-aids	*pensos*	**payn**-soosh
cold medicine	*remédio para*	reh-**meh**-dee-oo **pah**-rah
	constipação	kohnsh-tee-pah-**sow**
cough drops	*rebuçados*	reh-boo-**sah**-doosh
	da tosse	dah **tos**-seh
decongestant	*descongestio-*	dish-kohn-zhish-tee-oh-
	nante	**nahn**-teh
disinfectant	*desinfetante*	dehz-een-feh-**tahn**-teh
first-aid cream	*creme*	**kreh**-meh
	desinfetante	dehz-een-feh-**tahn**-teh
gauze / tape	*gaze / adesivo*	**gah**-zeh / ah-deh-**zee**-voo
	médico	**may**-dee-koo
laxative	*laxativo*	lak-sah-**tee**-voo
medicine for	*remédio para*	reh-**meh**-dee-oo **pah**-rah
diarrhea	*a diarréia*	ah dee-ah-**ray**-ah
moleskin	*sinal*	see-**nahl**

HEALTH

pain killer	*comprimidos*	koh<u>n</u>-pree-**mee**-doosh
	para as dores	**pah**-rah ahsh **doh**-rish
Preparation H	*Preparação H*	preh-pah-rah-**sow** eh-**gah**
support bandage	*ligadora*	lee-gah-**doo**-rah
thermometer	*termometro*	tehr-**mow**-may-troo
Vaseline	*vasilina*	vah-zee-**lee**-nah
vitamins	*vitaminas*	vee-tah-**mee**-nahsh

HEALTH

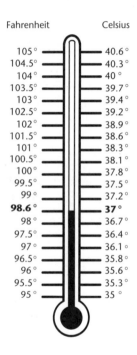

Fahrenheit	Celsius
105°	40.6°
104.5°	40.3°
104°	40°
103.5°	39.7°
103°	39.4°
102.5°	39.2°
102°	38.9°
101.5°	38.6°
101°	38.3°
100.5°	38.1°
100°	37.8°
99.5°	37.5°
99°	37.2°
98.6°	**37°**
98°	36.7°
97.5°	36.4°
97°	36.1°
96.5°	35.8°
96°	35.6°
95.5°	35.3°
95°	35°

Contacts and Glasses

glasses	ocúlos	oo-**koo**-loosh
sunglasses	ocúlos de sol	oo-**koo**-loosh deh sohl
prescription	receita	reh-**say**-tah
contact lenses...	lentes de contacto...	**lehn**-tish deh koh<u>n</u>-**tahk**-too
...soft	...flexibeis	fleh-**shee**-baysh
...hard	...rigidas	ree-**zhee**-dahs
solution...	solução...	soo-loo-**sow**
...cleaning	...de limpeza	deh leem-**pay**-zah
...soaking	...para molhar	**pah**-rah mool-**yar**
all-purpose solution	solução para limpeza e tratamento	soo-loo-**sow pah**-rah leem-**pay**-zah ee trah-tah-**mayn**-too
20/20 vision	visão vinte sobre vinte	vee-**zow veen**-teh **soh**-breh **veen**-teh
I've lost / I've swallowed my contact lens.	Perdi / Engoli minha lente de contacto.	pehr-**dee** / ay<u>n</u>-goo-**lee meen**-yah **lehn**-teh deh koh<u>n</u>-**tahk**-too

Toiletries

comb	pente	**payn**-teh
conditioner (for hair)	condicionador (para o cabelo)	koh<u>n</u>-dee-see-oh-nah-**door** (**pah**-rah oo kah-**behl**-oo)
condoms	preservativos	pray-zehr-vah-**tee**-voosh
dental floss	fio dental	**fee**-oo day<u>n</u>-**tahl**
deodorant	desodorizante	deh-zoo-dor-ee-**zayn**-teh
facial tissue	lenços de papel	**layn**-soosh deh pah-**pehl**
hairbrush	escova do cabelo	ish-**koh**-vah doo kah-**beh**-loo
hand lotion	creme para as mãos	**kreh**-meh **pah**-rah ahsh **mowsh**
lip salve	batão de cierio	bah-**tow** deh see-**yay**-roo
mirror	espelho	ish-**payl**-yoo

HEALTH

nail clipper	*cortas-unhas*	**kor**-tah **oon**-yahsh
razor	*lâmina*	**lah**-mee-nah
sanitary napkins	*pensos*	**payn**-soosh
	higiénicos	ee-zhee-**ehn**-ee-koosh
scissors	*tesoura*	teh-**zoh**-rah
shampoo	*shampoo*	"shampoo"
shaving cream	*creme de barbear*	**kreh**-meh deh bar-**behr**
soap	*sabão*	sah-**bow**
sunscreen	*protector solar*	proo-tehk-**tor** soo-**lar**
tampons	*tampões*	tahn-**powsh**
	higiénicos	ee-zhee-**ehn**-ee-koosh
tissues	*lenços de papel*	**layn**-soosh deh pah-**pehl**
toilet paper	*papel*	pah-**pehl**
	higiénico	ee-zhee-**ehn**-ee-koo
toothbrush	*escova de*	ish-**koh**-vah deh
	dentes	**dayn**-tish
toothpaste	*pasta dos*	**pahsh**-tah doosh
	dentes,	**dayn**-tish,
	dentifrice	dayn-tee-**free**-seh
tweezers	*pinça*	**peen**-sah

Makeup

blush	*blush*	"blush"
eye shadow	*sombra*	**sohn**-brah
eyeliner	*lápis para os*	**lah**-peesh **pah**-rah ooz
	olhos,	**ohl**-yoosh,
	delineador	deh-leen-eh-ah-**door**
face cleanser	*produto para*	proh-**doo**-too **pah**-rah
	a limpeza	ah leem-**pay**-zah
	do rosto	doo **rohsh**-too
face powder	*pó para o rosto*	poh **pah**-rah oo **rohsh**-too
foundation	*base*	**bah**-zeh
lipstick	*baton*	bah-**tohn**
makeup	*maquiagem*	mah-kee-**ah**-zhayn
mascara	*rimel*	**ree**-mehl

moisturizer...	*hidratante...*	eed-rah-**tahn**-teh
...with sun block	*...com proteção solar*	koh<u>n</u> proh-tehk-**sow** soh-**lar**
nail polish	*verniz para as unhas*	vehr-**neezh pah**-rah ahz **oon**-yahsh
nail polish remover	*acetona*	ah-seh-**toh**-nah
perfume	*perfume*	pehr-**foo**-meh

For Babies

baby	*bebé*	bay-**bay**
baby food	*comida para bebés*	koo-**mee**-dah **pah**-rah bay-**baysh**
bib	*babete*	bah-**beh**-teh
bottle	*bibron*	beeb-**roh<u>n</u>**
diaper(s)	*fralda(s)*	**frahl**-dah(sh)
diaper wipes	*lenço húmido para fraldas*	**layn**-soo **oo**-mee-doo **pah**-rah **frahl**-dahsh
diaper ointment	*creme para fraldas*	**kreh**-meh **pah**-rah **frahl**-dahsh
formula...	*alimento suplementar...*	ah-lee-**mehn**-too soo-pleh-mehn-**tar**
...powdered	*...em pó*	ay<u>n</u> poh
...liquid	*...em liquido*	ay<u>n</u> **lee**-kee-doo
...soy	*...em soja*	ay<u>n</u> **soh**-zhah
medication for...	*medicação para...*	meh-dee-kah-**sow pah**-rah
...diaper rash	*...assadura das fraldas*	ah-sah-**doo**-rah dahsh **frahl**-dahsh
...teething	*...dentição*	dehn-tee-**sow**
nipple	*bico do peito*	**bee**-koo doo **pay**-too
pacifier	*chupeta*	shoo-**pay**-tah
Will you refrigerate this?	*Pode por no frigorifico?*	**pod**-eh poor noo free-goh-**ree**-fee-koo
Will you warm... for a baby?	*Pode aquecer... para o bebé?*	**pod**-eh ah-keh-**sehr**... **pah**-rah oo bay-**bay**
...this	*...isto*	**eesh**-too

HEALTH

...some water	...um pouco de água	oon **poh**-koo deh **ah**-gwah
...some milk	...um pouco de leite	oon **poh**-koo deh **lay**-teh
Not too hot, please.	Não muito quente, por favor.	no<u>w</u> **mween**-too **kayn**-teh poor fah-**vor**

More Baby Things

backpack to carry baby	saco para levar o bebé nas costas	**sah**-koo **pah**-rah leh-**vahr** oo bay-**bay** nahsh **kosh**-tahsh
booster seat	suporte para cadeira	soo-**por**-teh **pah**-rah kah-**day**-rah
car seat	cadeira de carro para o bebé	kah-**day**-rah deh **kah**-roo **pah**-rah oo bay-**bay**
high chair	cadeira alta	kah-**day**-rah **ahl**-tah
playpen	parque	**par**-keh
stroller	carrinho de bebê	kar-**een**-yoo deh bay-**bay**

CHATTING

English	Portuguese	Pronunciation
My name is ___.	Chamo-me ___.	**shah**-moo-meh ___
What's your name?	Como se chama?	**koh**-moo seh **shah**-mah
Pleased to meet you.	Prazer em conhecer.	**p**rah-**zehr** ay<u>n</u> koh<u>n</u>-yeh-**sehr**
This is ___. (informal)	Esta é ___.	**ehsh**-tah eh ___
This is ___. (formal)	Apregento-lhe ___.	ah-preh-**zhehn**-tool-yeh
How are you?	Como está?	**koh**-moo ish-**tah**
Very well, thanks.	Muito bem, obrigado[a].	**mween**-too bay<u>n</u> oh-bree-**gah**-doo
Where are you from?	De onde é que você é?	deh **oh<u>n</u>**-deh eh keh voh-**say** eh
What city?	De que cidade?	deh keh see-**dah**-deh
What country?	De que pais?	deh keh pah-**eesh**
What planet?	De que planeta?	deh keh plah-**nay**-tah
I am...	Sou...	soh
...American.	...Americano[a].	ah-meh-ree-**kah**-noo
...Canadian.	...Canadiano[a].	kah-nah-dee-**ah**-noo
...a pest.	...terrível.	teh-**ree**-vehl
Where are you going?	Onde vai?	**oh<u>n</u>**-deh vī
I'm going to ___.	Vou para ___.	voh **pah**-rah
We're going to ___.	Vamos para ___.	**vah**-moosh **pah**-rah

Will you take my / our photo?	*Pode tirar a minha foto / a nossa foto?*	**pod**-eh tee-**rar** ah **meen**-yah **foh**-too / ah **noh**-sah **foh**-too
Can I take a photo of you?	*Posso tirar-lhe uma foto?*	**pos**-soh tee-**rar**-leh **oo**-mah **foh**-too
Smile!	*Sorria!*	soh-**ree**-ah

Nothing More Than Feelings...

I am / You are...	*Eu estou / Você está...*	**eh**-oo ish-**toh** / voh-**say** ish-**tah**
He is / She is...	*Ele está / Ela está...*	**eh**-leh ish-**tah** / **eh**-lah ish-**tah**
...happy.	*...feliz.*	feh-**leesh**
...sad.	*...triste.*	**treesh**-teh
...tired.	*...cansado[a].*	kah<u>n</u>-**sah**-doo
...thirsty.	*...com sede.*	koh<u>n</u> **say**-deh
...hungry.	*...com fome.*	koh<u>n</u> **fah**-meh
...lucky.	*...afortunado[a].*	ah-for-too-**nah**-doo
...homesick.	*...com saudades de casa.*	koh<u>n</u> soh-**dah**-dish deh **kah**-zah
...cold.	*...com frio.*	koh<u>n</u> **free**-oh
...hot.	*...com calor.*	koh<u>n</u> kah-**lor**

Who's Who

My... (male / female)	*O meu / A minha...*	oo **meh**-oo / ah **meen**-yah
...male friend / female friend.	*...amigo / amiga.*	ah-**mee**-goo / ah-**mee**-gah
...boyfriend / girlfriend.	*...namorado / namorada.*	nah-moo-**rah**-doo / nah-moo-**rah**-dah
...husband / wife.	*...marido / mulher.*	mah-**ree**-doo / mool-**yehr**
...son / daughter.	*...filho / filha.*	**feel**-yoo / **feel**-yah
...brother / sister.	*...irmão / irmã.*	eer-**mow** / eer-**mayn**
...father / mother.	*...pai / mãe.*	pī / **mayn**-eh
...uncle / aunt.	*...tio / tia.*	**tee**-oo / **tee**-ah

...nephew / niece.	...sobrinho / sobrinha.	soo-**breen**-yoo / soo-**breen**-yah
...male / female cousin.	...primo / prima.	**pree**-moo / **pree**-mah
...grandpa / grandma.	...avô / avó.	ah-**voh** / ah-**vah**
...grandson / granddaughter.	...neto / neta.	**nay**-too / **nay**-tah

Family

Are you married? (asked of a man)	É casado?	eh kah-**zah**-doo
Are you married? (asked of a woman)	É casada?	eh kah-**zah**-dah
Do you have children?	Tem algumas crianças?	tay<u>n</u> ahl-**goo**-mahsh kree-**ahn**-sahsh
How many boys / girls?	Quantos rapazes / raparigas?	**kwahn**-toosh rah-**pah**-zish / rah-pah-**ree**-gahsh
Do you have photos?	Tem fotos?	tay<u>n</u> **foh**-toosh
How old is your child?	Que idade tem a sua criança?	keh ee-**dah**-deh tay<u>n</u> ah **soo**-ah kree-**ahn**-sah
Beautiful child!	Linda criança!	**leen**-dah kree-**ahn**-sah
Beautiful children!	Lindas crianças!	**leen**-dahsh kree-**ahn**-sahsh

Work

What is your occupation?	Qual é a sua profissão?	kwahl eh ah **soo**-ah proo-fee-**sow**
Do you like your work?	Gosta do seu trabalho?	**gohsh**-tah doo **seh**-oo trah-**bahl**-yoo
I work...	Eu trabalho...	**eh**-oo trah-**bahl**-yoo
I'm studying to work...	Estou a estudar para trabalhar...	ish-**toh** ah ish-too-**dar** **pah**-rah trah-bahl-**yar**
I used to work...	Trabalhava...	trah-bahl-**yah**-vah
I want a job...	Quero um emprego...	**kay**-roo oo<u>n</u> ay<u>n</u>-**preh**-goo

CHATING

...in accounting.	...em contabilidade.	ayn kohn-tah-bee-lee-**dah**-deh
...in the medical field.	...no campo médico.	noo **kahm**-poo **may**-dee-koo
...in social services.	...em serviços sociais.	ayn sehr-**vee**-soosh soh-see-**ish**
...in the legal profession.	...em profição juridical.	ayn proh-fee-**sow** zhoo-ree-dee-**kahl**
...in banking.	...no banco.	noo **bang**-koo
...in business.	...nos negócios.	noosh neh-**gah**-see-oosh
...in government.	...no governo.	noo goh-**vehr**-noo
...in engineering.	...em engenharia.	ayn ayn-zhehn-yah-**ree**-ah
...in public relations.	...em relações publicas.	ayn reh-lah-**sowsh** **poob**-lee-kahsh
...in science.	...no campo da ciência.	noo **kahm**-poo dah see-**ayn**-see-ah
...in teaching.	...na educação.	nah ee-doo-kah-**sow**
...in the computer field.	...na área dos computadores.	nah **ah**-reh-ah doosh kohm-poo-tah-**dor**-ish
...in the travel industry.	...no turismo.	noo too-**reezh**-moo
...in the arts.	...nas artes.	nahz **ar**-tehsh
...in journalism.	...no jornalismo.	noo zhoor-nah-**leezh**-moo
...in a restaurant.	...no restaurante.	noo rish-toh-**rahn**-teh
...in a store.	...numa loja.	**noo**-mah **lah**-zhah
...in a factory.	...numa fabrica.	**noo**-mah **fah**-bree-kah
I am...	Estou...	ish-**toh**
...unemployed.	...desempregado[a].	dehz-ayn-preh-**gah**-doo
...retired.	...reformado[a].	reh-for-**mah**-doo
I'm a professional traveler.	Sou viajante professional.	soh vee-ah-**zhahn**-teh proo-feh-see-oo-**nahl**
Do you have a...?	Você tem um...?	voh-**say** tayn oon
Here is my / our...	Aqui está o meu / nosso...	ah-**kee** ish-**tah** oo **meh**-oo / **noh**-soo
...business card	...cartão	kar-**tow**
...e-mail address	...endereço eletrônico	ayn-deh-**ray**-soo eh-leh-**troh**-nee-koo

KEY PHRASES: CHATTING

My name is ___.	Chamo-me ___.	**shah**-moo-meh ___
What's your name?	Como se chama?	**koh**-moo seh **shah**-mah
Pleased to meet you.	Prazer em conhecer.	prah-**zehr** ay<u>n</u> koh<u>n</u>-yeh-**sehr**
Where are you from?	De onde é que você é?	deh **ohn**-deh eh keh voh-**say** eh
I'm from ___.	Eu sou de ___.	**eh**-oo soh de
Where are you going?	Onde vai?	**ohn**-deh vī
I'm going to ___.	Vou para ___.	voh **pah**-rah
I like...	Gosto...	**gohsh**-too
Do you like...?	Você gosta?	voh-**say gohsh**-tah
Thank you very much.	Muito obrigado[a].	**mween**-too oh-bree-**gah**-doo
Have a good trip!	Boa-viagem!	boh-ah-vee-**ah**-zhay<u>n</u>

Chatting With Children

What's your name?	Como te chamas?	**koh**-moo teh **shah**-mahsh
My name is ___.	Chamo-me ___.	**shah**-moo-meh ___
How old are you?	Que idade tens?	keh ee-**dah**-deh tay<u>n</u>sh
Do you have brothers and sisters?	Tens irmãos e irmãs?	tay<u>n</u>sh eer-**mowsh** ee eer-**mahsh**
Do you like school?	Gostas da escola?	**gohsh**-tahsh dah ish-**koh**-lah
What are you studying?	O que é que estuda?	oo keh eh keh ish-**too**-dah
I'm studying...	Estou a estudar...	ish-**toh** ah ish-too-**dar**
What's your favorite subject?	Qual é a tua disciplina preferida?	kwahl eh oo **too**-ah dee-shee-**plee**-nah pray-feh-**ree**-dah
Do you have pets?	Tens animais de estimação?	tay<u>n</u>sh ah-nee-**mīsh** deh ish-tee-mah-**sow**
I have / We have a...	Eu tenho / Nós temos um...	**eh**-oo tay<u>n</u>-yoo / nohsh **teh**-moosh oo<u>n</u>

English	Portuguese	Pronunciation
...cat / dog / fish / bird.	...gato / cão / peixe / pássaro	**gah**-too / ko<u>w</u> / **pay**-sheh / **pah**-sah-roo
What is this?	O que é isto?	oo keh eh **eesh**-too
Will you teach me...?	Ensina-me...?	ay<u>n</u>-**see**-nah-meh
Will you teach us...?	Ensina-nos...?	ay<u>n</u>-**see**-nah-nohsh
...some Portuguese words	...algumas palavras em português	ahl-**goo**-mahsh pah-**lah**-vrahz ay<u>n</u> poor-too-**gaysh**
...a simple Portuguese song	uma canção portuguêsa	**oo**-mah kah<u>n</u>-**sow** poor-too-**gay**-zah
Guess which country I live in / we live in.	Adivinha em que país eu vivo / nós vivemos.	ah-dee-**veen**-yah ay<u>n</u> keh pah-**eez** eh-oo **vee**-voo / nohsh vee-**veh**-moosh
How old am I?	Quantos anos tenho?	**kwahn**-toosh **ah**-noosh **tayn**-yoo
I'm ___ years old.	Tenho ___ anos.	**tayn**-yoo ___ **ah**-noosh
Want to hear me burp?	Queres ouvir-me a arrotar?	**keh**-rish oh-**veer**-meh ah ah-roo-**tar**
Teach me a fun game.	Ensina-me um jogo engraçado.	ay<u>n</u>-**see**-nah-meh oo<u>n</u> **zhoh**-goo ay<u>n</u>-grah-**sah**-doo
Got any candy?	Tens um rebuçado?	tay<u>n</u>sh oo<u>n</u> reh-boo-**sah**-doo
Want to thumb wrestle?	Queres um braço de força?	**keh**-rehz oo<u>n</u> **brah**-soo deh **for**-sah
Gimme five.	Dá-me cinco.	**dah**-meh **seeng**-koo

If you do break into song, you'll find the words for Happy Birthday on page 23 and the national anthem on page 256.

Travel Talk

English	Portuguese	Pronunciation
I am / Are you...?	Estou / Está...?	ish-**toh** / ish-**tah**
...on vacation	...de férias	deh **feh**-ree-ahsh
...on business	...em negócios	ay<u>n</u> neh-**gos**-ee-oosh
How long have you been traveling?	Á quanto tempo é que tem estado a viajar?	ah **kwahn**-too **tayn**-poo eh keh tay<u>n</u> ish-**tah**-doo ah vee-ah-**zhar**

CHATTING

English	Portuguese	Pronunciation
day / week	dia / semana	**dee**-ah / seh-**mah**-nah
month / year	mês / ano	maysh / **ah**-noo
When are you going home?	Quando é que vai voltar para casa?	**kwahn**-doo eh keh vī vohl-**tar pah**-rah **kah**-zah
This is my first time in ___.	Esta é a minha primeira vêz em ___.	**ehsh**-tah eh ah **meen**-yah pree-**may**-rah vaysh ayn
This is our first time in ___.	Esta é a nossa primeira vêz em ___.	**ehsh**-tah eh ah **noh**-sah pree-**may**-rah vaysh ayn
It is (not) a tourist trap.	(Não) é uma armadilha para turista.	(now) eh **oo**-mah ar-mah-**deel**-yah **pah**-rah too-**reesh**-tah
I'm happy here.	Estou contente aqui.	ish-**toh** kohn-**tehn**-teh ah-**kee**
This is paradise.	Isto é um paraíso.	**eesh**-too eh oon pah-rah-**ee**-zoo
Portugal is wonderful.	Portugal é maravilhoso.	poor-too-**gahl** eh mah-rah-veel-**yoh**-zoo
The Portuguese are friendly / boring / rude.	Os portuguêses são simpáticos / chatos / rudes.	oosh poor-too-**gay**-zish sow seeng-**pah**-tee-koosh / **shah**-toosh / **roo**-dish
So far...	Até agora...	ah-**teh** ah-**goh**-rah
Today...	Hoje...	**oh**-zheh
...I have seen / we have seen ___ and ___.	...eu vi / nós vimos ___ e ___.	**eh**-oo vee / nohsh **vee**-moosh ___ ee ___
Next...	Depois...	day-**pwaysh**
Tomorrow...	Amanhã...	ah-ming-**yah**
...I will see / we will see ___.	...eu vou ver / nós vamos ver ___.	**eh**-oo voh vehr / nohsh **vah**-moosh vehr
Yesterday...	Ontem...	**ohn**-tayn
...I saw / we saw ___.	...eu vi / nós vimos ___.	**eh**-oo vee / nohsh **vee**-moosh
My / Our vacation is ___ days long, starting in ___ and ending in ___.	Minhas / Nossas férias são de ___ dias, começando em ___ até ___.	**meen**-yahsh / **noh**-sahsh **feh**-ree-ahsh sow deh ___ **dee**-ahsh koh-meh-**sayn**-doo ayn ___ ah-**teh**

CHATTING

To travel is to live.	*A maneira de viver é viajar.*	ah mah-**nay**-rah deh vee-**vehr** eh vee-ah-**zhar**
Travel is enlightening.	*Viajar é agradavel.*	vee-ah-**zhar** eh ah-grah-**dah**-vehl
I wish all (American) politicians traveled.	*Desejo que todos os (americanos) politicos tivessem viajado.*	deh-**zeh**-zhoo keh **toh**-dooz ooz (ah-meh-ree-**kah**-noosh) poh-**lee**-tee-koosh tee-**veh**-sayn vee-ah-**zhah**-doo
Have a good trip!	*Boa-viagem!*	boh-ah-vee-**ah**-zhayn

Map Musings

Use the following maps to delve into family history and explore travel dreams.

I live here.	*Eu vivo aqui.*	**eh**-oo **vee**-voo ah-**kee**
We live here.	*Vivimos aqui.*	vee-**vee**-moosh ah-**kee**
I was born here.	*Eu nasci aqui.*	**eh**-oo **nahsh**-see ah-**kee**
My ancestors came from ___.	*Os meus antepassados vieram de ___.*	oosh **meh**-oosh ahn-teh-pah-**sah**-doosh vee-**eh**-rahm deh
I've traveled to ___.	*Já viajei a ___.*	zhah vee-**ah**-zhay ah
We've traveled to ___.	*Já viajamos a ___.*	zhah vee-ah-**zhah**-mooz ah
Next I'll go to ___.	*Em seguida irei ___.*	ayn sehg-**ee**-dah ee-**ray**
Next we'll go to ___.	*Em seguida iremos ___.*	ayn sehg-**ee**-dah ee-**ray**-moosh
I'd like / We'd like to go to ___.	*Gostaria / Gostaríamos de ir para ___.*	goosh-tah-**ree**-ah / goosh-tah-**ree**-ah-moosh deh eer **pah**-rah
Where do you live?	*A onde vive?*	ah **ohn**-deh **vee**-veh
Where were you born?	*A onde nasceu?*	ah **ohn**-deh nahsh-**seh**-oo
Where did your ancestors come from?	*De onde vieram os vossos antepassados?*	deh **ohn**-deh vee-**eh**-rahm oosh **voh**-soosh ahn-teh-pah-**sah**-doosh

Where have you traveled?	*A onde tem viajado?*	ah **ohn**-deh tayn vee-ah-**zhah**-doo
Where are you going?	*A onde vai?*	ah **ohn**-deh vī
Where would you like to go?	*A onde gostaria de ir?*	ah **ohn**-deh goosh-tah-**ree**-ah deh eer

PORTUGAL

EUROPE

THE UNITED STATES

THE WORLD

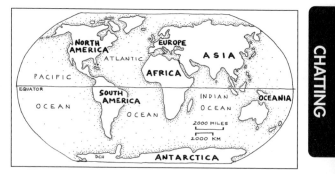

Favorite Things

What's your favorite...?	*Qual é o seu... favorito?*	kwahl eh oo **seh**-oo... fah-voo-**ree**-too
...hobby	*...passatempo*	pah-sah-**tayn**-poo
...ice cream	*...gelado*	zheh-**lah**-doo
...male singer	*...cantor*	kahn-**tor**
...male movie star	*...actor*	ah-**tor**
...male artist	*...artista*	ar-**teesh**-tah
...male author	*...escritor*	ish-kree-**tor**
...movie	*...filme*	**feel**-meh
...(kind of) book	*...(tipo de) livro*	(**tee**-poo deh) **leev**-roo
...sport	*...desporto*	dish-**por**-too
...vice	*...vício*	**vee**-see-oo
What's your favorite...?	*Qual é o sea... favorita?*	kwahl eh oo **seh**-ah... fah-voo-**ree**-tah
...food	*...comida*	koo-**mee**-dah
...art	*...arte*	**ar**-teh
...music	*...música*	**moo**-zee-kah
...female singer	*...cantora*	kahn-**toh**-rah
...female movie star	*...actriz*	ah-**treesh**
...female artist	*...artista*	ar-**teesh**-tah
...female author	*...escritora*	ish-kree-**toh**-rah
Can you recommend a good...?	*Pode recomendar um bom...?*	**pod**-eh reh-koh-mayn-**dar** oon bohn
...Portuguese CD	*...CD em português*	say day ayn poor-too-**gaysh**
...Portuguese book translated in English	*...livro português traduzido em inglês*	**lee**-vroo poor-too-**gaysh** trah-doo-**zee**-doo ayn een-**glaysh**

Weather

What will the weather be like tomorrow?	*Qual é o tempo para amanhã?*	kwahl eh oo **tayn**-poo **pah**-rah ah-ming-**yah**

sunny / cloudy	*sol / nublado*	sohl / noo-**blah**-doo
hot / cold	*quente / frio*	**kayn**-teh / **free**-oo
muggy / windy	*úmido / vento*	**oo**-mee-doo / **vayn**-too
rain / snow	*chuva / neve*	**shoo**-vah / **neh**-veh
Should I bring a jacket?	*Preciso trazer um casaco?*	preh-**see**-zoo trah-**zehr** oon kah-**zah**-koo

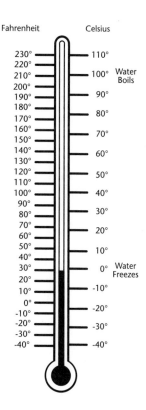

Fahrenheit   Celsius

- 230° — 110°
- 220°
- 210° — 100° Water Boils
- 200°
- 190° — 90°
- 180°
- 170° — 80°
- 160° — 70°
- 150°
- 140° — 60°
- 130°
- 120° — 50°
- 110°
- 100° — 40°
- 90°
- 80° — 30°
- 70° — 20°
- 60°
- 50° — 10°
- 40°
- 30° — 0° Water Freezes
- 20°
- 10° — -10°
- 0°
- -10° — -20°
- -20° — -30°
- -30°
- -40° — -40°

CHATING

188

Thanks a Million

Thank you very much.	Muito obrigado[a].	mween-too oh-bree-gah-doo
You are...	Você é...	voh-say eh
...kind.	...simpatico[a].	seeng-pah-tee-koo
...wonderful.	...maravilhoso[a].	mah-rah-veel-yoh-zoo
...generous.	...generouso[a].	zheh-neh-roh-zoo
You spoil me / us.	Mimou me / nos.	mee-moh meh / nohsh
You've been a great help.	Você foi uma grande ajuda.	voh-say foy oo-mah grahn-deh ah-zhoo-dah
I will remember you...	Vou lembrar-me de você...	voh lehm-brar-meh deh voh-say
We will remember you...	Vamos lembrar-nos de você...	vah-moosh lehm-brar-noosh deh voh-say
...always.	...sempre.	sayn-preh
...until Tuesday.	...até terça-feira.	ah-teh tehr-sah-fay-rah

Responses for All Occasions

I like that.	Gosto disto.	gohsh-too deesh-too
We like that.	Gostamos disto.	goosh-tah-moosh deesh-too
I like you.	Gosto de si.	gohsh-too deh see
We like you.	Gostamos de si.	goosh-tah-moosh deh see
Fantastic!	Fantástico!	fahn-tahsh-tee-koo
What a nice place.	Que sítio bonito.	keh see-tee-oo boh-nee-too
Perfect.	Perfeito.	pehr-fay-too
Funny.	Cómico.	kom-ee-koo
Interesting.	Interessante.	een-teh-reh-sahn-teh
Really?	A sério?	ah seh-ree-oo
Wow!	Fiche!	fee-sheh
Congratulations!	Parabéns!	pah-rah-baynsh
Well done!	Bem feito!	bayn fay-too
You're welcome.	Não tem de quê.	now tayn deh kay

CHATING

Bless you! (after sneeze)	Santinho!	sahn-**teen**-yoo
What a pity.	É uma pena.	eh **oo**-mah **pay**-nah
That's life.	É a vida.	eh ah **vee**-dah
No problem.	Não tem problema.	no<u>w</u> tay<u>n</u> proo-**blay**-mah
O.K.	Está bem.	ish-**tah** bay<u>n</u>
This is the good life!	Esta é a boa vida!	**ehsh**-tah eh ah **boh**-ah **vee**-dah
Have a good day!	Tenha um bom dia.	**tehn**-yah oo<u>n</u> boh<u>n</u> **dee**-ah
Good luck!	Boa-sorte!	boh-ah-**sor**-teh
Let's go!	Vamos!	**vah**-moosh

Smoking

Do you smoke?	Você fuma?	voh-**say foo**-mah
Do you smoke pot?	Você fuma ervas?	voh-**say foo**-mah **ehr**-vahsh
I (don't) smoke.	(Não) fumo.	(no<u>w</u>) **foo**-moo
We (don't) smoke.	(Não) fumamos.	(no<u>w</u>) foo-**mah**-moosh
lighter	esqueiro	ish-**kay**-roo
cigarettes	cigarros	see-**gah**-roosh
marijuana	erva, marijuana	**ehr**-vah, mah-ree-**zhwah**-nah
hash	hashishe	ah-**shee**-sheh
joint	baseado	bah-zeh-**ah**-doo
stoned	drogado[a]	droh-**gah**-doo
Wow!	Fiche!	**fee**-sheh

Conversing with Animals

rooster / cock-a-doodle-doo	galo / co-coro-cocó	**gah**-loo / koo-koo-roo-koo-**kah**
bird / tweet tweet	pássaro / piu piu	**pah**-sah-roo / pee-**oo** pee-**oo**
cat / meow	gato / miau	**gah**-too / **mee**-ow

CHATING

dog / woof woof	cão / ão ão	kow / ow ow
duck / quack quack	pato / quac quac	**pah**-too / kwahk kwahk
cow / moo	vaca / moo	**vah**-kah / moo
pig / oink oink	porco / orn orn	**por**-koo / orn orn
(or just snort)		

Profanity

People make animal noises, too. These words will help you understand what the more colorful locals are saying.

bastard	bastardo	bahsh-**tar**-doo
bitch	puta	**poo**-tah
breasts	mamas	**mah**-mahsh
penis	pénis	**peh**-neesh
shit	merda	**mehr**-dah
drunk	bêbado	**bay**-bah-doo
imbecile	parvo	**par**-voo
jerk	palerma	pah-**lehr**-mah
stupid	estúpido[a]	ish-**too**-pee-doo
Did someone fart?	Alguem deu um peido?	**ahl**-gayn **deh**-oo oon **pay**-doo
I burped.	En arrotei.	ayn ah-**roh**-tay
This sucks.	Isto é chato.	**eesh**-too eh **shah**-too
Go to hell!	Vá para o inferno!	vah **pah**-rah oo een-**fehr**-noo
Shove it up your ass.	Enfia no rabo.	ehn-**fee**-ah noh **rah**-boo
Bullshit.	Merda.	**mehr**-dah
You are...	Vôce é...	voh-**say** eh
Don't be...	Não seja...	now **seh**-zhah
...a son of a bitch.	...um filho da puta.	oon **feel**-yoo dah **poo**-tah
...an idiot.	...um idióta.	oon ee-dee-**ow**-dah
...a creep.	...um estranho.	oon ish-**trayn**-yoo
...a cretin.	...um cretino.	oon kreh-**tee**-noo
...a pig.	...um porco.	oon **por**-koo

Sweet Curses

My goodness.	*Meu deus.*	**meh**-oo **deh**-oosh
Goodness gracious.	*Deus nos vale.*	**deh**-oosh noosh **vah**-leh
Oh, my gosh.	*Ó nossa.*	oo **noh**-sah
Shoot.	*Força.*	**for**-sah
Darn it!	*Caramba!*	kah-**rahm**-bah

Create Your Own Conversation

Using these lists, you can have deep (or ridiculous) conversations with the locals.

Who

I / you	*eu / você*	**eh**-oo / voh-**say**
he / she	*ele / ela*	**eh**-leh / **eh**-lah
we / they	*nós / eles*	nohsh / **eh**-lish
my / your...	*meus / seus...*	**meh**-oosh / **seh**-oosh
...parents / children	*...pais / crianças*	pīsh / kree-**ahn**-sahsh
men / women	*homens / mulheres*	**ah**-maynsh / mool-**yeh**-rish
rich / poor	*rico / pobre*	**ree**-koo / **poh**-breh
young / middle-aged / old	*jovem / meia-idade / idoso*	**zhah**-vayn / **may**-ah-ee-**dah**-deh / ee-**doh**-zoo
Portuguese	*Portugueses*	poor-too-**gay**-zish
Spanish	*Espanhóis*	ish-pahn-**yoysh**
Austrians	*Austriacos*	owsh-tree-**ah**-koosh
Belgians	*Belgas*	**behl**-gahsh
British	*Britânicos*	bree-**tah**-nee-koosh

CHATING

Czechs	Checos	**cheh**-koosh
French	Franceses	frahn-**say**-zish
Germans	Alemães	ah-leh-**maynsh**
Irish	Irlandês	eer-lahn-**daysh**
Italians	Italianos	ee-tahl-**yah**-noosh
Moroccans	Marroquinos	mah-roo-**kee**-noosh
Swiss	Suiços	**swee**-soosh
Europeans	Europeus	eh-oo-roh-**pee**-oosh
EU	UE (União	oo eh (oo-nee-**ow**
(European Union)	Europeia)	eh-oo-roh-**peh**-ee-ah)
Americans	Americanos	ah-meh-ree-**kah**-noosh
liberals	liberais	lee-**beh**-raysh
conservatives	conservadores	kohn-sehr-vah-**doh**-rish
radicals	radicais	rah-**dee**-kaysh
terrorists	terroristas	teh-roh-**reesh**-tahsh
politicians	políticos	poo-**lee**-tee-koosh
big business	negócio grande	neh-**gos**-ee-oo **grahn**-deh
multinational	companhias	kohn-pahn-**yee**-ahsh
corporations	multinacionais	mool-tee-nah-see-oh-**nīsh**
military	militares	mee-lee-**tah**-rish
mafia	máfia	**mah**-fee-ah
refugees	refigiados	reh-fee-zhee-**ah**-doosh
travelers	vijantes	vee-**zhan**-tish
God	Deus	**deh**-oosh
Christians	cristãos	kreesh-**towsh**
Catholics	católicos	kah-**tal**-ee-koosh
Protestants	protestantes	proh-tish-**tayn**-tehsh
Jews	judeus	**zhoo**-deh-oosh
Muslims	mussulmanos	moo-sool-**mah**-noosh
everyone	todas as pessoas	**toh**-dahsh ahsh peh-**soh**-ahsh

What

buy / sell	comprar / vender	kohn-**prar** / vayn-**dar**
have / lack	ter / faltar	tehr / fahl-**tar**
help / abuse	ajudar / abusar	ah-zhoo-**dar** / ah-boo-**zar**

learn / fear	aprender / temer	ah-prayn-**dehr** / teh-**mehr**
love / hate	amar / odiar	ah-**mar** / oo-dee-**ar**
prosper / suffer	prósperar / sofrer	prahsh-peh-**rar** / soof-**rehr**
take / give	tirar / dar	tee-**rar** / dar
want / need	querer / precisar	keh-**rehr** / preh-see-**zar**
work / play	trabalhar / brincar	trah-bahl-**yar** / breen-**kar**

Why

(anti-)	(contra-)	(**kohn**-trah-)
globalization	globalização	gloh-bah-lee-zah-**sow**
class warfare	luta de classes	**loo**-tah deh **klah**-shish
corruption	corrupção	koo-roop-**sow**
democracy	democracia	deh-moo-krah-**see**-ah
education	instrucão	eensh-troo-**sow**
family	familia	fah-**meel**-yah
food	comida	koo-**mee**-dah
global perspective	perspectiva mundial	persh-pehk-**tee**-vah moon-dee-**ahl**
guns	pistolas	peesh-**toh**-lahsh
happiness	felicidade	feh-lee-see-**dah**-deh
health	saúde	sah-**oo**-deh
hope	esperança	ish-peh-**rahn**-sah
imperialism	imperialismo	eem-peh-ree-ah-**leezh**-moo
lies	mentiras	mayn-**tee**-rahsh
love / sex	amor / sexo	ah-**mor** / **sehk**-soo
marijuana	marijuana	mah-ree-**zhwah**-nah
money / power	dinheiro / poder	deen-**yay**-roo / poo-**dehr**
pollution	poluição	pool-wee-**sow**
racism	racismo	rah-**seesh**-moo
regime change	mudança de regime	moo-**dahn**-sah deh reh-**zhee**-meh
relaxation	descanso	dish-**kahn**-soo
religion	religião	ray-lee-**zhow**
respect	respeito	rish-**pay**-too
taxes	taxas	**tahsh**-ahsh

CHATTING

television	televisão	teh-leh-vee-**zow**
violence	violência	vee-oo-**layn**-see-ah
war / peace	guerra / paz	**geh**-rah / pahsh
work	trabalho	trah-**bahl**-yoo

You Be the Judge

(no) problem	(não) á problema	(no<u>w</u>) ah proo-**blay**-mah
(not) good	(não) bom	(no<u>w</u>) boh<u>n</u>
(not) dangerous	(não) perigoso	(no<u>w</u>) peh-ree-**goh**-zoo
(not) fair	(não) justo	(no<u>w</u>) **zhoosh**-too
(not) guilty	(não) culpado	(no<u>w</u>) kool-**pah**-doo
(not) powerful	(não) poderoso	(no<u>w</u>) poo-deh-**roh**-zoo
(not) stupid	(não) estúpido	(no<u>w</u>) ish-**too**-pee-doo
(not) happy	(não) feliz	(no<u>w</u>) feh-**leesh**
because / for	porque / para	**poor**-keh / **pah**-rah
and / or / from	e / ou / de	ee / oh / deh
too much	demasiado	deh-mah-zee-**ah**-doo
(never) enough	(nunca é) suficiente	(**noon**-kah eh) soo-fee-see-**ayn**-teh
same	mesmo	**mehsh**-moo
better / worse	melhor / pior	mil-**yor** / pee-**or**
here / everywhere	aqui / em toda parte	ah-**kee** / ay<u>n</u> toh-**dah par**-teh

Beginnings and Endings

I like...	Gosto...	**gohsh**-too
We like...	Nós gostamos...	nohsh goosh-**tah**-moosh
I don't like...	Não gosto...	no<u>w</u> **gohsh**-too
We don't like...	Não gostamos...	no<u>w</u> goosh-**tah**-moosh
Do you like...?	Você gosta...	voh-**say gohsh**-tah
In the past...	No passado...	noo pah-**sah**-doo
When I was younger, I thought...	Quando eu era jovem, pensava...	**kwahn**-doo eh-oo eh-rah **zhah**-vay<u>n</u> payn-**sah**-vah
Now, I think...	Agora penso...	ah-**goh**-rah **payn**-soo
I am / Are you...?	Eu sou / Você é...?	**eh**-oo soh / voh-**say** eh

CHATING

...an optimist / pessimist	...um optimista / pessimista	oo<u>n</u> **ohp**-tee-meesh-tah / **peh**-see-meesh-tah
I (don't) believe...	(Não) acredito...	(no<u>w</u>) ah-**kreh**-dee-too
Do you believe...?	Acredita...?	ah-kreh-**dee**-tah
...in God	...em Deus	ay<u>n</u> **deh**-oosh
...in life after death	...em vida depois da morte	ay<u>n</u> **vee**-dah day-**pwaysh** dah **mor**-teh
...in extra-terrestrial life	...que existe vida em outros planetas	keh ee-**zeesh**-teh **vee**-dah ay<u>n</u> **oh**-troosh plah-**nay**-tahsh
...in Santa Claus	...no Pai-Natal	noo pī-nah-**tahl**
Yes. / No.	Sim. / Não.	seeng / no<u>w</u>
Maybe. / I don't know.	Talvez. / Não sei.	**tahl**-vaysh / no<u>w</u> say
What's most important in life?	O que é a coisa mais importante na vida?	oo keh eh ah **koy**-zah mī sh eem-poor-**tahn**-teh nah **vee**-dah
The problem is...	O problema é...	oo proo-**blay**-mah eh
The answer is...	A resposta é...	ah rish-**pohsh**-tah eh
We have solved	Nós resolvemos	nohsh reh-zool-**vay**-moosh
the world's problems.	os problemas do mundo.	oosh proo-**blay**-mahsh doo **moon**-doo

A Portuguese Romance

Words of Love

I / me / you / we	*eu / mim / tú / nós*	**eh**-oo / meeng / too / nohsh
flirt	*namorar*	nah-moo-**rar**
kiss	*beijo*	**bay**-zhoo
hug	*abraço*	ah-**brah**-soo
love	*amor*	ah-**mor**
make love	*fazer amor*	fah-**zehr** ah-**mor**
condom	*preservativo*	preh-zehr-vah-**tee**-voo
contraceptive	*contraceptivo*	koh<u>n</u>-trah-sehp-**tee**-voo
safe sex	*sexo seguro*	**sehk**-soo say-**goo**-roo
sexy	*sexy*	"sexy"
romantic	*romântico*	roh-**mahn**-tee-koo
my tender love	*minha ternura*	**meen**-yah tehr-**noo**-rah
my darling (male / female)	*meu querido / minha querida*	**meh**-oo keh-**ree**-doo / **meen**-yah keh-**ree**-dah
my angel	*meu anjo*	**meh**-oo **ahn**-zhoo
baby	*bebé*	bay-**bay**
my soft thing (male / female)	*meu fofinho / minha fofinha*	**meh**-oo foh-**feen**-yoo / **meen**-yah foh-**feen**-yah

Ah, Amor

What's the matter?	*Que se passa?*	keh seh **pah**-sah
Nothing.	*Nada.*	**nah**-dah
I am / Are you...?	*Sou / És...?*	soh / ehsh
...straight	*...normal*	nor-**mahl**
...gay	*...gay*	"gay"
...bisexual	*...bissexual*	bee-sehk-**swahl**
...undecided	*...indeciso[a]*	een-day-**see**-zoo

...prudish	...puritano[a]	poo-ree-**tah**-noo
...horny	...excitado[a]	ish-see-**tah**-doo
We are on our honeymoon.	Nós estamos em lua de mel.	nohsh ish-**tah**-moosh ayn **loo**-ah deh mehl
I have...	Tenho...	**tayn**-yoo
...a boyfriend.	...um namorado.	oon nah-moo-**rah**-doo
...a girlfriend.	...uma namorada.	**oo**-mah nah-moo-**rah**-dah
I'm married.	Sou casado[a].	soh kah-**zah**-doo
I'm married but...	Sou casado[a] mas...	soh kah-**zah**-doo mahsh
I'm not married.	Não sou casado[a].	no<u>w</u> soh kah-**zah**-doo
Do you have a boyfriend / girlfriend?	Tens namorado / namorada?	tay<u>n</u>sh nah-moo-**rah**-doo / nah-moo-**rah**-dah
I'm adventurous.	Sou aventureiro[a].	soh ah-vehn-too-**ray**-roo
I'm lonely.	Sinto-me só.	**seeng**-too-meh soh
I'm lonely tonight.	Estou sozinho[a] hoje a noite.	ish-**toh** soh-**zeen**-yoo **oh**-zheh ah **noy**-teh
I'm rich and single.	Sou rico[a] e solteiro[a].	soh **ree**-koo ee sool-**tay**-roo
Do you mind if I sit here?	Importa-se se eu me sento aqui?	eem-**por**-tah-seh seh **eh**-oo meh **sehn**-too ah-**kee**
Would you like a drink?	Queres beber algo?	**keh**-rish beh-**behr** **ahl**-goo
Will you go out with me?	Queres sair comigo?	**keh**-rish sah-**eer** koh<u>n</u>-**mee**-goo
Would you like to go out tonight for...?	Queres sair hoje á noite por...?	**keh**-rish sah-**eer** **oh**-zheh ah **noy**-teh poor
...a walk	...um passeio	oon pah-**say**-oo
...dinner	...um jantar	oon zhan-**tar**
...a drink	...um copo	oon **koh**-poo
Where's the best place to dance nearby?	Onde é o melhor lugar para dançar por aqui?	**oh<u>n</u>**-deh ay oo mil-**yor** loo-**gar pah**-rah dah<u>n</u>-**sar** poor ah-**kee**
Do you want to dance?	Queres dançar?	**keh**-rish dah<u>n</u>-**sar**
Again?	Outra vez?	**oh**-trah vehz

CHATING

English	Portuguese	Pronunciation
Let's have a wild and crazy night!	Vamos nos divertir hoje a noite!	**vah**-moosh noosh dee-vehr-**teer oh**-zheh ah **noy**-teh
I have no diseases.	Não tenho nenhuma doença.	now **tayn**-yoo neen-**yoo**-mah doo-**ayn**-sah
I have many diseases.	Tenho muitas doenças.	**tayn**-yoo **mween**-tahsh doo-**ayn**-sahsh
I have only safe sex.	Só faço sexo com proteção.	soh **fah**-soo **sehk**-soo koh<u>n</u> proh-teh-**sow**
Can I take you home? (f / m)	Posso leva-la[o] para casa?	**pos**-soo **leh**-vah-lah **pah**-rah **kah**-zah
Why not?	Porque não?	poor-**kay** now
How can I change your mind?	Oque posso fazer para você mudar de idéia?	**oh**-keh **pos**-soo fah-**zehr pah**-rah voh-**say** moo-**dar** deh ee-**day**-yah
Kiss me.	Dê-me um beijo.	**deh**-meh oon **bay**-zhoo
May I kiss you?	Posso beijar?	**pos**-soo bay-**zhar**
Can I see you again?	Quando é que o / a posso ver?	**kwahn**-doo eh keh oo / ah **pos**-soo vehr
Your place or mine?	Na sua casa ou na minha?	nah **soo**-ah **kah**-zah oh nah **meen**-yah
How does this feel?	Como te fáz sentir?	**koh**-moo teh fahsh sehn-**teer**
Is this an aphrodisiac?	É isto um afrodisíaco?	eh **eesh**-too oon ah-froo-dee-**zee**-ah-koo
This is (not) my first time.	(Não) é a minha primeira vez.	(now) eh ah **meen**-yah pree-**may**-rah vaysh
You are my most beautiful souvenir.	Você é a minha melhor recordação.	voh-**say** ay ah **meen**-yah mil-**yor** reh-kor-dah-**sow**
Do you do this often?	Faz isto regularmente?	fahsh **eesh**-too reh-goo-lar-**mayn**-teh
Is my breath O.K.?	Tenho bom hálito?	**tayn**-yoo boh<u>n</u> **ah**-lee-too
Let's just be friends.	Vamos ser só amigos.	**vah**-moosh sehr soh ah-**mee**-goosh

I'll pay for my share.	*Pagarei a minha parte.*	pah-gah-**ray** ah **meen**-yah **par**-teh
Would you like a massage for...?	*Gostaria de uma massagem para...?*	goosh-tah-**ree**-ah deh **oo**-mah mah-**sah**-zhay<u>n</u> **pah**-rah
...your back	*...as tuas costas*	ahsh **too**-ahsh **kosh**-tahsh
...your feet	*...os seus pés*	oosh **seh**-oosh pehsh
Why not?	*Porquê não?*	poor-**kay** no<u>w</u>
Try it.	*Exprimente.*	ish-pree-**mayn**-teh
It tickles.	*Isso faz cócegas.*	**ee**-soo fahsh **kah**-see-gahsh
Oh my God!	*Ó meu Deus!*	ah **meh**-oo **deh**-oosh
I love you.	*Eu amo-te.*	**eh**-oo **ah**-moo-teh
Darling, will you marry me?	*Querida, queres casar comigo?*	keh-**ree**-dah **keh**-rish kah-**zar** koo-**mee**-goo

DICTIONARY

Portuguese/English

You'll see some of the words in the dictionary listed like this: *agressivo[a]*. Use the *a* ending (pronounced "ah") if you're talking about a female.

A

á	at	acima	above
á moda de casa	homemade	acordar	wake up
abaixo	down; below	acordo, de	agree
aberto	open (adj)	adega	cellar
abertor de latas	can opener	adesivo	tape (adhesive); band-aid
abôrto	abortion		
abôrto natural	miscarriage	adeus	goodbye
Abril	April	adulto	adult
abrir	open (v)	advogado[a]	lawyer
abstrato	abstract	aérea, linha	airline
abusar	abuse (v)	aéreo, correio	air mail
acabado	over (finished)	aeroporto	airport
acesso a Internet	Internet access	agência de viagens	travel agency
acetona	nail polish remover	agnóstico[a]	agnostic
acidente	accident	agora	now

Agosto	August	**amanhã**	tomorrow
agrafador	stapler	**amante**	lover
agressivo[a]	aggressive	**amar**	love (v)
água	water	**amarelo**	yellow
água da torneira	tap water	**ambulância**	ambulance
água mineral	mineral water	**amigo[a]**	friend
água potável	drinkable water	**amizade**	friendship
água, queda de	waterfall	**amor**	love (n)
agulha	needle	**andar**	walk (v); story (floor)
ajuda	help (n)	**animal de estimação**	pet (n)
ajudar	help (v)	**aniversário**	birthday
albergue de juventude	youth hostel	**ano**	year
		antepassado[a]	ancestor
alcool	alcohol	**antes**	before
alcunha	nickname	**antibiótico**	antibiotic
aldeia	village	**antigo**	ancient
aleijado[a]	handicapped	**antiguidades**	antiques
Alemanha	Germany	**antiquário**	antiques shop
alergias	allergies	**apanhar**	catch (v)
alérgico[a]	allergic	**apartamento**	apartment
alfândega	customs	**aperitivos**	appetizers
alfinete	pin	**apontamento**	appointment
alfinete de segurança	safety pin	**apontar**	point (v)
		aprender	learn
algodão	cotton	**apressar**	hurry (v)
alguma coisa	something	**apretado**	tight
coisa, alguma	something	**aproximada- mente**	approximately
alguns	some		
alicate	pliers	**aqui**	here
alimento suplementar	baby formula	**ar**	air
		ar condicionado	air-conditioned
almoço	lunch	**arco íris**	rainbow
almoço, pequeno	breakfast	**armários**	lockers
almofada	pillow	**arranha**	spider
alta, tensão	high blood pressure	**arranjar**	fix (v)
altar	altar	**arrepios**	chills
alto[a]	tall; high	**arrôba**	at sign (@)
alugar	rent (v)	**arte**	art

arte nova	Art Nouveau
artesanato	crafts
artista	artist
artrite	arthritis
árvore	tree
asa	wing
asma	asthma
aspirina	aspirin
assadura das fraldas	diaper rash
assento	seat
assinatura	signature
ateu	atheist
atirar	throw
atleta	athlete
atraente	attractive
atraso	delay (n)
através	through
atravessar	go through
audio guia	audioguide
auto serviço	self-service
autocarro	city bus
autoestrada	highway
automática, caixa	cash machine
avião	plane
avó	grandmother
avô	grandfather
azedo	sour
azul	blue

B

babeiro	bib
bagagem	baggage
bagagem	baggage claim
bagagem de mão	carry-on luggage
baixo	low
balde	bucket
balsa	raft
banco	bank
bandeira	flag
banheira	bathtub
banho	bath
banho, casa de	bathroom
barata	cockroach
barato	cheap
barba	beard
barbeiro	barber
barco	boat, ship (n), ferry
barco de passeio	rowboat
barco de vela	sailing
barulho[a]	noisy
base	foundation (makeup)
baseado	joint (marijuana)
basebol	baseball
basquetebol	basketball
batão de cierio	lip salve
bateria	battery
baton	lipstick
bêbado[a]	drunk
bebé	baby
beber	drink (v)
bebida	drink (n)
beijo	kiss (n)
Belgica	Belgium
beliches	bunk beds
bem-vindo	welcome
bexiga	bladder
biblioteca	library
bicicleta	bicycle
bife	beef
bigode	moustache
bilhete	ticket

bloco	block	cabelo	hair
blusa	blouse	cada	each
boca	mouth	cadeira	chair
bola	ball	cadeira de	baby car seat
boleia, pedir	hitchhike	carro para o bebé	
bolhas	blisters	cadeirinha alta	highchair
bolsa	purse	caderno	notebook
bolso	pocket	café	coffee; coffee shop
bom	good, fine	café Internet	Internet café
bomba	bomb; pump (n)	cãibra	cramps
bomba de	gas station	cair	fall (v)
gasolina		cais	platform (train)
bom-dia	good day	caixa	cashier; box
boné	cap	caixa	cash machine
boneca	doll	automática	
bonito[a]	pretty, handsome	caixão	crypt
borracha	eraser	calado[a]	quiet
botão	button	calção de banho	swim trunks
botas	boots	banho, calção de	swim trunks
braço	arm	calças	pants
branco	white	calções	shorts
brilho de sol	sunshine	calendário	calendar
sol, brilho de	sunshine	calor	heat (n)
brincos	earrings	caloria	calorie
brinquedo	toy	cama	bed
broche	brooch	camara	camera
broches	clothes pins	camarote	sleeper (train)
bronze	bronze	câmbio	exchange (n)
bronzeado	suntan (n)	caminho de ferro	railway
bronzear	sunbathe	camioneta	long-distance bus
buraco	hole	camisa	shirt
burro	donkey	camisa de dormir	nightgown
		campaínha	ring (n)
C		campeonato	championship
cabeça	head	campismo	camping; campsite
cabedal	leather	campo	countryside; field
cabelareiro	beauty salon	Canadá	Canada

canal	canal; channel
canção	song
cancelar	cancel
caneta	pen
canoa	canoe
cansado[a]	tired
cantar	sing
cantor[a]	singer
cão	dog
capela	chapel
capitão	captain
cara	face
carne	meat
caro	expensive
carpete	carpet, rug
carregar	carry
carrinho de bebê	stroller
carro	car
carruagem	train car
carruagem cama	sleeper car (train)
carruagem restaurante	dining car (train)
carta	letter
cartão	card (also businiss card)
cartão de crédito	credit card
cartão postal	postcard
cartão telefónico	telephone card
cartas	cards (deck)
carteira	wallet
carteirista	pickpocket
casa	house
casa de banho	bathroom
casa de ferragens	hardware store
casa de fotocopias	photocopy shop
casa, á moda de	homemade
casaco	jacket
casaco impermeável	raincoat
casado[a]	married
casamento	wedding
cassete	tape (cassette)
castanho	brown
castelo	castle
catedral	cathedral
Católico[a]	Catholic (adj)
cavaleiros	knights
cavalheiro	gentleman
cavalo	horse
cave	cave
cedo	soon; early
centro	center; downtown
centro comercial	shopping mall
ceramica	ceramic
certo[a]	right (correct)
cerveja	beer
cesto	basket
céu	sky; heaven
chaleira	kettle
chapéu	hat
charcutaria	delicatessen
chateado[a]	angry
chave	key
chave de parafusos	screwdriver
chávena	cup
chegadas	arrivals
chegar	arrive
cheio	no vacancy
cheiro	smell (n)

cheque	check	**comboio**	train
cheque de viagem	traveler's check	**começar**	begin
chinélos	slippers	**comer**	eat
chinês	Chinese (adj)	**comichão**	itch (n)
chorar	cry (v)	**comida**	food
chupeta	pacifier	**comida para bebés**	baby food
chuva	rain (n)	**como**	how
chuveiro	shower	**compact disco**	compact disc
cidade	city; town	**complicado**	complicated
ciência	science	**compras**	shopping
cientista	scientist	**comprimido**	pill
cigarro	cigarette	**comprimidos para as dores**	pain killer
cima, em	upstairs	**computador**	computer
cinto	belt	**concerto**	concert
cintura	waist	**concha**	shell
cinzeiro	ashtray	**condicionador**	conditioner (hair)
cinzento	gray	**condutor**	conductor; driver
claro	clear	**conduzir**	drive (v)
classe	class	**conexão**	connection (train)
classe, primeira	first class	**confeitaria**	sweets shop
classe, segunda	second class	**confirmar**	confirm
clássico	classical	**confortável**	comfortable; cozy
clinica médica	medical clinic	**congestão**	congestion (sinus)
clip	paper clip	**constipação**	cold (n)
cobre	copper	**construção na estrada**	construction (sign)
código pessoal	PIN code	**conta**	bill (payment)
código postal	zip code	**contador**	accountant
coelho	rabbit	**contagioso**	contagious
coisa	thing	**contracepçaõ**	condom
colete	vest	**convidado[a]**	guest
colher	spoon	**convite**	invitation
cólicas	menstrual cramps	**copiado**	copy
collants	nylons (panty hose)	**copo**	glass
com	with	**cor de laranja**	orange (color)
com gás	fizzy		
combinação	slip		

cor de rosa	pink
coração	heart
coral	choir
corbetor	blanket
corda	rope
cordão de sapatos	shoelaces
cordeiro	lamb
cores	colors
corpo	body
corredor	aisle; corridor
correia de ventoinha	fan belt
correio	mail (n)
correio aéreo	air mail
corrente	stream (n)
correr	run (v)
corrupção	corruption
corta unhas	nail clipper
corte de cabelo	haircut
costa	coast
costas	back
cotovelo	elbow
coxa	thigh
cozinha	kitchen
cozinhar	cook (v)
crédito	credit
crédito, cartão de	credit card
creme	cream; lotion
creme de barbear	shaving cream
creme desinfetante	first-aid cream
creme para as mãos	hand lotion
criado	waiter
criança	child
crianças	children
Cristão	Christian (adj)

cru	raw
cruz	cross
cruzamento	intersection
cruzeta	coat hanger
cuecas	underpants
cuidadoso	careful
culpado[a]	guilty
cúpula	dome
curto[a]	short
custa, quanto	how much ($)

D

dançar	dance (v)
dar	give
de	of; from
de acordo	agree
de repente	suddenly
debaixo	under
declarar	declare (customs)
dedo	finger
dedo do pé	toe
delicioso	delicious
delineador	eyeliner
demasiado	too (much)
democracia	democracy
dente, dor de	toothache
dentes	teeth
dentição	teething (baby)
dentista	dentist
depois	after; afterwards
depois de amanhã	day after tomorrow
depósito	deposit
descanso	relaxation
descongestionante	decongestant
desconto	discount

desculpa	apology
desculpe	sorry; excuse me
desejo	wish (v)
desempregado[a]	unemployed
desinfetante	disinfectant
desodorizante	deodorant
despertador	alarm clock
desporto	sport
desventurado[a]	unfortunate
desvio	detour
detergente	laundry detergent
detrás	behind
deus	God
Dezembro	December
dia	day
diabético[a]	diabetic
diafragma	diaphragm (birth control)
diamante	diamond
diarreia	diarrhea
dicionário	dictionary
difícil	difficult
dinheiro	money; cash
direção	direction
directo	direct
direita	right (direction)
disco voador	Frisbee
divertido[a]	funny; fun (adj)
divorciado[a]	divorced
dobrar	double
doce	sweet (adj); candy
doença	disease
doença venéria	venereal disease
doente	sick
domingo	Sunday
donde	where

dono[a]	owner
dor	pain; cramps
dor de cabeça	headache
dor de dente	toothache
dor de estômago	stomachache
dor de garganta	sore throat
dor de ouvido	earache
dor no peito	chest pains
dormir	sleep (v)
dormitorio	dormitory
doutor[a]	doctor
drogado[a]	stoned
dúzia	dozen

E

e	and
ela	she
ele	he
eles	they
elevador	elevator
eliminar	delete
em	in
em cima	upstairs
em frente	straight
em vez de	instead
embaixada	embassy
embalagem	package
embrulhar	wrap (v)
ementa	menu
emergência	emergency
emergência, saída de	emergency exit
emergência, sala de	emergency room
emprestar	borrow; lend
empurrar	push
encantador[a]	charming

encher	refill (n)	esfomeado[a]	hungry
endereço	address	esgotado[a]	exhausted
endereço eletrônico	e-mail address	Espanha	Spain
		especialidade	specialty
enfermeiro[a]	nurse	espectáculo	show (n)
engenheiro	engineer	espelho	mirror
engolir	swallow (v)	espera, sala de	waiting room
enicologista	gynecologist	esperança	hope
entender	understand	esperar	wait (v)
entrada	entrance	espirro	sneeze (n)
entrada	entrance (road)	esposa	wife
entrada do metro	subway entrance	esquecer	forget
		esquerda	left (direction)
envenanamento alimentar	food poisoning	esqui aquático	waterskiing
		esquiar	ski (v); skiing
enviar	send, ship (v)	esquina	corner
enxaqueca	migraine	esta noite	tonight
epilepcia	epilepsy	estação	station
equipa	team	estação de metro	subway station
erro	mistake		
erupção	rash	estacas de tenda	tent pegs
erva	marijuana	estacionamento, parque de	parking lot
escada	ladder		
escadas	stairs	estacionar	park (v)
Escandinavia	Scandinavia	estado	state
escandulo	scandalous	Estados Unidos	United States
escola	school	estanho	pewter
escorregadio	slippery	este	east
escova	brush	estilo	style
escova de cabelo	hairbrush	estômago	stomach
escova de dentes	toothbrush	estômago, dor de	stomachache
escrever	write		
escritório	office	estranho[a]	strange
escultor[a]	sculptor	estrangeiro[a]	foreign
escultura	sculpture	estreito	narrow
escuro	dark	estrela	star (in sky)
escutar	listen	estudante	student

estúpido[a]	stupid	**feriado**	holiday
eu	I	**férias**	vacation
Europa	Europe	**ferido[a]**	injured
exactamente	exactly	**fervido**	boiled
excelente	excellent	**festa**	party
excepto	except	**festival**	festival
excursão	tour	**Fevereiro**	February
exemplo	example	**fevre**	fever
explicar	explain	**ficha**	token
		filha	daughter

F

		filho	son
fábrica	factory	**filme**	movie
faca	knife	**fio**	string; necklace
fácil	easy	**fio dental**	dental floss
falar	talk, speak	**fita cola**	scotch tape
falésia	cliff	**flor**	flower
falso	false	**fogo**	fire
familia	family	**fogo de artificio**	fireworks
famoso[a]	famous	**fonte**	fountain
fantástico[a]	fantastic	**forno**	oven
farmácia	pharmacy	**forte**	strong
faróis da frente	headlights	**fortificação**	wall, fortified
fatia	slice	**fosforos**	matches
fato de banho	swimsuit	**fosso**	moat
banho, fato de	swimsuit	**fotocopia**	photocopy
favor, por	please	**fotografia**	photo
fazer	make (v)	**frágil**	fragile
febre dos fenos	hay fever	**fraldas**	diaper
fechado	closed	**França**	France
fechadura	lock (n)	**frente, em**	straight
fechar	lock (v)	**fresco**	fresh; cool
fecho	zipper	**frio[a]**	cold (adj)
feio[a]	ugly	**fronteira**	border
feira	flea market	**fruta**	fruit
felicidade	happiness	**fumador**	smoking
feliz	happy	**fumador, não**	non-smoking
feminino	female	**fumo**	smoke

fundo	bottom
fussil	fuses
futebol	soccer
futebol americano	American football
futuro	future

G

gaivota	paddleboat
galeria	gallery
galeria de arte	art gallery
galinha	chicken
garagem	garage
garantia	guarantee
garfo	fork
garganta	throat
garganta, dor de	sore throat
garrafa	bottle
gás	gas
gás, com	fizzy (water)
gastar	spend
gato	cat
gaze	bandage; gauze
gelado	ice cream
gelo	ice
gêmeos	twins
generouso[a]	generous
genuíno	genuine
gerente	manager
Gilete	razor
ginastica	gymnastics
golfe	golf
gordo[a]	fat (adj)
gordura	fat (n)
gorduroso	greasy
gostar	enjoy, like (v)
gótico	Gothic

Grã-Bretanha	Britain
gramática	grammar
grande	big
grande armazen	department store
granjeiro[a]	farmer
grátis	free (no cost)
grátis, taxa	toll-free
grávida	pregnant
gravidez	pregnancy
Grécia	Greece
gripe	flu
grosso	thick
guarda-chuva	umbrella
guardanapo	napkin
guardar	keep; save (computer)
guerra	war
guia, um (m)	guidebook
guia, uma (f)	guide
guitarra	guitar

H

halito	breath
hashishe	hash (drug)
hemorróidas	hemorrhoids
hidratante	moisturizer
hidroplano	hydrofoil
hífen	hyphen (-)
história	history
hoje	today
Holanda	Netherlands
homen	man
homosexual	gay
honesto[a]	honest
hóquei	hockey
hora	hour

horário	opening hours; timetable
horrível	horrible
humilhante	embarrassing

I

ida e volta	roundtrip
ida, uma	one way (ticket)
idade	age
igreija	church
ilha	island
imediatamente	immediately
imobilizado	stuck
importado	imported
importante	important
impossível	impossible
imposto não pago	duty free
impressionista	Impressionist
imprimir	print (v)
inacreditável	incredible
inchado	swelling (n)
incluido	included
incomudar	disturb
inconciente	unconscious
independente	independent
indigestão	indigestion
industria	industry
infecção	infection
infecção urinaria	urinary infection
inflamação	inflammation
informação	information
Inglaterra	Great Britain
inglês	English
inocente	innocent
insecto	insect
insolação	sunstroke

instante	instant
instrucão	education
inteligente	intelligent
interior	inside
interresante	interesting
intestino	intestines
inverno	winter
iodo	iodine
ir	go
Irlanda	Ireland
irmã	sister
irmão	brother
isqueiro	lighter (n)
Itália	Italy

J

já	already
Janeiro	January
janela	window
jantar	dinner
jardim	garden
jardinagem	gardening
jarro	carafe
jeans	jeans
joalheria	jewelry; jewelry shop
joelho	knee
jogar	play (v)
jogo	game
jornal	newspaper
jovem	young; teenager
jovens	youths
Judeu	Jewish
Julho	July
Junho	June
juntos	together
justo	fair (just)
juventude	youth

juventude, albergue de	youth hostel	litro	liter
kitchenete	kitchenette	livraria	book shop
		livre	vacant
		livro	book
L		local	local
lã	wool	local da Web	Web site
lábio	lip	loja	store; shop (n)
ladrão	thief	loja de brinquedos	toy store
lago	lake		
lâmpada	light bulb	loja de lembranças	souvenir shop
lanterna a pilhas	flashlight		
lápis	pencil	loja de roupa	clothing boutique
lápis para os olhos	eyeliner	loja de telemóveis	cell phone shop
laranja	orange (fruit)		
lata	can (n)	loja de vinhos	wine shop
latão	brass	loja fotográfica	camera shop
lavandaria	launderette	longe	far
lavar	wash	louro[a]	blond
lavatório	sink	lua	moon
laxativo	laxative	lua de mel	honeymoon
lenço	scarf	lugar	seat
lençol	sheet	lugar sentado	berth (train)
lençol de cama	bedsheet	luta	fight (n)
lenços de papel	facial tissue	lutar	fight (v)
lentes de contacto	contact lenses	luvas	gloves
		luz	light (n)
lento[a]	slow	luzes traseiras	tail lights
levar, para	take out (food)		
ligadora	bandage, support	**M**	
limpo[a]	clean (adj)	macho	macho
lindo[a]	beautiful	madeira	wood
língua	language	maduro	ripe
linha	track (train); thread	mãe	mother
linha aérea	airline	magnifico[a]	great
linha de roupas	clothesline	magro[a]	thin
linho	linen	Maio	May
lista	list	mais	more

mais tarde	later	melhor	best
mala	suitcase	Menina	Miss
malenten-dido	misunderstanding	menina	waitress
		menstruação	menstruation; period
mangas	sleeves		
manhã	morning	mentiras	lies
mão	hand	mercado	market
mão, bagagem de	carry-on luggage	mercado de flores	flower market
mapa	map	mercado municipal	open-air market
mapa do metro	subway map		
maquiagem	makeup	mercearia	grocery store
máquina de lavar roupa	washer	mês	month
		mesa	table
mar	sea	mesmo	same
Março	March	mesquita	mosque
marido	husband	metal	metal
marisco	seafood	metro	subway
mármore	marble (material)	meu	my
mas	but	militares	military
masculino	male	minimo	minimum
masmorra	dungeon	minutos	minutes
matar	kill	missa	mass
mau	bad	mista	mix (n)
maxila	jaw	mobilias	furniture
máximo	maximum	mochila	backpack
mecânico[a]	mechanic	moda	fashion
mediaval	medieval	moda de casa, á	homemade
medicina	medicine	moderno	modern
medidor	taxi meter	moedas	coins
médio	medium	molhado	wet
medo[a]	afraid	momento	moment
meia de vidro	nylons (panty hose)	monestério	monastery
		montanha	mountain
meia-noite	midnight	montar a cavalo	horse riding
meias	socks	monumento	monument
meio-dia	noon	morrer	die

morto[a]	dead	**noite**	night
mosquito	mosquito	**noite, esta**	tonight
mosteiro	cloister	**noitecer**	evening
mostrar	show (v)	**nome**	name
mota	motorcycle	**normal**	normal
motocicleta	motor scooter	**norte**	north
Muçulmano[a]	Muslim (adj)	**nós**	we; us
mudar	change (v);	**Novembro**	November
	transfer (v)	**novo**	new
muito	many; much; very	**nunca**	never
mulher	woman	**nuo[a]**	naked
mulheres	women		
Multibanco	cash machine	**O**	
multidão	crowd (n)	**o quê**	what
mundo	world	**quê, o**	what
músculo	muscle	**O.K.**	O.K.
museu	museum	**obrigado**	thanks
música	music	**oceano**	ocean
		oculista	optician
N		**ocúlos**	glasses (eye)
nacionalidade	nationality	**óculos de sol**	sunglasses
nada	nothing	**ocupado**	occupied
nadar	swim	**odiar**	hate
não	no; not	**oeste**	west
não fumador	non-smoking	**olá**	hello
nariz	nose	**óleo**	oil (n)
nascer do sol	sunrise	**óleo de**	transmission fluid
Natal	Christmas	**transmissão**	
natureza	nature	**olhar**	look; watch (v)
náusea	nausea	**olho**	eye
nebuloso	cloudy	**Olímpicos**	Olympics
necessário	necessary	**ombros**	shoulder
necessitar	need	**ontem**	yesterday
negócio	business	**ópera**	opera
nervoso[a]	nervous	**operador**	operator
neto[a]	grandchild	**orelha**	ear
nevoeiro	fog	**orgão**	organ

ou	or	parque de diversões	playground
ouro	gold		
outono	autumn	parque de estacionamento	parking lot
outra vez	again		
outro	other; another	partidas	departures
Outubro	October	partido	broken
ouvido, dor de	earache	partir	depart
ouvir	hear	Pascoa	Easter
		passado	past

P

		passageiro[a]	passenger
padaria	bakery	passaporte	passport
padre	priest	pássaro	bird
pagar	pay	passatempo	hobby
página	page	pasta de dentes	toothpaste
pai	father	pastelaria	pastry shop
Pai-Natal	Santa Claus	pastilha elástica	gum
pais	parents	patinagem	skating
país	country	patins	roller skates
palácio	palace	patrão	boss
palavra	word	paz	peace
palito	toothpick	pé	foot
pão	bread	pé de atleta	athlete's foot
papel	paper	peão	pedestrian
papel higiénico	toilet paper	pedaço	piece
papelaria	office supplies store	pedir boleia	hitchhike
para	for; to	peito	chest; breast
para levar	take out (food)	peito, dor no	chest pains
parabéns	congratulations	peixe	fish (n)
para-brisas	windshield wipers	pele	skin
paragem	stop (n, train or bus)	pena, que	it's a pity
paragem de autocarro	bus stop	pénis	penis
		pensar	think
paragem do metro	subway stop	pensos higiénicos	sanitary napkins
		pente	comb (n)
parar	stop (v)	pequeno almoço	breakfast
parque	park (garden); playpen	pequeno[a]	small

percento	percent	pobre	poor
perdido[a]	lost	poder	can (v); power
perfeito	perfect (adj)	poderoso[a]	powerful
pergunta	question (n)	podre	rotten
perguntar	ask	polícia	police
perigo	danger	poliester	polyester
perigoso[a]	dangerous	políticos	politicians
período	period (of time)	poluição	pollution
perna	leg	ponte	bridge
perservativo	condom	ponto	dot (computer)
perto	near	pontual	on time
pesado	heavy	pôr do sol	sunset
pescar	fish (v)	por favor	please
pescoço	neck	porão	basement
peso	weight	porcelana	porcelain
pessoa	person	porco	pig, pork
pessoas	people	porquê	why; because
pessoas de	seniors	porta	door
terceira idade		portagem	toll
petisco	snack	porto	harbor
piada	joke (n)	possível	possible
pijamas	pajamas	possuir	own (v)
pilula	birth control pill	pouco	few
anticoncepcional		praça	square (town)
pinsa	tweezers	praia	beach
pintura	painting	prancha	surfboard
pior	worst	prata	silver
piquenique	picnic	prático[a]	practical
pisca-pisca	turn signal	prato	plate
piscina	swimming pool	preço	cost, price
pistola	gun	prédio	building
planta	plant	preguiçoso[a]	lazy
plástico	plastic	prenda	gift
pneu	tire (n)	Preparação H	Preparation H
pó	powder	presente	present (gift)
pó de talco	talcum powder	preto	black
pó para o rosto	face powder	primavera	spring (n)

primeira classe	first class
primeiro	first
primo[a]	cousin
principal	main
prisão de ventre	constipation
privado	private
problema	problem, trouble
problema no coração	heart condition
produto para a limpeza do rosto	face cleanser
professor	teacher
profissão	occupation
proibido	forbidden
pronto socorro	first aid
pronto[a]	ready
pronúncia	pronunciation
prósperar	prosper
protector solar	sunscreen
solar, protector	sunscreen
Protestante	Protestant (adj)
provar	taste (try)
próximo[a]	next
público	public
pulga	flea
pullover	sweater
pulmões	lungs
púlpito	pulpit
pulsação	pulse
pulseira	bracelet
pulso	wrist
puxador	handle (n)

Q

qualidade	quality
quando	when
quanto	how many
quanto custa	how much ($)
quarta-feira	Wednesday
quarto	room; bedroom; quarter (1/4)
quartos	vacancy sign
que pena	it's a pity
queda de água	waterfall
queijo	cheese
queimadura	burn (n)
queimadura solar	sunburn
queixar	complain
quem	who
quente	warm; hot (adj)
querer	want
quinta	farm
quinta-feira	Thursday
quiosque	newsstand

R

rabo	tail
rabuçados da tosse	cough drops
racismo	racism
radiador	radiator
rádio	radio
rainha	queen
raio X	X-ray
rapariga	girl
rapaz	boy
reboque	tow truck
recado	message
receber	receive
receita	recipe
receita médica	prescription
recepcionista	receptionist
recibo	receipt
recomendar	recommend

recordar	remember	roda	wheel
recto	rectum	rodas-acesso	wheelchair-accessible
rede	cot		
reembolso	refund (n)	rolha	cork
refigiados	refugees	românico	Romanesque
reformado[a]	retired	romântico[a]	romantic; Romantic
rei	king		
relaxar	relax	rotunda	roundabout
rélica	relic	roubado[a]	robbed
religião	religion	roulote	R.V. (camper)
relógio	clock; watch (n)	roupa	clothes
remédio	medicine	roxo	purple
remédio para a diarréia	diarrhea medicine	rua	street
		ruidoso[a]	loud
remédio para azia	antacid	ruínas	ruins
remédio para constipação	cold medicine		

S

renascimento	Renaissance)	sábado	Saturday
renda	lace	sabão	soap
reparar	repair	saber	know
repelente de insectos	insect repellant	sabor	taste (n); flavor (n)
		sacarolhas	corkscrew
repente, de	suddenly	saco	bag
Republica Checa	Czech Republic	saco de dormir	sleeping bag
		saco plástico	plastic bag
reserva	reservation	saco plástico com fecho	zip-lock bag
reservar	reserve		
respeito	respect (n)	saia	skirt
resposta	answer	saída	exit
ressonar	snore	saída de emergência	emergency exit
revista	magazine		
rico[a]	rich	saída do metro	subway exit
rimel	mascara	sair	leave
rio	river	sala	hall (big room)
rir	laugh (v)	sala de emergência	emergency room
robe	bathrobe		
rock	rock (n)	sala de espera	waiting room

saldos	sale	senhora	waitress
saltar	jump	senhoras	ladies
salvagem	wild	sentido único	one-way street
sandálias	sandals	separado	separate
sandálias de dedo	flip-flops	ser	is
sande	sandwich	sério	serious
sangrar	bleeding	serviço	service
sangre	blood	Setembro	September
santo[a]	saint	sexo	sex
sapatos	shoes	sexta-feira	Friday
sapatos de ténis	tennis shoes	sexy	sexy
saudade	homesick	SIDA	AIDS
saudavel	healthy	silêncio	silence
saúde	health	sim	yes
Saúde!	Cheers!	similar	similar
se	if	simpático[a]	nice; kind
secador	dryer	simples	simple; plain
secar	dry (v)	sinagoga	synagogue
seco	dry (adj)	sinal	sign; moleskin
século	century	sinal de luz	stoplight
seda	silk	sinos	bells
sede	thirsty	sinosite	sinus problems
segredo	secret	sintético	synthetic
segunda	second	slide	slide (photo)
segunda classe	second class	só	only
segunda-feira	Monday	sobre	on
seguro	insurance	sobremesa	dessert
seguro de saúde	health insurance	sobrinha	niece
		sobrinho	nephew
seguro[a]	safe; insured	sofrer	suffer
selo	stamp	sol	sun; sunny
sem	without	sol, nascer do	sunrise
semana	week	sol, óculos de	sunglasses
sempre	always	sol, pôr do	sunset
Senhor	Mr.	solar, queimadura	sunburn
senhor	sir	sólido	sturdy
Senhora	Mrs.	solteiro[a]	single

sombra	eye shadow
sonhar	dream (v)
sonho	dream (n)
sonolento[a]	sleepy
sorriso	smile (n)
sorte	luck
soutien	bra
sozinho[a]	alone
suar	sweat (v)
subida	up; hill
sublinhar	underscore (_)
substituto para aspirina	non-aspirin substitute
suficiente	enough
Suiça	Switzerland
sujo	dirty
sul	south
sumo	juice
supermercado	supermarket
suplemento	supplement
suporte para cadeira	booster seat
surfista	surfer
surpresa	surprise (n)

T

talvez	maybe
tamanho	size
tampa para lava louça	sink stopper
tampões	tampons
tampões de ouvido	earplugs
tarde	late; afternoon
tarde, mais	later
taxa	tax
taxa grátis	toll-free
teatro	theater

tecido	cloth
telefone	telephone (n)
telefone publico	phone booth
telefónico, cartão	telephone card
telemóvel	cell phone
televisão	television
telhado	roof
temer	fear (v)
temperatura	temperature
tempestada	storm
tempo	weather
tenda	tent
ténis	tennis
tenro	tender
tensão alta	high blood pressure
tépido	lukewarm
ter	have
terça-feira	Tuesday
terceira idade, pessoas de	seniors
terminal das camionetas	bus station
terminar	finish (v)
termómetro	thermometer
terra	earth
terrível	terrible
terroristas	terrorists
tesoraria	treasury
tesouras	scissors
teste de gravidez	pregnancy test
testículos	testicles
tia	aunt
tijela	bowl
tímido[a]	shy

tio	uncle	universidade	university
tirar	pull	uretra	urethra
toalha	towel	urgente	urgent
todo	every	usar	use (v)
tomada	electrical adapter	útero	uterus
tomar	take		
tonturas	dizziness		

V

torneira	faucet	vaca	cow
tornozelo	ankle	vale	valley
torre	tower	validade	validate
tosse	cough (n)	válido	valid
tosser	cough (v)	varanda	balcony
total	total	vasilina	Vaseline
trabalhar	work (v)	vazio	empty
trabalho	job; work (n)	vegetariano[a]	vegetarian
tradicional	traditional	vela	candle
traduzir	translate	velas	sparkplugs
tráfico	traffic	veleiro	sailboat
transferência	download	velho[a]	old
traseiro	buttocks	velocidade	speed
travões	brakes	veludo	velvet
tripé	tripod	vender	sell
triste	sad	vento	wind; windy
troca	change (n)	ver	see
tu	you (informal)	verão	summer
tubo para mergulho	snorkel	verde	green
tudo	everything	vermelho	red
túnel	tunnel	verniz para	nail polish
turista	tourist	as unhas	
Turkia	Turkey	vestido	dress (n)
		vez de, em	instead
		vez, outra	again

U

último[a]	last	vez, uma	once
uma ida	one way (ticket)	via	by (via)
uma vez	once	viagem	trip
úmido	muggy	viagem,	traveler's check
unha	fingernail	cheque de	

viajar	travel (v)
vida	life
vídeo	video
vijantes	travelers
vinhedo	vineyard
vinho	wine
violação	rape (n)
violência	violence
vir	come
vírus	virus
visita	visit (n)
visita guiada	guided tour
visitar	visit (v)
vista	view
vitaminas	vitamins
viúva	widow
viúvo	widower
viver	live (v)
voar	fly (v)
você	you (formal)
volta, ida e	roundtrip
vomitar	vomit
voo	flight
voz	voice

X

xampú	shampoo

English/Portuguese

You'll see some of the words in the dictionary listed like this: *agresivo[a]*. Use the *a* ending (pronounced "ah") if you're talking about a female.

A

abortion	aborto	alcohol	alcool
above	acima	allergic	alérgico[a]
abstract	abstrato	allergies	alergias
abuse (v)	abusar	alone	sozinho[a]
accident	acidente	already	já
accountant	contador	altar	altar
adapter, electrical	tomada	always	sempre
address	endereço	ambulance	ambulancia
address, e-mail	endereço eletronico	ancestor	antepassado[a]
		ancient	antigo
adult	adulto	and	e
afraid	medo[a]	angry	chateado[a]
Africa	Africa	animal	animal
after	depois	ankle	tornozelo
afternoon	tarde	another	outro
afterwards	depois	answer	resposta
again	outra vez	antacid	remédio para azia
age	idade	antibiotic	antibiótico
aggressive	agressivo[a]	antiques	antiguidades
agnostic	agnóstico[a]	antiques shop	antiquário
agree	de acordo	apartment	apartamento
AIDS	SIDA	apology	desculpa
air	ar	appetizers	aperitivos
air mail	correio aéreo	appointment	apontamento
air-conditioned	ar condicionado	approximately	aproximadmente
airline	linha aérea		
airport	aeroporto	April	Abril
aisle	corredor	arm	braço
alarm clock	despertador	arrivals	chegadas

arrive	chegar	bad	mau
art	arte	bag	saco
art gallery	galeria de arte	bag, plastic	saco plástico
Art Nouveau	arte nova	bag,	saco plástico
arthritis	artrite	zip-lock	com fecho
artificial	artificial	baggage	bagagem
artist	artista	baggage claim	bagagem
ashtray	cinzeiro	bakery	padaria
ask	perguntar	balcony	varanda
aspirin	aspirina	ball	bola
asthma	asma	bandage	gaze
at	á	bandage, support	ligadora
at sign (@)	arroba	band-aid	adesivo
atheist	ateu	bank	banco
athlete	atleta	barber	barbeiro
athlete's foot	pé de atleta	baseball	basebol
attractive	atraente	basement	porão
audioguide	audio guia	basket	cesto
August	Agosto	basketball	basquetebol
aunt	tia	bath	banho
Austria	Austria	bathrobe	robe
autumn	outono	bathroom	casa de banho
		bathtub	banheira
		battery	bateria

B

baby	bebé	beach	praia
baby	suporte para cadeira	beard	barba
booster seat		beautiful	lindo[a]
baby	cadeira de carro	beauty salon	cabelareiro
car seat	para o bebé	because	porque
baby food	comida para bebés	bed	cama
baby	alimento suplementar	bedroom	quarto
formula		bedsheet	lençol de cama
babysitter	babysitter	beef	bife
babysitting	serviços de ajuda	beer	cerveja
service	com as crianças	before	antes
back	costas	begin	começar
backpack	mochila	behind	detrás

Belgium	Belgica	**borrow**	emprestar
bells	sinos	**boss**	patrão
below	abaixo	**bottle**	garrafa
belt	cinto	**bottom**	fundo
berth (train)	lugar sentado	**boutique,**	loja de roupa
best	melhor	**clothing**	
bib	babeiro	**bowl**	tijela
bicycle	bicicleta	**box**	caixa
big	grande	**boy**	rapaz
bill (payment)	conta	**bra**	soutien
bird	pássaro	**bracelet**	pulseira
birth	pilula	**brakes**	travões
control pills	anticoncepcional	**brass**	latão
birthday	aniversário	**bread**	pão
black	preto	**breakfast**	pequeno almoço
bladder	bexiga	**breast**	peito
blanket	corbetor	**breath**	halito
bleeding	sangrar	**bridge**	ponte
blisters	bolhas	**Britain**	Grã-Bretanha
block	bloco	**broken**	partido
blond	louro[a]	**bronze**	bronze
blood	sangre	**brooch**	broche
blood pressure,	tensão alta	**brother**	irmão
high		**brown**	castanho
blouse	blusa	**bucket**	balde
blue	azul	**building**	prédio
blush (makeup)	blush	**bulb, light**	lampada
boat	barco	**bunk beds**	beliches
body	corpo	**burn (n)**	queimadura
boiled	fervido	**bus**	autocarro
bomb	bomba	**bus**	terminal das camionetas
book	livro	**station**	
book shop	livraria	**bus**	paragem de autocarro
booster	suporte para cadeira	**stop**	
seat		**bus, city**	autocarro
boots	botas	**bus, long-distance**	camioneta
border	fronteira	**business**	negócio

but	mas	**cards (deck)**	cartas
buttocks	traseiro	**careful**	cuidadoso
button	botão	**carpet**	carpete
by (via)	via	**carry**	carregar
		carry-on	bagagem de mão
C		**luggage**	
calendar	calendário	**cash**	dinheiro
calorie	caloria	**cash**	caixa automática,
camera	camara	**machine**	Multibanco
camera shop	loja fotográfica	**cashier**	caixa
camper (R.V.)	roulote	**cassette**	cassete
camping	campismo	**castle**	castelo
campsite	campismo	**cat**	gato
can (n)	lata	**catch (v)**	apanhar
can (v)	poder	**cathedral**	catedral
can opener	abertor de latas	**Catholic (adj)**	Católico[a]
Canada	Canadá	**cave**	cave
canal	canal	**cell phone**	telemóvel
cancel	cancelar	**cell phone**	loja de telemóveis
candle	vela	**shop**	
candy	doce	**cellar**	adega
canoe	canoa	**center**	centro
cap	boné	**century**	século
captain	capitão	**ceramic**	ceramica
car	carro	**chair**	cadeira
car (train)	carruagem	**championship**	campeonato
car seat	cadeira de carro	**change (n)**	troca
(baby)	para o bebe	**change (v)**	mudar
car, dining	carruagem	**chapel**	capela
(train)	restaurante	**charming**	encantador[a]
car, sleeper	carruagem cama	**cheap**	barato
(train)		**check**	cheque
carafe	jarro	**Cheers!**	Saúde!
card	cartão	**cheese**	queijo
(also businiss card)		**chest**	peito
card,	cartão telefónico	**chest pains**	dor no peito
telephone		**chicken**	galinha

child	criança	coins	moedas
children	crianças	cold (adj)	frio[a]
chills	arrepios	cold (n)	constipação
Chinese (adj)	chines	cold	remédio para
chocolate	chocolate	medicine	constipação
choir	coral	colors	cores
Christian (adj)	Cristão	comb (n)	pente
Christmas	Natal	come	vir
church	igreija	comfortable	confortável
church service	serviço	compact disc	compact disco
cigarette	cigarro	complain	queixar
cinema	cinema	complicated	complicado
city	cidade	computer	computador
class	classe	concert	concerto
class, first	primeira classe	conditioner	condicionador
class, second	segunda classe	(hair)	
classical	clássico	condom	perservativo
clean (adj)	limpo[a]	conductor	condutor
clear	claro	confirm	confirmar
cliff	falésia	congestion (sinus)	congestão
clinic, medical	clinica médica	congratulations	parabéns
clock	relógio	connection (train)	conexão
clock, alarm	despertador	constipation	prisão de ventre
cloister	mosteiro	construction	construção
closed	fechado	(sign)	na estrada
cloth	tecido	contact	lentes de contacto
clothes	roupa	lenses	
clothes pins	broches	contagious	contagioso
clothesline	linha de roupas	contraceptives	contracepção
clothing	loja de roupa	cook (v)	cozinhar
boutique		cool	fresco
cloudy	nebuloso	copper	cobre
coast	costa	copy	copiado
coat hanger	cruzeta	copy shop	casa de fotocopias
cockroach	barata	cork	rolha
coffee	café	corkscrew	sacarolhas
coffee shop	café	corner	esquina

corridor	corredor	**day**	dia
corruption	corrupção	**day after tomorrow**	depois de amanhã
cost	preço		
cot	rede	**dead**	morto[a]
cotton	algodão	**December**	Dezembro
cough (n)	tosse	**declare (customs)**	declarar
cough (v)	tosser	**decongestant**	descongestionante
cough drops	rabuçados da tosse		
country	país	**delay (n)**	atraso
countryside	campo	**delete**	eliminar
cousin	primo[a]	**delicatessen**	charcutaria
cow	vaca	**delicious**	delicioso
cozy	confortável	**democracy**	democracia
crafts	artesanato	**dental floss**	fio dental
cramps	dor, cãibra	**dentist**	dentista
cramps, menstrual	cólicas	**deodorant**	desodorizante
cream, first-aid	creme desinfetante	**depart**	partir
		department store	grande armazen
credit card	cartão de crédito	**departures**	partidas
cross	cruz	**deposit**	depósito
crowd (n)	multidão	**dessert**	sobremesa
cry (v)	chorar	**detergent**	detergente
crypt	caixão	**detour**	desvio
cup	chávena	**diabetes**	diabetes
customs	alfandega	**diabetic**	diabético[a]
Czech Republic	Republica Checa	**diamond**	diamante
		diaper	fraldas
		diaper rash	assadura das fraldas

D

dad	pai	**diaphragm (birth control)**	diafragma
dance (v)	dançar		
danger	perigo	**diarrhea**	diarreia
dangerous	perigoso[a]	**diarrhea medicine**	remédio para a diarréia
dark	escuro		
dash (-)	hífen	**dictionary**	dicionário
daughter	filha	**die**	morrer

difficult	difícil	dry (v)	secar
dining car	carruagem	dryer	secador
(train)	restaurante	dungeon	masmorra
dinner	jantar	duty free	imposto não pago:
direct	directo		tax free
direction	direção		
dirty	sujo	**E**	
discount	desconto	each	cada
disease	doença	ear	orelha
disease,	doença venéria	earache	dor de ouvido
venereal		early	cedo[a]
disinfectant	desinfetante	earplugs	tampões de ouvido
disturb	incomudar	earrings	brincos
divorced	divorciado[a]	earth	terra
dizziness	tonturas	east	este
doctor	doutor[a]	Easter	Pascoa
dog	cão	easy	fácil
doll	boneca	eat	comer
dome	cúpula	education	instrução
donkey	burro	elbow	cotovelo
door	porta	electrical adapter	tomada
dormitory	dormitorio	elevator	elevador
dot (computer)	ponto	e-mail	e-mail
double	dobrar	e-mail	endereço eletronico
down	abaixo	address	
download	transferencia	embarrassing	humilhante
downtown	centro	embassy	embaixada
dozen	dúzia	emergency	emergencia
dream (n)	sonho	emergency	saída de
dream (v)	sonhar	exit	emergencia
dress (n)	vestido	emergency	sala de
drink (n)	bebida	room	emergencia
drink (v)	beber	empty	vazio
drive (v)	conduzir	engineer	engenheiro
driver	condutor	English	ingles
drunk	bebado[a]	enjoy	gostar
dry (adj)	seco	enough	suficiente

entrance	entrada	famous	famoso[a]
entrance (road)	entrada	fan belt	correia de ventoinha
envelope	envelope	fantastic	fantástico[a]
epilepsy	epilepcia	far	longe
eraser	borracha	farm	quinta
Europe	Europa	farmer	granjeiro[a]
evening	noitecer	fashion	moda
every	todo	fat (adj)	gordo[a]
everything	tudo	fat (n)	gordura
exactly	exactamente	father	pai
example	exemplo	faucet	torneira
excellent	excelente	fax	fax
except	excepto	fear (v)	temer
exchange (n)	cambio	February	Fevereiro
excuse me	desculpe	female	feminino
exhausted	esgotado[a]	ferry	barco
exit	saída	festival	festival
exit,	saída de	fever	fevre
emergency	emergencia	few	pouco
expensive	caro	field	campo
explain	explicar	fight (n)	luta
eye	olho	fight (v)	lutar
eye shadow	sombra	fine (good)	bom
eyeliner	lápis para os olhos,	finger	dedo
	delineador	fingernail	unha
		finish (v)	terminar
		fire	fogo
F		fireworks	fogo de artificio
face	cara	first	primeiro
face	produto para	first aid	pronto socorro
cleanser	a limpeza do rosto	first class	primeira classe
face powder	pó para o rosto	first-aid	creme desinfetante
facial tissue	lenços de papel	cream	
factory	fábrica	fish (n)	peixe
fair (just)	justo	fish (v)	pescar
fall (v)	cair	fix (v)	arranjar
false	falso	fizzy	com gás
family	familia		

flag	bandeira	friendship	amizade
flash (camera)	flash	Frisbee	disco voador
flashlight	lanterna a pilhas	from	de
flavor (n)	sabor	fruit	fruta
flea	pulga	fun (adj)	divertido[a]
flea market	feira	funeral	funeral
flight	voo	funny	divertido[a]
flip-flops	sandálias de dedo	furniture	mobilias
floss, dental	fio dental	fuses	fussil
flower	flor	future	futuro
flower market	mercado de flores		

G

flu	gripe	gallery	galeria
fly (v)	voar	game	jogo
fog	nevoeiro	garage	garagem
food	comida	garden	jardim
food poisoning	envenanamento alimentar	gardening	jardinagem
foot	pé	gas	gás
football (soccer)	futebol	gas station	bomba de gasolina
football, American	futebol americano	gauze	gaze
for	para	gay	gay
forbidden	proibido	generous	generouso[a]
foreign	estranjeiro[a]	gentleman	cavalheiro
forget	esquecer	genuine	genuíno[a]
fork	garfo	Germany	Alemanha
formula (for baby)	alimento suplementar	gift	prenda
		girl	rapariga
foundation (makeup)	base	give	dar
fountain	fonte	glass	copo
fragile	frágil	glasses (eye)	óculos
France	França	gloves	luvas
free (no cost)	grátis	go	ir
fresh	fresco	go through	atravessar
Friday	sexta-feira	God	deus
friend	amigo[a]	gold	ouro
		golf	golfe

good	bom	handle (n)	puxador
good day	bom-dia	handsome	bonito[a]
goodbye	adeus	happiness	felicidade
Gothic	gótico	happy	feliz
grammar	gramática	harbor	porto
grandchild	neto[a]	hard	difícil
grandfather	avo	hardware store	casa de ferragens
grandmother	avó		
gray	cinzento	hash (drug)	hashishe
greasy	gorduroso	hat	chapéu
great	magnifico[a]	hate	odiar
Great Britain	Inglaterra	have	ter
Greece	Grécia	hay fever	febre dos fenos
green	verde	he	ele
grocery store	mercearia	head	cabeça
guarantee	garantia	headache	dor de cabeça
guest	convidado[a]	headlights	faróis da frente
guide	uma guia	health	saúde
guidebook	um guia	health insurance	seguro de saúde
guided tour	visita guiada		
guilty	culpado[a]	healthy	saudavel
guitar	guitarra	hear	ouvir
gum	pastilha elástica	heart	coração
gun	pistola	heart condition	problema no coração
gymnastics	ginastica		
gynecologist	enicologista	heat (n)	calor
		heaven	céu
H		heavy	pesado
hair	cabelo	hello	olá
hairbrush	escova de cabelo	help (n)	ajuda
haircut	corte de cabelo	help (v)	ajudar
hall (big room)	sala	hemorrhoids	hemorróidas
hand	mão	here	aqui
hand lotion	creme para as mãos	hi	olá
		high	alto
handicapped	aleijado[a]	high blood pressure	tensão alta
handicrafts	artesanato		

highchair	cadeirinha alta	**immediately**	imediatamente
highway	autoestrada	**important**	importante
hill	subida	**imported**	importado
history	história	**impossible**	impossível
hitchhike	pedir boleia	**Impressionist**	impressionista
hobby	passatempo	**in**	em
hockey	hóquei	**included**	incluido
hole	buraco	**incredible**	inacreditável
holiday	feriado	**independent**	independente
homemade	á moda de casa	**indigestion**	indigestão
homesick	saudade	**industry**	industria
honest	honesto[a]	**infection**	infecção
honeymoon	lua de mel	**infection, urinary**	infecção urinaria
hope	esperança		
horrible	horrível	**inflammation**	inflamação
horse	cavalo	**information**	informação
horse riding	montar a cavalo	**injured**	ferido[a]
hospital	hospital	**innocent**	inocente
hot	quente	**insect**	insecto
hotel	hotel	**insect repellant**	repelente de insectos
hour	hora		
house	casa	**inside**	interior
how	como	**instant**	instante
how many	quanto	**instead**	em vez de
how much ($)	quanto custa	**insurance**	seguro
hungry	esfomeado[a]	**insurance, health**	seguro de saúde
hurry (v)	apressar		
husband	marido	**insured**	seguro[a]
hydrofoil	hidroplano	**intelligent**	inteligente
hyphen (-)	hífen	**interesting**	interresante
		Internet	Internet
I		**Internet access**	acesso a Internet
I	eu		
ice	gelo	**Internet café**	café Internet
ice cream	gelado	**intersection**	cruzamento
if	se	**intestines**	intestino
ill	doente	**invitation**	convite

iodine	iodo
Ireland	Irlanda
is	sér
island	ilha
Italy	Itália
itch (n)	comichão

J

jacket	casaco
January	Janeiro
jaw	maxila
jeans	jeans
jewelry	joalheria
jewelry shop	joalheria
Jewish	Judeu
job	trabalho
jogging	jogging
joint (marijuana)	baseado
joke (n)	piada
journey	viagem
juice	sumo
July	Julho
jump	saltar
June	Junho

K

keep	guardar
kettle	chaleira
key	chave
kill	matar
kind	simpático[a]
king	rei
kiss (n)	beijo
kitchen	cozinha
kitchenette	kitchenete
knee	joelho
knife	faca
knights	cavaleiros
know	saber

L

lace	renda
ladder	escada
ladies	senhoras
lake	lago
lamb	cordeiro
language	língua
large	grande
last	último[a]
late	tarde
later	mais tarde
laugh (v)	rir
launderette	lavandaria
laundry soap	detergente
lawyer	advogado[a]
laxative	laxativo
lazy	preguiçoso[a]
learn	aprender
leather	cabedal
leave	sair
left (direction)	esquerda
leg	perna
lend	emprestar
lenses, contact	lentes de contacto
letter	carta
library	biblioteca
lies	mentiras
life	vida
light (n)	luz
light bulb	lampada
lighter (n)	isqueiro
like (v)	gostar
linen	linho

lip	lábio	mall (shopping)	centro comercial
lip salve	batão de cierio	man	homen
lipstick	baton	manager	gerente
list	lista	many	muito
listen	escutar	map	mapa
liter	litro	marble (material)	mármore
little	pequeno	March	Março
live (v)	viver	marijuana	erva, marijuana
local	local	market	mercado
lock (n)	fechadura	market, flea	feira
lock (v)	fechar	market, flower	mercado de flores
lockers	armários	market, open-air	mercado municipal
look	olhar	married	casado[a]
lost	perdido[a]	mascara	rimel
lotion, hand	creme para as mãos	mass	missa
loud	ruidoso[a]	matches	fosforos
love (n)	amor	maximum	máximo
love (v)	amar	May	Maio
lover	amante	maybe	talvez
low	baixo	meat	carne
luck	sorte	mechanic	mecanico[a]
luggage	bagagem	medicine	medicina
luggage, carry-on	bagagem de mão	medicine for a cold	remédio para constipação
lukewarm	tépido	medicine, non-aspirin substitute	substituto para aspirina
lungs	pulmões	medieval	mediaval

M

macho	macho	medium	médio
mad	chateado[a]	men	homens
magazine	revista	menstrual cramps	cólicas
mail (n)	correio	menstruation	menstruação
main	principal	menu	ementa
make (v)	fazer	message	recado
makeup	maquiagem	metal	metal
male	masculino		

meter, taxi	medidor	**movie**	filme
midnight	meia-noite	**Mr.**	Senhor
migraine	enxaqueca	**Mrs.**	Senhora
military	militares	**much**	muito
mineral water	água mineral	**muggy**	úmido
minimum	minimo	**muscle**	músculo
minutes	minutos	**museum**	museu
mirror	espelho	**music**	música
miscarriage	aborto natural	**Muslim (adj)**	Muçulmano[a]
Miss	Menina	**my**	meu
mistake	erro		
misunder- standing	malentendido	**N**	
mix (n)	mista	**nail (finger)**	unha
moat	fosso	**nail clipper**	corta unhas
modem	modem	**nail polish**	verniz para as unhas
modern	moderno	**nail polish remover**	acetona
moisturizer	hidratante	**naked**	nuo[a]
moleskin	sinal	**name**	nome
mom	mãe	**napkin**	guardanapo
moment	momento	**narrow**	estreito
monastery	monestério	**nationality**	nacionalidade
Monday	segunda-feira	**natural**	natural
money	dinheiro	**nature**	natureza
month	mes	**nausea**	náusea
monument	monumento	**near**	perto
moon	lua	**necessary**	necessário
more	mais	**neck**	pescoço
morning	manhã	**necklace**	fio
mosque	mesquita	**need**	necessitar
mosquito	mosquito	**needle**	agulha
mother	mãe	**nephew**	sobrinho
motor scooter	motocicleta	**nervous**	nervoso[a]
motorcycle	mota	**Netherlands**	Holanda
mountain	montanha	**never**	nunca
moustache	bigode	**new**	novo
mouth	boca	**newspaper**	jornal

newsstand	quiosque	old	velho[a]
next	próximo[a]	Olympics	Olímpicos
nice	simpático[a]	on	sobre
nickname	alcunha	on time	pontual
niece	sobrinha	once	uma vez
night	noite	one way (street)	sentido único
nightgown	camisa de dormir	one way (ticket)	uma ida
no	não	one-way street	sentido único
no vacancy	cheio	only	só
noisy	barulho[a]	open (adj)	aberto
non-aspirin	substituto para	open (v)	abrir
substitute	aspirina	open-air	mercado municipal
non-smoking	não fumador	market	
noon	meio-dia	opening hours	horário
normal	normal	opera	ópera
north	norte	operator	operador
nose	nariz	optician	oculista
not	não	or	ou
notebook	caderno	orange (color)	cor de laranja
nothing	nada	orange (fruit)	laranja
November	Novembro	organ	orgão
now	agora	original	original
nurse	enfermeiro[a]	other	outro
nylon (material)	nylon	oven	forno
nylons	meia de vidro,	over (finished)	acabado
(panty hose)	collants	own (v)	possuir
		owner	dono[a]

O

O.K.	O.K.
occupation	profissão
occupied	ocupado
ocean	oceano
October	Outubro
of	de
office	escritório
office supplies store	papelaria
oil (n)	óleo

P

pacifier	chupeta
package	embalagem
paddleboat	gaivota
page	página
pail	balde
pain	dor
pain	comprimidos
killer	para as dores

pains, chest	dor no peito	photo	fotografia
painting	pintura	photocopy	fotocopia
pajamas	pijamas	photocopy shop	casa de fotocopias
palace	palácio		
panties	cuecas	pickpocket	carteirista
pants	calças	picnic	piquenique
paper	papel	piece	pedaço
paper clip	clip	pig	porco
parents	pais	pill	comprimido
park (garden)	parque	pill, birth control	pilula anticoncepcional
park (v)	estacionar		
parking lot	(parque de) estacionamento	pillow	almofada
		pin	alfinete
party	festa	PIN code	código pessoal
passenger	passageiro[a]	pink	cor de rosa
passport	passaporte	pity, it's a	que pena
past	passado	pizza	pizza
pastry shop	pastelaria	plain	simples
pay	pagar	plane	avião
peace	paz	plant	planta
pedestrian	peão	plastic	plástico
pen	caneta	plastic bag	saco plástico
pencil	lápis	plate	prato
penis	pénis	platform (train)	cais
people	pessoas	play (v)	jogar
percent	percento	playground	parque de diversões
perfect (adj)	perfeito		
perfume	perfume	playpen	parque
period (of time)	período	please	por favor
period	menstruação	pliers	alicate
person	pessoa	pneumonia	pneumonia
pet (n)	animal de estimação	pocket	bolso
pewter	estanho	point (v)	apontar
pharmacy	farmácia	police	polícia
phone (n)	telefone	politicians	políticos
phone booth	telefone publico	pollution	poluição
phone, mobile	telemóvel	polyester	poliester

poor	pobre
porcelain	porcelana
pork	porco
Portugal	Portugal
possible	possível
postcard	cartão postal
poster	poster
power	poder
powerful	poderoso[a]
practical	prático[a]
pregnancy	gravidez
pregnancy test	teste de gravidez
pregnant	grávida
Preparation H	Preparação H
prescription	receita médica
present (gift)	presente
pretty	bonito[a]
price	preço
priest	padre
print (v)	imprimir
private	privado
problem	problema
profession	profissão
prohibited	proibido
pronunciation	pronúncia
prosper	prósperar
Protestant (adj)	Protestante
public	público
pull	tirar
pulpit	púlpito
pulse	pulsação
pump (n)	bomba
punctual	pontual
purple	roxo
purse	bolsa
push	empurrar

Q

quality	qualidade
quarter (1/4)	quarto
queen	rainha
question (n)	pergunta
quiet	calado[a]

R

R.V. (camper)	roulote
rabbit	coelho
racism	racismo
radiator	radiador
radio	rádio
raft	balsa
railway	caminho de ferro
rain (n)	chuva
rainbow	arco íris
raincoat	casaco impermeável
rape (n)	violação
rash	erupção
rash, diaper	assadura das fraldas
raw	cru
razor	Gilete
ready	pronto[a]
receipt	recibo
receive	receber
receptionist	recepcionista
recipe	receita
recommend	recomendar
rectum	recto
red	vermelho
refill (n)	encher
refugees	refigiados
refund (n)	reembolso
relax	relaxar

relaxation	descanso
relic	rélica
religion	religião
remember	recordar
Renaissance	renascimento
rent (v)	alugar
repair	reparar
reservation	reserva
reserve	reservar
respect (n)	respeito
retired	reformado[a]
rich	rico[a]
right (correct)	certo[a]
right (direction)	direita
ring (n)	campaínha
ripe	maduro
river	rio
robbed	roubado[a]
rock (n)	rock
roller skates	patins
Romanesque	romanico
Romantic	romantico
romantic	romantico[a]
roof	telhado
room	quarto
rope	corda
rotten	podre
roundabout	rotunda
roundtrip	ida e volta
rowboat	barco de passeio
rucksack	mochila
rug	carpete
ruins	ruínas
run (v)	correr
Russia	Russia

S

sad	triste
safe	seguro[a]
safety pin	alfinete de segurança
sailboat	veleiro
sailing	barco de vela
saint	santo[a]
sale	saldos
same	mesmo
sandals	sandálias
sandwich	sande
sanitary napkins	pensos higiénicos
Santa Claus	Pai-Natal
Saturday	sábado
save (computer)	guardar
scandalous	escandulo
Scandinavia	Escandinavia
scarf	lenço
school	escola
science	ciencia
scientist	cientista
scissors	tesouras
scotch tape	fita cola
screwdriver	chave de parafusos
sculptor	escultor[a]
sculpture	escultura
sea	mar
seafood	marisco
seat	lugar, assento
second	segunda
second class	segunda classe
secret	segredo
see	ver

self-service	auto serviço	shop, sweets	confeitaria
sell	vender	shop, wine	loja de vinhos
send	enviar	shopping	compras
seniors	pessoas de terceira idade	shopping mall	centro comercial
separate	separado	short	curto[a]
September	Setembro	shorts	calções
serious	sério	shoulder	ombros
service	serviço	show (n)	espectáculo
service (church)	serviço	show (v)	mostrar
sex	sexo	shower	chuveiro
sexy	sexy	shy	tímido[a]
shampoo	xampú	sick	doente
shaving cream	creme de barbear	sign	sinal
		signature	assinatura
she	ela	silence	silencio
sheet	lençol	silk	seda
shell	concha	silver	prata
ship (n)	barco	similar	similar
ship (v)	enviar	simple	simples
shirt	camisa	sing	cantar
shoelaces	cordão de sapatos	singer	cantor[a]
shoes	sapatos	single	solteiro[a]
shoes, tennis	sapatos de ténis	sink	lavatório
shop (n)	loja	sink stopper	tampa para lava louça
shop, antique	antiquário		
shop, barber	barbeiro	sinus problems	sinosite
shop, camera	loja fotográfica	sir	senhor
shop, cell phone	loja de telemóveis	sister	irmã
		size	tamanho
shop, coffee	café	skating	patinagem
shop, jewelry	joalheria	ski (v)	esquiar
shop, pastry	pastelaria	skiing	esquiar
shop, photocopy	casa de fotocopias	skin	pele
		skinny	magro[a]
shop, souvenir	loja de lembranças	skirt	saia
		sky	céu

sleep (v)	dormir	Spain	Espanha
sleeper (train)	camarote	sparkplugs	velas
sleeper car (train)	carruagem cama	speak	falar
		specialty	especialidade
sleeping bag	saco de dormir	speed	velocidade
sleepy	sonolento[a]	spend	gastar
sleeves	mangas	spider	arranha
slice	fatia	spoon	colher
slide (photo)	slide	sport	desporto
slip	combinação	spring (n)	primavera
slippers	chinélos	square (town)	praça
slippery	escorregadio	stairs	escadas
slow	lento[a]	stamp	selo
small	pequeno[a]	stapler	agrafador
smell (n)	cheiro	star (in sky)	estrela
smile (n)	sorriso	state	estado
smoke	fumo	station	estação
smoking	fumador	stomach	estomago
snack	petisco	stomachache	dor de estomago
sneeze (n)	espirro	stoned	drogado[a]
snore	ressonar	stop (n, train or bus)	paragem
snorkel	tubo para mergulho	stop (v)	parar
soap	sabão	stoplight	sinal de luz
soap, laundry	detergente	stopper, sink	tampa para lava louça
soccer	futebol	store	loja
socks	meias	store, department	grande armazen
some	alguns		
something	alguma coisa	store, hardware	casa de ferragens
son	filho		
song	canção	store, office supplies	papelaria
soon	cedo		
sore throat	dor de garganta	store, toy	loja de brinquedos
sorry	desculpe	storm	tempestada
sour	azedo	story (floor)	andar
south	sul	straight	em frente
souvenir shop	loja de lembranças	strange	estranho[a]

stream (n)	corrente	surfboard	prancha
street	rua	surfer	surfista
string	fio	surprise (n)	surpresa
stroller	carrinho de bebe	swallow (v)	engolir
strong	forte	sweat (v)	suar
stuck	imobilizado	sweater	pullover
student	estudante	sweet	doce
stupid	estúpido[a]	sweets shop	confeitaria
sturdy	sólido	swelling (n)	inchado
style	estilo	swim	nadar
subway	metro	swim suit	fato de banho
subway entrance	entrada do metro	swim trunks	calção de banho
		swimming pool	piscina
subway exit	saída do metro	Switzerland	Suiça
subway map	mapa do metro	synagogue	sinagoga
subway station	estação de metro	synthetic	sintético

T

subway stop	paragem do metro	table	mesa
suddenly	de repente	tail	rabo
suffer	sofrer	tail lights	luzes traseiras
suitcase	mala	take	tomar
summer	verão	take out (food)	para levar
sun	sol	talcum powder	pó de talco
sunbathe	bronzear	talk	falar
sunburn	queimadura solar	tall	alto[a]
Sunday	domingo	tampons	tampões
sunglasses	óculos de sol	tape (adhesive)	adesivo
sunny	sol	tape (cassette)	cassete
sunrise	nascer do sol	taste (n)	sabor
sunscreen	protector solar	taste (try)	provar
sunset	por do sol	tax	taxa
sunshine	brilho de sol	taxi meter	medidor
sunstroke	insolação	teacher	professor
suntan (n)	bronzeado	team	equipa
supermarket	supermercado	teenager	jovem
supplement	suplemento	teeth	dentes

teething (baby)	dentição	tires	pneus
telephone (n)	telefone	tissue, facial	lenços de papel
telephone card	cartão telefónico	to	para
		today	hoje
television	televisão	toe	dedo do pé
temperature	temperatura	together	juntos
tender	tenro	toilet	casa de banho
tennis	ténis	toilet paper	papel higiénico
tennis shoes	sapatos de ténis	token	ficha
tent	tenda	toll	portagem
tent pegs	estacas de tenda	toll-free	taxa grátis
terrible	terrível	tomorrow	amanhã
terrorists	terroristas	tomorrow, day after	depois de amanhã
testicles	testículos	tonight	esta noite
thanks	obrigado	too (much)	demasiado
theater	teatro	tooth	dente
thermometer	termómetro	toothache	dor de dente
they	eles	toothbrush	escova de dentes
thick	grosso	toothpaste	pasta de dentes
thief	ladrão	toothpick	palito
thigh	coxa	total	total
thin	magro[a]	tour	excursão
thing	coisa	tour, guided	visita guiada
think	pensar	tourist	turista
thirsty	sede	tow truck	reboque
thread	linha	towel	toalha
throat	garganta	tower	torre
through	através	town	cidade
throw	atirar	toy	brinquedo
Thursday	quinta-feira	toy store	loja de brinquedos
ticket	bilhete	track (train)	linha
tight	apretado	traditional	tradicional
time, on	pontual	traffic	tráfico
timetable	horário	train	comboio
tire (n)	pneu	train car	carruagem
tired	cansado[a]	transfer (v)	mudar

translate	traduzir	urethra	uretra
transmission fluid	óleo de transmissão	urgent	urgente
		urinary infection	infecção urinaria
travel (v)	viajar		
travel agency	agencia de viagens	us	nós
		use (v)	usar
traveler's check	cheque de viagem	uterus	útero

V

travelers	vijantes	vacancy sign	quartos
treasury	tesoraria	vacancy, no	cheio
tree	árvore	vacant	livre
trip	viagem	vacation	férias
tripod	tripé	vagina	vagina
trouble	problema	valid	válido
T-shirt	T-shirt	validate	validade
Tuesday	terça-feira	valley	vale
tunnel	túnel	Vaseline	vasilina
Turkey	Turkia	vegetarian	vegetariano[a]
turn signal	pisca-pisca	velvet	veludo
tweezers	pinsa	venereal disease	doença venéria
twins	gemeos		
		very	muito

U

		vest	colete
ugly	feio[a]	video	vídeo
umbrella	guarda-chuva	video camera	video camera
uncle	tio	view	vista
unconscious	inconciente	village	aldeia
under	debaixo	vineyard	vinhedo
underpants	cuecas	violence	violencia
underscore (_)	sublinhar	virus	vírus
understand	entender	visit (n)	visita
unemployed	desempregado[a]	visit (v)	visitar
unfortunate	desventurado[a]	vitamins	vitaminas
United States	Estados Unidos	voice	voz
university	universidade	vomit	vomitar
up	subida		
upstairs	em cima		

W

waist	cintura
wait (v)	esperar
waiter	criado
waiting room	sala de espera
waitress	senhora, menina
wake up	acordar
walk (v)	andar
wall, fortified	fortificação
wallet	carteira
want	querer
war	guerra
warm (adj)	quente
wash	lavar
washer	máquina de lavar roupa
watch (n)	relógio
watch (v)	olhar
water	água
water, drinkable	água potável
water, tap	água da torneira
waterfall	queda de água
waterskiing	esqui aquático
we	nós
weather	tempo
Web site	local da Web
wedding	casamento
Wednesday	quarta-feira
week	semana
weight	peso
welcome	bem-vindo
west	oeste
wet	molhado
what	o que
wheel	roda

wheelchair-accessible	rodas-acesso
when	quando
where	donde
white	branco
who	quem
why	porque
widow	viúva
widower	viúvo
wife	esposa
wild	salvagem
wind	vento
window	janela
windshield wipers	para-brisas
windsurfing	windsurfing
windy	vento
wine	vinho
wine shop	loja de vinhos
wing	asa
winter	inverno
wish (v)	desejo
with	com
without	sem
woman	mulher
women	mulheres
wood	madeira
wool	lã
word	palavra
work (n)	trabalho
work (v)	trabalhar
world	mundo
worst	pior
wrap (v)	embrulhar
wrist	pulso
write	escrever

X

X-ray	raio X

Y

year	ano
yellow	amarelo
yes	sim
yesterday	ontem
you (formal)	voçe
you (informal)	tu
young	jovem
youth	juventude
youth hostel	albergue de juventude
youths	jovens

Z

zero	zero
zip code	código postal
zip-lock bag	saco plástico com fecho
zipper	fecho
zoo	zoo

TIPS FOR HURDLING
THE LANGUAGE BARRIER

Don't Be Afraid to Communicate

Don't be afraid to communicate. Even the best phrase book won't satisfy your needs in every situation. To really hurdle the language barrier, you need to leap beyond the printed page, and dive into contact with the locals. Never allow your lack of foreign language skills to isolate you from the people and cultures you traveled halfway around the world to experience. Remember that in every country you visit, you're surrounded by expert, native-speaking tutors. Spend bus and train rides letting them teach you.

Start conversations by asking politely in the local language, "Do you speak English?" When you speak English with someone from another country, talk slowly, clearly, and with carefully chosen words. Use what the Voice of America calls "simple English." You're talking to people who are wishing it was written down, hoping to see each letter as it tumbles out of your mouth. Pronounce each letter, avoiding all contractions and slang. For bad examples, listen to other tourists.

Keep things caveman-simple. Make single nouns work as entire sentences ("Photo?"). Use internationally-understood words ("Self-service" works in Lisbon). Butcher the language if you must. The important thing is to make the effort. To get air mail stamps, you can flap your wings and say "tweet, tweet." If you want milk, moo and pull two imaginary udders. Risk looking like a fool.

If you're short on words, make your picnic a potluck. Pull out a map and point out your journey. Draw what you mean. Bring photos from home and introduce your family. Play cards or toss a Frisbee. Fold an origami bird for kids or dazzle 'em with sleight-of-hand magic.

Go ahead and make educated guesses. Many situations are easy-to-fake multiple choice questions. Practice. Read timetables, concert posters, and newspaper headlines. Listen to each language on a multilingual tour. Be melodramatic. Exaggerate the local accent. Self-consciousness is the deadliest communication-killer.

Choose multilingual people to communicate with, such as students, business people, urbanites, young well-dressed people, or anyone in the tourist trade. Use a small note pad to jot down handy phrases and to help you communicate more clearly with the locals by scribbling down numbers, maps, and so on. Some travelers carry important messages written on a small card: allergic to nuts, strict vegetarian, your finest ice cream.

International Words

As our world shrinks, more and more words hop across their linguistic boundaries and become international. Savvy travelers develop a knack for choosing words most likely to be universally understood ("auto" instead of "car," "kaput" instead of "broken," "photo" not "picture"). Internationalize your pronunciation . "University," if you play around with its sound (oo-nee-vehr-see-tay), will be understood anywhere. The average American is a real flunky in this area. Be creative.

Here are a few internationally understood words. Remember, cut out the Yankee accent and give each word a pan-European sound.

Amigo	Communist	Mañana	Restaurant
Attila	Computer	McDonald's	Rock 'n' roll
(mean, crude)	Disco	Michael Jackson	Self-service
Auto	Disneyland	Michelangelo	Sex / Sexy
Autobus	(wonderland)	(artistic)	Sport
("booos")	Elephant	Moment	Stop
Bank	(big clod)	No	Super
Beer	English	No problem	Taxi
Bill Gates	("Engleesh")	Nuclear	Tea
Bon voyage	Europa	OK	Telephone
Bye-bye	Fascist	Oo la la	Toilet
Camping	Hello	Pardon	Tourist
Casanova	Hercules	Passport	U.S. profanity
(romantic)	(strong)	Photo	University
Central	Hotel	Photocopy	Vino
Chocolate	Information	Picnic	Yankee,
Ciao	Internet	Police	Americano
Coffee	Kaput	Post	
Coke, Coca-Cola	Mama mia	Rambo	

Portuguese Verbs

These conjugated verbs will help you construct a caveman sentence in a pinch.

Portuguese has two different verbs that correspond to the English "to be"—*ser* and *estar*. Generally speaking, *ser* is used to describe a condition that is permanent or longer-lasting, and *estar* is used for something that is temporary. Which verb you use can determine the meaning of the sentence. For example, "*Ricardo é contente*," using *ser*, means that Ricardo is a happy, content person (as a permanent personality trait). "*Ricardo está contente*," using *estar*, means that Ricardo is currently happy (temporarily in a good mood).

TO BE (permanent)	*SER*	sehr
I am	*eu sou*	**eh**-oo soh
you are (formal)	*você é*	voh-**say** eh
you are (informal)	*tú és*	too ehsh
he / she is	*ele / ela é*	**eh**-leh / **eh**-lah eh
we are	*nós somos*	nohsh **soh**-moosh
you (plural, formal)	*vocês são*	voh-**saysh** so<u>w</u>
they are	*eles / elas são*	**eh**-lish / **eh**-lahsh so<u>w</u>
(males or coed / females only)		

TO BE (temporary)	*ESTAR*	ish-**tar**
I am	*eu estou*	**eh**-oo ish-**toh**
you are (formal)	*você está*	voh-**say** ish-**tah**
you are (informal)	*tú estás*	too ish-**tahsh**
he / she is	*ele / ela está*	**eh**-leh / **eh**-lah ish-**tah**
we are	*nós estamos*	nohz ish-**tah**-moosh
you (plural, formal)	*vocês estão*	voh-**sayz** ish-**to**<u>w</u>
they are	*eles / elas estão*	**eh**-liz / **eh**-lahz ish-**to**<u>w</u>
(males or coed / females only)		

TO GO	IR	eer
I go	eu vou	**eh**-oo voh
you go (formal)	você vai	voh-**say** vī
you go (informal)	tú vais	too vī sh
he / she goes	ele / ela vai	**eh**-leh / **eh**-lah vī
we go	nós vamos	nohsh **vah**-moosh
you go (plural, formal)	vocês vão	voh-**saysh** vo<u>w</u>
they go (males or coed / females only)	eles / elas vão	**eh**-lish / **eh**-lahsh vo<u>w</u>

TO DO, TO MAKE	FAZER	fah-**zehr**
I do	eu faço	**eh**-oo **fah**-soo
you do (formal)	você fáz	voh-**say** fahsh
you do (informal)	tú fazes	too **fah**-zish
he / she does	ele / ela faz	**eh**-leh / **eh**-lah fahsh
we do	nós fazemos	nohsh fah-**zeh**-moosh
you do (plural, formal)	vocês fazem	voh-**saysh fah**-zay<u>n</u>
they do (males or coed / females only)	eles / elas fazem	**eh**-lish / **eh**-lahsh **fah**-zay<u>n</u>

TO HAVE	TER	tehr
I have	eu tenho	**eh**-oo **tayn**-yoo
you have (formal)	você tem	voh-**say** tay<u>n</u>
you have (informal)	tú tens	too taynsh
he / she has	ele / ela tem	**eh**-leh / **eh**-lah tay<u>n</u>
we have	nós temos	nohsh **tay**-moosh
you have (plural, formal)	vocês têm	voh-**saysh** tay<u>n</u>
they have (males or coed / females only)	eles / elas têm	**eh**-lish / **eh**-lahsh tay<u>n</u>

TO SEE	VER	vehr
I see	eu vejo	**eh**-oo **veh**-zhoo
you see (formal)	você vê	voh-**say** veh
you see (informal)	tú vês	too vehsh
he / she sees	ele / ela vê	**eh**-leh / **eh**-lah veh
we see	nós vemos	nohsh **veh**-moosh

| you see (plural, formal) | vocês vêem | voh-**saysh veh**-ay<u>n</u> |
| they see (males or coed / females only) | vocês vêem | **eh**-lish / **eh**-lahsh **veh**-ay<u>n</u> |

TO SPEAK	*FALAR*	fah-**lar**
I speak	*eu falo*	**eh**-oo **fah**-loo
you speak (formal)	*você fala*	voh-**say fah**-lah
you speak (informal)	*tú falas*	too **fah**-lahsh
he / she speaks	*ele / ela fala*	**eh**-leh / **eh**-lah **fah**-lah
we speak	*nós falamos*	nohsh fah-**lah**-moosh
you speak (plural, formal)	*vocês falam*	voh-**saysh fah**-lahm
they speak (males or coed / females only)	*eles / elas falam*	**eh**-lish / **eh**-lahsh **fah**-lahm

TO WALK	*ANDAR*	ahn-**dar**
I walk	*eu ando*	**eh**-oo **ahn**-doo
you walk (formal)	*você anda*	voh-**say ahn**-dah
you walk (informal)	*tú andas*	too **ahn**-dahsh
he / she walks	*ele / ela anda*	**eh**-leh / **eh**-lah **ahn**-dah
we walk	*nós andamos*	nohz ahn-**dah**-moosh
you walk (plural, formal)	*vocês andam*	voh-**sayz ahn**-dahm
they walk (males or coed / females only)	*eles / elas andam*	**eh**-liz / **eh**-lahz **ahn**-dahm

TO LIKE	*GOSTAR*	goosh-**tar**
I like	*eu gusto*	**eh**-oo **gohsh**-toh
you like (formal)	*você gosta*	voh-**say gohsh**-tah
you like (informal)	*tú gostas*	too **gohsh**-tahsh
he / she likes	*ele / ela gosta*	**eh**-leh / **eh**-lah **gohsh**-tah
we like	*nós gostamos*	nohsh goosh-**tah**-moosh
you like (plural, formal)	*vocês gostam*	voh-**saysh gohsh**-tahm
they like (males or coed / females only)	*eles / elas gostam*	**eh**-lish / **eh**-lahsh **gohsh**-tahm

TO WANT	*QUERER*	keh-**rehr**
I want	*eu quero*	**eh**-oo **kay**-roo
you want (formal)	*você quer*	voh-**say** kehr
you want (informal)	*tú queres*	too **keh**-rish
he / she wants	*ele / ela quer*	**eh**-leh / **eh**-lah kehr
we want	*nós queremos*	nohsh keh-**ray**-moosh
you want (plural, formal)	*vocês querem*	voh-**saysh keh**-rayn
they want (males or coed / females only)	*eles / elas querem*	**eh**-lish / **eh**-lahsh **keh**-rayn

TO NEED	*PRECISAR*	preh-see-**zar**
I need	*eu preciso*	**eh**-oo preh-**see**-zoo
you need (formal)	*você precisa*	voh-**say** preh-**see**-zah
you need (informal)	*tú precisas*	too preh-**see**-zahsh
he / she needs	*ele / ela precisa*	**eh**-leh / **eh**-lah preh-**see**-zah
we need	*nós precisamos*	nohsh preh-see-**zah**-moosh
you need (plural, formal)	*vocês precisam*	voh-**saysh** preh-**see**-zahm
they need (males or coed / females only)	*eles / elas precisam*	**eh**-lish / **eh**-lahsh preh-**see**-zahm

Portuguese Tongue Twisters

Tongue twisters are a great way to practice a language and break the ice with locals. Here are a few Portuguese tongue twisters that are sure to challenge you and amuse your hosts.

O rato roeu a roupa do rei de Roma.

The mouse nibbled the clothes of the king of Rome.

Um tigre, dois tigres, três tigres.

One tiger, two tigers, three tigers.

Se cá nevasse fazia-se cá ski, mas como cá não neva não se faz cá ski.

If the snow would fall, we'd ski, but since it doesn't, we don't.

English Tongue Twisters

After your Portuguese friends have laughed at you, let them try these tongue twisters in English.

If neither he sells seashells,
 nor she sells seashells,
 who shall sell seashells?
 Shall seashells be sold?

Peter Piper picked a peck
 of pickled peppers.

Rugged rubber baby
 buggy bumpers.

The sixth sick sheik's
 sixth sheep's sick.

Red bug's blood and
 black bug's blood.

Soldiers' shoulders.
Thieves seize skis.

I'm a pleasant mother
 pheasant plucker. I pluck
 mother pheasants. I'm
 the most pleasant mother
 pheasant plucker that ever
 plucked a mother pheasant.

Portuguese National Anthem

If you ever hear the Portuguese national anthem and you'd like to sing along, here's a little help:

A PORTUGUESA

—Music by Alfredo Keil, lyrics by
Henrique Lopes de Mendonça, 1981

Heróis do mar, nobre Povo,	Heroes of the sea, noble people,
Nação valente, imortal,	Valiant and immortal nation,
Levantai hoje de novo,	Raise up today again
O esplendor de Portugal!	The splendor of Portugal!
Entre as brumas da memória,	From out of the mists of memory,
Ó Pátria sente-se a voz	Oh homeland, we hear the voices
Dos teus egrégios avós	Of your great forefathers
Que há-de guiar-te à vitória.	That shall lead you on to victory!
Às armas! Às armas!	To arms! To arms!
Sobre a terra, sobre o mar!	On land and sea!
Às armas! Às armas!	To arms! To arms!
Pela Pátria lutar!	To fight for our homeland!
Contra os canhões	Against the enemy cannons,
marchar, marchar!	march, march!

Numbers and Stumblers

- Europeans write a few of their numbers differently than we do. 1 = 1, 4 = 4, 7 = 7.
- Europeans write the date in this order: day/month/year.
- Commas are decimal points and decimals are commas. A dollar and a half is 1,50 and there are 5.280 feet in a mile.
- The European "first floor" isn't the ground floor, but the first floor up.
- When counting with your fingers, start with your thumb. If you hold up only your first finger, you'll probably get two of something.

APPENDIX

Let's Talk
Telephones

Making Calls within a European Country: About half of all European countries use area codes (like we do); the other half uses a direct-dial system without area codes.

To make calls within a country that uses a direct-dial system (Belgium, Czech Republic, Denmark, France, Italy, Portugal, Norway, Spain, and Switzerland), you dial the same number whether you're calling across the country or across the street.

In countries that use area codes (such as Austria, Britain, Finland, Germany, Ireland, the Netherlands, and Sweden), you dial the local number when calling within a city, and you add the area code if calling long-distance within the country.

Making International Calls: You always start with the international access code (011 if you're calling from America or Canada, or 00 from Europe), then dial the country code of the country you're calling (see codes below).

What you dial next depends on the phone system of the country you're calling. If the country uses area codes, drop the initial zero of the area code, then dial the rest of the number.

Countries that use direct-dial systems (no area codes) vary in how they're accessed internationally by phone. You always start by dialing the international access code, followed by the country code. Then, if you're calling the Czech Republic, Denmark, Italy, Norway, Portugal, or Spain, simply dial the phone number in its entirety. But if you're calling Belgium, France, or Switzerland, drop the initial zero of the phone number.

Country Codes

After you've dialed the international access code, dial the code of the country you're calling.

Austria—43	Belgium—32
Britain—44	Canada—1
Czech Rep.—420	Denmark—45
Estonia—372	Finland—358
France—33	Germany—49
Gibraltar—350	Greece—30
Ireland—353	Italy—39
Morocco—212	Netherlands—31
Norway—47	Portugal—351
Spain—34	Sweden—46
Switzerland—41	United States—1

APPENDIX

Directory Assistance

Dial 118 for local numbers and 177 for international numbers.

Embassies

American Embassy
- tel. 217-273-300,
- Avenida das Forças Armadas, **Lisbon**
- www.american-embassy.pt

Tear-Out Cheat Sheet

Keep this sheet of survival phrases in your pocket, handy to memorize or use if you're caught without your phrase book.

Good day.	*Bom dia.*	boh<u>n</u> **dee**-ah
Do you speak English?	*Fala inglês?*	**fah**-lah een-**glaysh**
Yes. / No.	*Sim. / Não.*	seeng / no<u>w</u>
I don't understand.	*Não compreendo.*	no<u>w</u> koh<u>n</u>-pree-**ayn**-doo
Please.	*Por favor.*	poor fah-**vor**
Thank you.	*Obrigado[a].**	oh-bree-**gah**-doo
You're welcome.	*De nada.*	deh **nah**-dah
I'm sorry.	*Desculpe[a].*	dish-**kool**-peh
Excuse me (to get attention).	*Desculpe[a].*	dish-**kool**-peh
Excuse me (to pass).	*Com licença.*	koh<u>n</u> li-**sehn**-sah
(No) problem.	*(Não) á problema.*	(no<u>w</u>) ah proo-**blay**-mah
Good.	*Bom.*	boh<u>n</u>
Goodbye.	*Adeus.*	ah-**deh**-oosh
How much is it?	*Quanto custa?*	**kwahn**-too **koosh**-tah
Write it?	*Escreva?*	ish-**kray**-vah
euro (€)	*euro*	**yoo**-roh
one / two	*um / dois*	oo<u>n</u> / doysh
three / four	*três / quarto*	traysh / **kwah**-troo
five / six	*cinco / seis*	**seeng**-koo / saysh
seven / eight	*sete / oito*	**seh**-teh / **oy**-too
nine / ten	*nove / dez*	**nah**-veh / **dehsh**
20	*vinte*	**veen**-teh
30	*trinta*	**treen**-tah
40	*quarenta*	kwah-**rayn**-tah
50	*cinquenta*	seeng-**kwayn**-tah

* If you're male, use the "o" ending (*obrigado*); if you're female, use the "a" ending (*obrigada*).

60	*sessenta*	seh-**sayn**-tah
70	*setenta*	seh-**tayn**-tah
80	*oitenta*	oy-**tayn**-tah
90	*noventa*	noh-**vayn**-tah
100	*cem*	say<u>n</u>
I would like...	*Gostaria...*	goosh-tah-**ree**-ah
We would like...	*Gostaríamos...*	goosh-tah-**ree**-ah-moosh
...this.	*...isto.*	**eesh**-too
...more.	*...mais.*	mī sh
...a ticket.	*...um bilhete.*	oo<u>n</u> beel-**yeh**-teh
...a room.	*...um quarto.*	oo<u>n</u> **kwar**-too
...the bill.	*...a conta.*	ah **kohn**-tah
Is it possible?	*É possível?*	eh poo-**see**-vehl
Where is the toilet?	*Onde é que é a casa de banho?*	**ohn**-deh eh keh eh ah **kah**-zah deh **bahn**-yoo
men / women	*homens / mulheres*	**ah**-may<u>n</u>sh / mool-**yeh**-rish
entrance / exit	*entrada / saída*	ay<u>n</u>-**trah**-dah / sah-**ee**-dah
no entry	*proibido a entrada*	proy-**bee**-doo ah ay<u>n</u>-**trah**-dah
open / closed	*aberto / fechado*	ah-**behr**-too / feh-**shah**-doo
What time does this open / close?	*A que horas é que abre / fecha?*	ah kee **oh**-rahsh eh keh **ah**-breh / **fay**-shah
At what time?	*A que horas?*	ah kee **oh**-rahsh
Just a moment.	*Um momento.*	oo<u>n</u> moo-**mayn**-too
Now.	*Agora.*	ah-**goh**-rah
Soon.	*Breve.*	**bray**-veh
Later.	*Mais tarde.*	mī sh **tar**-deh
Today.	*Hoje.*	**oh**-zheh
Tomorrow.	*Amanhã.*	ah-ming-**yah**
Monday	*segunda-feira*	seh-goon-dah-**fay**-rah
Tuesday	*terça-feira*	tehr-sah-**fay**-rah
Wednesday	*quarta-feira*	kwar-tah-**fay**-rah
Thursday	*quinta-feira*	keen-tah-**fay**-rah
Friday	*sexta-feira*	saysh-tah-**fay**-rah
Saturday	*sábado*	**sah**-bah-doo
Sunday	*domingo*	doo-**meeng**-goo

MAKING YOUR HOTEL RESERVATION

Most hotel managers know basic "hotel English." E-mailing or faxing are the preferred methods for reserving a room. They're clearer and more foolproof than telephoning. Photocopy and enlarge this form, or find it online at www.ricksteves.com/reservation.

- -

One-Page Fax

To: _____ @ _____
        hotel   fax

From: _____ @ _____
          name   fax

Today's date: _____ / _____ / _____
                       day   month   year

Dear Hotel_____

Please make this reservation for me:

Name: _____

Total # of people: _____ # of rooms: _____ # of nights: _____

Arriving: _____ / _____ / _____   Arrival time: (24-hr clock): _____
                day   month   year   (I will telephone if I will be late)

Departing: _____ / _____ / _____
                 day   month   year

Room(s): Single____ Double____ Twin____ Triple____ Quad____ Quint____

With: Toilet____ Shower____ Bathtub____ Sink only____

Special needs: View____ Quiet____ Cheapest____ Ground floor____

Credit card: Visa____ Mastercard____ American Express____

Card #: _____

Expiration date: _____

Name on card: _____

If a deposit is necessary, you may charge me for the first night. Please e-mail, fax, or mail me confirmation of my reservation, along with the type of room reserved, the price, and whether the price includes break-fast. Please also inform me of your cancellation policy. Thank you.

Signature _____

Name _____

Address _____

City_____ State ____ Zip Code _____ Country_____

E-mail address _____

The perfect complement
to your phrase book

Travel with Rick Steves' candid, up-to-date advice on the best places to eat and sleep, the must-see sights, getting off the beaten path—and getting the most out of every mile, minute, and dollar while you're in Europe.

Take a trip to ricksteves.com

Our website is bursting with free information to boost your Travel I.Q. and liven up your European adventure. Here's a sampling of what you'll find…

▼ The latest from Rick on where he's been and what's hot in Europe.

▼ Excerpts from Rick's books, including self-guided tours.

▼ Rick's comprehensive **Guide to European Railpasses**, complete with maps.

▼ Frequently asked travel questions and years of archived newsletter articles.

▼ Streaming video previews from the all-new season of **Rick Steves' Europe**.

▼ Full itineraries and seat availability for our free-spirited tours.

▼ A directory of the best travel websites.

▼ Our **Rick Steves Travel Store** features fast, secure, user-friendly online ordering for all your favorite travel bags, accessories, books and videos— with frequent money-saving specials.

Free, fresh travel tips, all year long.

Visit **www.ricksteves.com**
to get Rick's free
64-page newsletter... and more!